The Politically Incorrect Joke Book

The Politically Incorrect Joke Book

George Coote

Gap Publishing

THE POLITICALLY INCORRECT JOKE BOOK
© G. COOTE 1996

Published in 1996 by
GAP PUBLISHING
44 Wendell St
Norman Park
Queensland 4170
Australia
Reprinted 1997 (twice)

Printed in Australia by
Australian Print Group
Maryborough, Victoria

ISBN 0 947163 26 3

CONTENTS

FOREWORD

George Coote

POLITICALLY CORRECT
versus
FREEDOM OF SPEECH

WE survive the tragedies of life by seeing the funny side.

We laugh to preserve our sanity.

Credited as the first comedy writer the great scribe, Aristophanes, began poking fun at the pompous officials and their institutions around 400 BC. The Thought Police of the day were assigned to get him.

Today we find another crusade antagonistic to free speech under the guise of being Politically Correct. It is mounted by the usual scoundrels, the jingoist patriots and the priests who still wish they could burn heretics at the stake.

If an anti-Irish, or an anti-Jewish joke is banned, who decides when an anti-Nazi joke is offensive? And who decides when anti-politician jokes are forbidden? The politicians?

Ethnic humour is here to stay as long as we divide ourselves into national, religious, racial and cultural groups. That of course includes all of us?

AN official for Political Correctness phoned the city council and told the chief librarian that the library had 23,000 books with the word "wog" in them and that all these books would have to removed from the shelves.

The librarian protested. "We have twice that many volumes with the word 'bastard' in them."

"I know," said the PC official, "but you bastards are not organised."

No doubt the bastards rushed off to join the ever-lengthening queue seeking political protection.

The author just happens to be multi-national.

He's part Irish and part Italian. (That's Irish from his mother's side, and Italian by a friend of his father's).

To set the mood we will start with a few multi-cultural items which give many nationalities a spray before we satirize Australians.

The discovery of a fly in the soup can mean different responses to different diners in different countries.

In France the soup is eaten and the fly is left high and dry on the side of the plate.

In England the fly is quietly and discreetly removed and hidden under a serviette.

In Australia the soup is sent back to the kitchen, the fly is removed and the same soup returned.

In America the soup and the fly are subpoenaed as evidence for the ensuing litigation.

In Italy the diner storms into the kitchen and cuts up the chef.

In the Orient the fly is eaten first and washed down by the soup.

In Scotland the fly is wrung out and then the soup is consumed.

In Israel the bill is quickly amended. The fly is extra.

In India the diner complains: "Waiter, what's this? Only one fly?"

HELL happens to be multi-cultural:
The Germans are the police force,
The Italians the defence force,
The Indonesians are in charge of housing,
The Indians run the railways.
The Irish make the laws,
The English are the cooks
... and the common language is Dutch.

AUSTRALIANS

AUSTRALIAN humour probably started when two aboriginals saw Captain Cook and his party landing at Botany Bay. They watched for a while before one said: "Well, there goes the neighbourhood."

Australian humour has gone through the laconic Dad and Dave stage which identified it with the hard life in the Outback. Today Australians still have a unique sense of humour, but the nation is multicultural which means they have to take their turn on the rough end of the pineapple.

AFTER a month's holiday in Australia Paddy returned to Ireland where the family wanted to know all about his trip.

He said Australians were the most hospitable people he had ever met. "They'll share their house, they'll share their grog, they'll even share their women." he said.

"It's the white bastards you have to watch!"

*   *   *

AH, for the Good Old Days.

There was a time when there was no violence, no street gangs, no muggings, no graffiti, no vandals, no burglaries...

Then along came Captain Cook.

*   *   *

HOW do you make an Aussie laugh on Monday morning?

Tell him a joke on Friday night.

* * *

AUSSIES don't clock in for work ...

They sign the Visitor's Book.

* * *

WHAT do you call an Aussie with half a brain?

Gifted.

* * *

WHEN their car broke down a Jew, an Indian and an Australian knocked on a farmer's door to ask for accommodation for the night.

"One will have to sleep in the barn," said the farmer.

"I will," volunteered the Jew.

But five minutes later there was a knock on the door.

"There's a pig in the barn," said the Jew.

"Okay, I'll go," said the Indian.

Five minutes later there was a knock on the door.

"There is an un-sacred cow in the barn," he said.

"Bugger yers, I'll go," said the Aussie.

Five minutes later there was yet another knock on the door. It was the pig and the cow.

* * *

WHY do Queenslanders call their beer XXXX?

Because they can't spell BEER.

* * *

BLUEY, the typical Australian Ocker was enjoying a few beers at his local when a cold hand landed on his shoulder and he turned to see the Grim Reaper.

"Time's up," said Grim.

Bluey was prepared to take it like a man and told Grim so. "But just let me have one last tumble in the cot. Just one more shag with Cheryl and I'll go quietly," he said.

Mr Grim admired the audacity so characteristic of Australians and agreed to the short reprieve.

Bluey raced home. "Quick Cheryl," he said, "I've only got a few moments to live. This is our last root." And with that he humps her on the bedroom floor and comes within a minute as he hears the dreaded voice boom: "Time's up."

True to his word Bluey hops up and walks towards the door.

"Bloody typical," roars Cheryl, "What about my orgasm?"

* * *

WHAT is an Aussie lover's idea of foreplay?

"Hey Cheryl. Wake up!"

* * *

WHAT is an Aussie lover's idea of foreplay?

"Brace yourself, Sheila."

* * *

THE young woman looked at the Aussie's beer gut with disgust.

"If that stomach was on a woman, she would be pregnant," she said.

"It was and she is," replied the Ocker.

* * *

CHERYL was about to be married and went to confession with a problem on her mind.

"Dear Father," she said, "I believe an open and honest relationship is the foundation for every marriage and I will need your blessing to admit to my fiance that my family is not perfect. For example," she said, "there is my father who has long been a member of the Liberal Party, my mother has always been working the streets, my eldest brother is still touching up little boys and of course, brother Ned who fled to England to beat a murder charge, got married and is hiding there under another name.

"My main problem, Father, is should I tell my fiance that my brother is married to a Pom?"

* * *

HOW can you tell when an Australian is formally dressed?

He's wearing black thongs.

* * *

BLUEY, the typical Australian Ocker was enjoying a few beers at his local when a cold hand landed on his shoulder and he turned to see the Grim Reaper.

"Time's up," said Grim.

Bluey was prepared to take it like a man and told Grim so. "But just let me have one last tumble in the cot. Just one more shag with Cheryl and I'll go quietly," he said.

Mr Grim admired the audacity so characteristic of Australians and agreed to the short reprieve.

Bluey raced home. "Quick Cheryl," he said, "I've only got a few moments to live. This is our last root." And with that he humps her on the bedroom floor and comes within a minute as he hears the dreaded voice boom: "Time's up."

True to his word Bluey hops up and walks towards the door.

"Bloody typical," says Cheryl, "What about my orgasm?"

* * *

HOW many Australian men does it take to lower a toilet seat?

None. They've never seen it done before.

* * *

BRUCE stood on the edge of the cliff with a budgie strapped to each shoulder. He took a mighty leap, and plummeted straight down to the rocks below.

"Jeeze, mate," he said to Kevin who was already there, "this budgie jumping isn't all it's cracked up to be."

* * *

AN Aussie who shows wise planning for future contingencies is the bloke who buys two slabs of beer instead of one.

* * *

WORDS were the big topic of the million dollar television quiz show where Professor Geewhizz challenged the audience to stump him with a word he couldn't put into a sentence.

"Garn!" shouted a bloke in the third row.

"Garn?" said the professor, "Garn? It's not a swear word is it?"

"No," said the punter in the third row, "Garn."

Time elapsed, the buzzer went and the crowd applauded.

"You've stumped him," said the MC, "How do you use the word, sir?"

"Garn get fucked," said the punter who was immediately thrown out and the show closed until further notice.

It took the network twelve months to get over it. Finally they had the gumption to start it up again with

the proviso that they would have to screen the audience in future.

On the opening night they scrutinised each member
of the public as they arrived before asking for the first
word.

A man in the third row wearing a vicar's collar and
a beard put his hand up. "Smee," he said.

"Smee?" said the professor, "Smee?" The seconds
ticked away and he was forced to concede on the very
first word.

After the applause had died down the MC asked the
punter, "How do you use the word?"

The punter stood up, pulled his false beard off and
said "Smee again. Garn get fucked!"

*   *   *

WHAT is a typical Australian seven-course meal?

A pie and a six pack.

*   *   *

THE drought was so severe this year the local shire
closed two lanes of the municipal pool.

*   *   *

THE difference between an Australian wedding and
an Australian funeral is one less drunk.

*   *   *

IT was a typical Outback wedding and the celebrations
had been raging for two days in the shearing shed
before Ned finally arrived with his present. He was
about to enter when he encountered his mate Joe
hurriedly leaving the party.

"Don't go in," warned Joe. "There's bound to be
strife. They've run out of beer and the best man has
just rooted the bride."

Ned didn't need a picture to explain the trouble

which was about to erupt. He turned and headed back towards his car.

They were about to leave when another guest came out of the hall and shouted: "Don't go you blokes. No problems. There's another keg on the way and the best man has apologised."

* * *

AT the same wedding all the speeches were done and the dancing begun. A young couple were pressed together, dancing cheek to cheek. "Come outside and let's get in the car," she whispered.

He declined. He said the tune the band was playing was his favourite number. She pressed closer again, "But I know you want to take me outside. C'mon."

He finally agreed. When they left the hall it was pitch black and he produced a torch from his pocket.

She said: "Have you had that in your pocket all night?"

"Yes," he said.

"Let's go back to the dance then," she said.

* * *

DID you hear about the Irishman who built a bridge over the Nullabor Plain?

They had to pull it down because too many Aussies were fishing from it.

* * *

TWO wheat farmers finally sold their properties and decided to retire from the land. They surprised each other by buying a four-wheel-drive each and announcing that they intended to drive around Australia.

"What route are you taking?" said one.

"Ar, I think I'll take the missus. She stuck by me through the drought."

A WOMBAT goes on his first holiday abroad and lands in Paris where he is soon picked up by a lady of the night.

She takes him home cooks him a splendid meal and takes him to bed. Despite the language difficulty they eventually make ends meet.

After breakfast in bed the wombat gets up, puts his hat on and swaggers towards the door.

Suspecting the wombat doesn't understand the purpose of the preceding evening's exercise the woman grabs a dictionary and shows him the definition of prostitute; n, a woman who performs sexual favours for money.

Unperturbed, the wombat flicks a few pages and shows her the definition of wombat; n, peculiar to Australia, eats roots and leaves.

* * *

AUSSIES are well-known for their romance and sensitivity so it was no surprise to Cheryl when her husband rushed in and shouted: "Chessa! Pack your things. I've just won a million in the lottery."

"Shall I pack for warm weather or cold?" she asked.

"I don't care," he said, "just as long as you're out of the house by noon."

* * *

TWO builders' labourers were walking home from a party.

One said: "Basil, as soon as I get home I am going to rip the wife's knickers off."

"Why's that, Trevor?"

"'Cos the bloody elastic is killing me," he said.

* * *

WHEN Harry Bloggs arrived at the building site he was told "no ticket, no start," but Harry said it was against his principles to join the union.

They argued with him, the union organiser was called, even the boss who didn't want trouble on the site tried to cajole him to join the union. Harry wouldn't have it.

He was working on the scaffolding on the 52nd level, high over Collins St, when Big Norm, the union delegate, arrived.

"I will only tell you once, Harry," he said. "If you don't join the union I will pick up that piece of timber, wrap it around your neck and throw you right off this platform onto the tram tracks below."

Later, when they asked Harry why he joined, he said: "I had never had it explained so succinctly before."

*   *   *

THE gang of Painters and Dockers was having a smoko on the waterfront when a leading hand said to his boss, "Hey, that new bloke you hired this morning; he's not a spy is he?"

"No, I think he checked out okay, why?"

"Well, he just stubbed his toe on a crate of pig-iron and said, 'Oh, the perversity of inanimate objects!'"

*   *   *

AN American business tycoon had just arrived at a Melbourne hotel. "I am a man of few words," he said to the porter. "If I beckon with my finger that means come."

"I'm a man of few words myself," said the porter. "If I shakes me head that means I aint coming."

*   *   *

9

THE Chamber of Commerce was host to a United States business delegation and at the height of the dinner one of the Americans at the head table asked the waiter for some more butter.

"Sorry, just one pat of butter per person," said the waiter.

The chamber president was embarrassed to overhear this and called the waiter aside. "Do you know who that man is?" he said angrily. "He is in charge of the American delegation."

"And do you know who I am?" said the waiter. "I am in charge of the butter."

* * *

HAVE you heard about the Aussie punter who lost $100 on the Melbourne Cup and $500 on the replay?

* * *

A MOTORIST had been picked up on a traffic infringement and had given his name as Fred Shagbreak and his place of employment. When the cop arrived to deliver the summons he asked the girl at the enquiry desk: "Have you got a Shagbreak here?"

She replied: "You must be joking, the union has battled for two years just to get a coffee break."

* * *

MANAGER to boss: "The workers are demanding shorter hours."

"Right, well cut their lunch hour to 30 minutes!"

* * *

JAKE the plumber was on a house job and noted that the lady of the house was quite a woman. By mid afternoon they were having a tumble in the bedroom when the phone rang.

"That's my husband," she said. "He is coming home

now because he has a meeting tonight. Why don't you come back then and we can continue where we left off."

"What?" said the plumber. "On my own time?"

*　*　*

TWO Aussies wearing black singlets, shorts and thongs arrived at the Pearly Gates. St Peter took one look at them and said, "Nick off. You look like wharfies. We know all about you thieving Aussies. Pinch anything that wasn't nailed down. Piss off."

St Peter informed God he had just got rid of two Aussies. God went berserk. "You can't do that. Everyone is entitled to get to Heaven. Go and get them back."

St Peter went off to do His bidding but soon returned. "They've gone," he said.

"Who?" The Aussies?"

"No, the bloody Pearly Gates," said St Peter.

*　*　*

BRUCE detected that there was something troubling his mate Dennis. "C'mon, tell me all about it," he said.

A worried Dennis began by reminding his mate that they had been together for a long time, "but I've just gotta tell ya," he said.

"It's your wife, Beryl. I was in the local brothel the other night and there she was. Bruce, I hate to tell ya this but your wife is a prostitute."

"Oh no, you've got it wrong," said Bruce. "She's a substitute. She's only there on week-ends."

*　*　*

THE secretary of the Patchywallock bush racing club was worried about falling attendances. On the morning of the Patchywallock Cup race meeting he got a phone call from Sydney. "I'm bringing a coach-load of people," said the voice, "What time is the first race?"

"What time can you get here," replied the secretary.

* * *

THE drover looked over the field at the Oodnadatta Races and reckoned his nag could beat anything in the mounting yard, so he entered him for the main race.

"But what's his pedigree?" asked the steward.

"What d'yer mean, his pedigree?"

"What is he by, and what is he out of?" insisted the steward.

"He's by that bloody gum tree and out in that bloody paddock."

* * *

AN American tourist on a trip to Ayers Rock suddenly yelled "Stop the Bus" and scrambled to the front to get off. On a track just off the main road he had spotted an Aborigine with his ear to the ground.

"He must be one of those famous black-trackers they have out here," said the Yank as he ran back to the Aborigine.

"Can you tell me about the last people to pass this way?" enquired the Yank.

"Yeah," answered the Aborigine, and pointing to the wheel tracks he said "It was a Ford utility."

This didn't impress the Yank much. "Anything else?" he said.

"Yeah. There was ten people in it. Three in the front and seven in the back."

Now the Yank was really impressed. "Anything else?"

"Yeah. The three in the front were blokes, and there

were four women and three kids in the back and the truck was red with yellow wheel caps."

This amazed the Yank. "You can tell all that just by putting your ear to the ground?"

"Not really," said the Aborigine. "I just fell off the bloody thing!"

* * *

THE census taker told the mayor of the little bush town that he was puzzled about the town's population. For the past five years he had been on the job the population was the same, 1,503. "Must be something wrong."

"No," said the mayor. "It's always been 1,503."

"But don't you have babies?"

"Yep," said the mayor, "and every time we do some bloke has to leave town."

* * *

HOW does an Aussie woman gain her man's attention?

She drops her handkerchief .....after wrapping it round a can of beer.

* * *

DAVE was courting Mabel who lived on a neighbouring farm.

They were sitting on the porch one evening in a romantic setting watching the sun go down when the silhouette of a bull humping a cow seemed to put the finishing touch to the Utopian rural scene.

Dave watched the bull on the job for a time and took it as an omen to put the hard word on Mabel. He whispered in her ear: "I'd sure like to be doing what that bull is doing."

"Well, why don't you," she whispered back, "it's your cow."

* * *

ADDRESSING the little girl in plaits the teacher said: "Mary, come up to the map and point out Tasmania to me."

Mary did so.

"And now Ned," she said to a little kid in the front row, "Who discovered Tasmania?"

"Mary did," he said.

* * *

AUSSIE football can be tough, but when little Johnny came home from a footy match with a bleeding nose and a bruised ear his mother complained to her husband.

"Don't worry," he replied, "it used to happen to me too."

"Yes, but he doesn't know which kids they belong to," insisted his wife.

* * *

"HEY Mum," he said as he rushed in from school. "I've got the biggest dick in grade five."

"Well so you should. You will be 21 next August."

* * *

THE Frenchman, the Italian and the Australian were arguing as to who was best lover.

"When I am in bed with my wife I prepare such tender foreplay and technique that she levitates and rises a foot off the bed," said the Frenchman.

Not to be outdone the Italian said he whispers love-talk to his wife and employs such sensuous procedure she moans and rises two feet off the bed.

"That's nothing," said the Australian, "After I've

finished a good nookie with the missus I wipe my old fella on the curtains and she hits the roof."

* * *

ON his first night in London Kevin had won a date, but he was a little annoyed when she stopped making love, propped herself on one elbow and lit a fag.

"What's wrong," he said.

"I'm afraid your organ is not big enough," she said.

"Forgive me," said Kev, "but it wasn't meant to be played in a cathedral."

* * *

HOW do you tell a well-balanced Aussie?

He's got a chip on both shoulders.

* * *

THE seat-belt sign switched off and the three men seated together settled down for a long flight.

The distinguished man in the middle began the introductions with himself: "General, Australian Army, married, two sons, both lawyers."

The second took the cue: "General, Artillery, married, two sons, one a surgeon the other a judge."

There was an embarrassing silence until the third responded, "Petty Officer, Australian Navy, never married, two sons, both generals."

* * *

PRIVATE Curly was on patrol in the jungle when he discovered a quiet pool by the edge of the river. He stripped off for a swim and was later standing by the bank when a shot rang out.

He woke up in hospital.

"What happened?" he said to the medical team around him.

"Actually, to come to the point old man," said the

chief medic, "a sniper's bullet has shot your balls off. Neatly off I might add. We just had to sew up the wound."

Curly surveyed the damage.

"Could have been worse," he said, "Lucky I was thinking of me wife's younger sister when it happened."

*　*　*

ON the morning of his execution Kevin was visited by the chaplain.

"They are going to give an hour's grace," he said.

Kev shrugged. "That aint long. But what the hell, send her in."

*　*　*

AN Australian had been wandering the Outback for months. He finally came to a farm where a pretty girl met him at the gate.

"D'yer root?" he said.

"No," she replied, "but you've talked me into it you silver-tongued bastard."

*　*　*

A KELPIE sheep dog went in to an Outback post office, took down a blank form and wrote, "woof, woof, woof, woof-woof, woof, woof, woof-woof, woof, woof-woof."

He handed it to the clerk who studied it for a while.

"You have nine words here. You can have another word for the same price."

"Yeah," said the kelpie, "but it wouldn't make any bloody sense, would it."

*　*　*

TWO drovers were leaning on the rail outside the bush pub with pots in their hands. Nearby a kelpie sheepdog was sitting in the shade licking its knackers.

"You know, Jake," said one of the drovers watching the dog, "I'd like to be able to do that."

"Well why don't ya," said his mate. "But I'd pat him first."

*   *   *

WHENEVER two drovers get together there is the inevitable argument about who has the best kelpie. So the merits of their respective dogs was the subject of the debate at the bar.

"My dog's so smart," said one, "I can give him five instructions at the same time and he will carry them out to perfection."

"That's nothing," said his mate. "I only whistle and point and Bluey anticipates the whole exercise."

Finally they decided to put their dogs to the test. The first drover whistled his dog and told him to dash to the saleyards, select the oldest ram, bring him back into town and load it into the ute which was parked outside the pub.

The dog sped off in a cloud of dust and ten minutes later was seen bringing a large ram down the main street. He jumped into the ute, dropped the tail gate and hunted the ram in.

"Well that's not bad," conceded the second drover. "But watch this."

"Bluey, what about some tucker?"

In a cloud of dust Bluey streaked down the main street to a farm five kilometres out of town. The dog raced on to the chook house, nudged a hen off the nest and gently picked up an egg.

The dog then sped back to town and gently placed the egg at his master's feet. But without waiting for a pat on the head the mutt gathered a few sticks and lit a fire, grabbed a billy in its teeth and dashed to the creek, set the billy on the fire and dropped the egg into the simmering water.

After exactly three minutes, Bluey rolled the billy off the fire, laid the boiled egg at his master's feet and stood on his head.

"Well, that beats all," conceded the first drover, "But why is he standing on his head?"

"Well he knows I haven't got an egg cup," said the proud owner.

* * *

THEY were camping in the Outback and enjoying a few beers when Kev got up to go for a leak. When he returned he had forgotten to do up the fly in his shorts and as he sat down Dave told him that a big snake had just wriggled through the camp.

"It was one of the biggest I've seen," enthused Dave. "It was right near your chair. Heck! There it is, I can see the head there now," and reaching for a beer bottle said, "Hold still, I'll kill it."

Dave brought the bottle crashing down and Kev let out a wail.

"Hit it again," screamed Kev, "It just bit me."

* * *

THERE is a notice outside a Lion Safari Park in Australia which reads: Coaches $50, private cars $5, Pommies on bikes, free."

* * *

AN Englishman, a Scot and an Australian went for a job. The boss asked them all the same question: What is the capital of Ireland?

"New York," said the Scot.

"No. It's Vancouver," said the Englishman.

"Fools," said the Australian, "anybody knows the capital of Ireland is Brussels."

The Australian got the job because he was closest.

*   *   *

A LION in the London Zoo was lazing in the sun and licking its arse when a visitor turned to the keeper and said, "that's a docile old thing isn't it?"

"No way," said the keeper, "it is the most ferocious beast in the zoo. Why just an hour ago it dragged an Australian tourist into the cage and completely devoured him."

"Hardly seems possible," said the astonished visitor, "but why is he lying there licking his arse?"

"The poor thing is trying to get the taste out of his mouth," said the keeper.

*   *   *

KEVIN and Bruce had overstayed their English holiday and were in desperate need of a job, so the advertisement they saw in the "Times" was most appropriate. It read: "Two butlers needed for Scottish country manor. References a must."

The references were an initial problem, but was solved with simple Aussie ingenuity. Kevin wrote Bruce's reference and Bruce gave Kevin a splendid wrap.

When they were ushered before the lady of the manor they proffered their references but she waved them aside. "Later," she said, "First, I'd like to check your knees. Formal wear here means wearing kilts so if you would be so kind as to drop the tweeds ..."

The lads thought it a little strange, but they did so.

"Not bad," she said. "Now you can show me your testimonials."

When they picked themselves up from the gravel driveway, Kevin said: "With a little more education we would have got that job."

* * *

AN Aussie on holiday in Ireland was given a piece of advice by his Irish wife before the aircraft landed at Shannon Airport. She told him not to tell religious jokes or to be critical of Catholics.

He was in a pub the very next night playing a darts match with the locals when a television bulletin reported that the Pope was sick, and near death. The locals all gathered around the television set.

"C'mon you fellas, bugger the Pope let's get on with the game," he said.

When he woke up in hospital with his wife sitting beside him he said "Nobody told me the Pope was a Catholic."

* * *

A SCOT, an Irishman and an Australian were each sentenced to five years in prison and were allowed one request.

The Scot asked for all the great books so he could study and learn.

The Irishman asked if his wife could stay with him so he could start a family.

The Australian did a quick calculation and asked the equivalent of five packets of cigarettes a day for the five years.

At the end of the term the Scot emerged as an erudite scholar. The Irishman emerged from prison with a family of five kids.

The Australian emerged looking a little frustrated. "Anybody got a match?" he said.

* * *

A MIGRANT went for a job and was told he would have to pass an IQ test. When he asked what an IQ was the employer explained that anyone with an IQ of 150 would be admitted to university, but a bloke with an IQ of 50 would have trouble tieing his shoe laces.

"Oh," said the migrant, "So that's why so many Australians wear thongs."

* * *

WHY do Australian men piss in the bushes at parties?

Because there's always someone throwing up in the toilet.

* * *

AN Aussie on a flight to Rome got talking to the fellow seated beside him and couldn't help noticing he had one heck of a stutter. He was even more astonished when his new acquaintance told him, with difficulty, that he was going for an audition as an announcer for Radio Vatican.

"How do you rate your chances?" asked the Aussie.

"Ner, ner, ner, not too good," he replied. "They will per-per probably ger-ger give the job ter-ter some ber-bloody Catholic!"

* * *

AS the old stockman lay dying she sat beside him wiping his fevered brow. Raising himself up on one elbow he turned to her and spoke:

"Ethel, you've been with me through it all. Remember the time when I got trampled in the stampede? You were there.

"And when I lost all that money at the cattle sale. You were at my side.

"And now I've been shot by a rustler, here you are again. You know, Ethel, I'm beginning to think you're bad luck!"

* * *

THE salesman was travelling in the Outback late at night when his car blew a tyre and he realised he didn't have a jack. It was miles from anywhere, but across the field he could see a farmhouse in silhouette against the rising moon.

"He could lend me a jack," mused the salesman as he set off towards the farm.

As he stumbled across the paddocks in the dark he wondered if farmers still had the hospitality for which they were renowned.

"It's late," he thought. "He probably won't be too pleased about being woken up. He has probably had a hard day in the field and was looking forward to a bit of rest." He approached the farmhouse and knocked on the door.

While he waited his thoughts continued: "The poor bloke is most likely getting out of bed now. His wife could be nagging him. He will be upset. He could even put the dogs onto me."

When the farmer opened the door the traveller said: "You can stick the jack up your arse!"

* * *

SID, the Aussie battler, was told if he didn't sell more toothbrushes he would be fired. One month later his

22

sales record had soared and the manager called him in to explain the dramatic turnaround.

Sid explained that he got sick of calling on pharmacies. He said he set up a little table at Flinders St Station with some dry biscuits and a new dip.

"Try my dip," he would say, and a constant stream of people did so. When they enquired about the ingredients of the dip Sid told them: "It's garlic and chook shit!"

They would go "Aaaargh!" and spit it out.

Then Sid would say: "Would you like to buy a toothbrush?"

* * *

TWO Ockers from the same town met in London. "Fancy meeting you over here," said Bruce to Merv. "Listen mate, you've got to come over to my flat tomorrow night. We're having a small gathering."

Merv said he'd be in like Flynn.

"Get the tube to Earl's Court, straight down the High Street, second on the right, number 35 and you can ring the bell with your elbows."

"What's with the elbows bit?" said Merv.

"Well you're not coming without bottles are ya?"

* * *

THE lad from Dubbo got quite a buzz walking down Fifth Avenue in the heart of the Big Apple. He was looking up at the skyscrapers when he felt somebody bump him slightly.

With a jolt he remembered he was in New York and reached for his wallet. It was gone. And the youth who bumped him was hurrying down the street.

Our lad sprinted after him, grabbed him by the shirt-front and backed him against the wall. "Okay

23

pal. You've met your match. You're dealing with an Aussie. Hand over that wallet."

The youth produced the wallet, ducked out of the grip and ran. It wasn't until our Ocker got back to his room that he saw his own wallet where he had left it beside the bed.

*　*　*

AT the Ockers picnic they were selling coffee at 50 cents a mug. The queue of mugs stretched back around the corner.

*　*　*

BRUCE said: "I know a bloke who has got more brains in his head than you've got in your little finger."

*　*　*

AN Australian girl phoned her boyfriend.

"Trevor, I've just been to the doctor and he tells me I'm up the duff. Trevor, if you don't marry me I will drown myself."

"Hell, Cheryl, that's bloody decent of you. Not only are you a good root, you're a good sport too."

*　*　*

KEVIN and Keith were a little cheesed off when the gates of the sports ground were slammed shut. It was full to capacity for the grand final.

The ground was so crowded the toilet facilities could not cope and at half time many fans were forced to head for the perimeter fence and find a knot hole.

The two lads were still outside muttering about their bad luck when Kev noticed the odd dick being poked through the fence.

"Here's a chance to make some money," he said. He grabbed a dick and shouted: "Throw a fiver over or I'll cutcha cock off."

They were delighted to see a note flutter over the fence.

"We're on to something here," said Kev "you go that way and I'll meet you back here when we go right around the ground."

Ten minutes later they met. "I've got near on fifty dollars," said Kev, "How did you go?"

"Not so good," said Keith, "I got forty-five dollars. But I've got half a dozen cocks!"

*   *   *

WHY do Australian men suffer from premature ejaculation?

Because they can't wait long enough to get down the pub and boast to their mates.

*   *   *

HE couldn't believe it himself, but there he was, shipwrecked with Miss Australia.

There would be no hanky panky of course because he was a married man and she was too famous to have her reputation damaged. So they made a pact.

He said: "You stay this side of the island and I will keep to the other. We will meet in a week to check on provisions and rescue prospects." She agreed.

But of course when they met a week later they were as horny as hell.

"We might never be rescued," he said, "so why don't we do it?"

They virtually tore each others clothes off and went at it hammer and tongs. In fact it was so good they promised each other to meet the next night, same time, same place.

"But could you do me a favour," said the Aussie.

"What's that?"

"Could you dress up as a man?" he said. "I have salvaged some shirts and trousers."

Miss Australia looked at him askancè. "You're not kinky are you?"

"No. Nothing like that."

She reluctantly agreed. And next evening she was walking along the beach looking for all the world like a bloke when he fell into step beside her.

"G'day mate," he said slapping an arm around her shoulder, "You'll never guess who I screwed."

* * *

HE saw himself as a maker and shaker but was having trouble clinching the deal with two executives he had tried to impress over lunch.

He saw Rupert Murdoch pass by on the way to the gents, and quickly excused himself to follow. He lined up beside the tycoon and introduced himself. "My name's Peter. I have been a fan of yours for a long time, Mr Murdoch. I have always admired your style. Could you do me one great favour, little cost to you but forever appreciated by me if you just say hello to me as you pass my table. It would help me clinch the deal,"

"Not at all," said Rupert.

Sure enough, our yuppie had got settled and had resumed his spiel when Murdoch came by and said, "Hi Peter, How's it going?"

"Piss off, Rupe, can't you see I'm talking business!"

* * *

THEY were out in the rainforest of Northern Queensland when Smithy walked into the bush for a leak and a tree snake bit him on the donger.

Smithy let out such a scream his mate Joe was quickly on the scene.

First they panicked, then Smithy realised Joe had a mobile phone and urged him to ring a doctor.

Joe rang an emergency number and finally got advice from the top man in the field. Joe described the snake and was told that it was a taipan, the deadliest snake in Australia.

"The only thing you can do," said the doctor, "is to suck the poison out, otherwise your friend will be dead in an hour."

"What did he say? What did he say?" said Smithy.

"He said you're gonna be dead in an hour."

* * *

THE husband came home from work dejected because a boyhood friend was about to be executed for murder and his mood wasn't improved when his harpy wife began to nag him about being late.

"That's enough," he said finally, "Poor Jack Wright is going to die tonight and all you can do is bitch. I'm going to bed."

Alone and watching television the wife began to regret her conduct when a newsreader announced that the condemned man had been granted a reprieve.

She rushed into the bathroom where her husband was taking a shower. She pulled the curtain aside and shouted: "They are not hanging Wright tonight!"

"Dammit, woman. Isn't there anything about me that satisfies you?"

* * *

AUSTRALIAN technology is at its best in telecommunications. Tom, Dick and Harry were in the pub drinking together when a phone rang. "Excuse me fellows," said Tom drawing his right hand from his pocket to take the call. He put his thumb in his ear and spoke into the end of his little finger.

His yuppie mates were impressed.

Tom explained that a had a silicon chip inserted into his thumb and another in his finger. "Saves carrying those clumsy mobile phones around," he said.

A month later they were at the same bar and the phone rang. Tom said "Excuse me," and took the call merely by talking. When he "hung up" he explained that he had a chip inserted in his ear and another in his tooth, a vast advancement on the old thumb-and-finger phone.

However, about ten minutes later Tom grimaced as if he had cramps in the stomach. He lent forward, legs slightly apart and put both hands on the bar.

"Are you okay?" asked his mates.

"Yes, I'll be alright," he grunted, "It's just a fax coming through."

* * *

CHERYL knew all Aussie men thought a lot of their dicks and even gave them pet names.

"What do you call yours?" she asked the big life-saver on their first date.

"I don't call mine anything," he said. "It always comes without being called."

* * *

OF course Aussie men give their dicks names because they don't want a stranger making 99 per cent of their decisions for them.

* * *

CHERYL said her current boyfriend had no need to call his organ Willie, Peter or Dick. "He calls it Confidence," she confided to her girlfriend.

"Is that because he has no trouble getting it up?"

"No," she replied, "It's because he likes instilling it in me."

* * *

IN Sydney she was Rhonda
She was Patsy out in Perth
In Brisbane she was Brenda
The sweetest girl on earth.
In Wagga she was Wendy
The pick of all the bunch
But down on his expenses
They were petrol, oil and lunch.

* * *

THERE was a young man from Australia
Who painted his arse like a dahlia
The drawing was fine, the colour divine,
But the scent, ah, that was a failure.

AMERICANS

AFTER the Ark had been three weeks at sea one of Noah's sons came to him with a problem.

"What will we do with all the shit piling up in the bull's pen?"

"Push it over the side," said Noah.

They did.

And a few thousand years later it was discovered by Christopher Columbus.

* * *

WHAT is a nigger?

A black man who has just left the room.

* * *

WHAT do you call a nigger with a gun?

Sir!

* * *

WHO killed more Indians than the US Cavalry?

Union Carbide.

* * *

DID you know that former US Vice President Spiro Agnew was an anagram for "Grow a Penis?"

* * *

THERE is a variety of accents in America too.

When one woman complained that "horny men are all alike," her Southern belle friend agreed: "Horny men are all Ah like, too."

* * *

HE watched the blonde at the bar order a martini then swallow it in one gulp. Then she ordered another and did the same. Fascinated by her capacity to drink he watched a third and fourth go down. "Would five make you dizzy?" he asked her.

"The price is alright," she replied, "but the name is Daisy."

*   *   *

AMERICAN lawyers are the most ruthless in the world. One was approached by the Devil who told him that he could fix all his court cases so that he would never lose, double his fees and guarantee he would become a millionaire before he was 30 and live to be a hundred.

"All I want is your soul," said the Devil, "your parents' soul, your wife's soul and your children's soul."

"Okay, it's a deal," said the lawyer, "but what's the catch?"

*   *   *

DIVORCE is big in America so when Mickey Mouse filed for divorce from Minnie the judge knocked him back.

"I've read the psychiatrist's report," said the judge, "and you have no grounds to claim your wife is insane."

"I didn't say my wife was insane," protested Mickey, "I said she was fucking Goofy!"

*   *   *

AROUND the same time Donald Duck split with Daisy and soon found his way to the brothel.

"I'm down for a good time," he said, "and you can stick it on my bill."

AFTER his notorious case O.J. Simpson surprised everybody by saying he was going to get married again.

"Might as well have another stab at it," he said.

* * *

TWO young women who had not met for years were recounting their experiences since their school days.

"I'm delighted to say I married an American lawyer, and an honest man," said one.

"Isn't that bigamy?" asked the other.

* * *

THE notorious case where Lorina Bobbitt cut off her husband's penis gained worldwide publicity which overshadowed a minor detail of the incident.

Actually, she cut it off when they were driving along the highway and she flung it out the window.

With a resounding splatt it hit the windscreen of a car travelling in the opposite direction which contained two nuns.

One said: "Jeez, did you see the cock on that gnat?"

* * *

APPROACHING a woman in a New York singles bar he said: "Hi, chick, what about a date?"

"Forget it," she said, "I never go out with perfect strangers."

"We're both in luck then," he said, "I'm far from perfect."

* * *

THE bank manager was amazed at the new clerk's skill with figures.

"Where did you do your training?"

"Yale," said the teller.

"And how long have you been with us?"

"Yust since Yanuary," he said.

* * *

AN American couple had been successfully smuggling native birds out of Australia to the States for years.

The husband suggested they could double their earnings by smuggling some American wildlife on the return trips.

"For example," he said. "I've got a squirrel here and I am going to hide it by stuffing it down the front of my trousers."

"And this is for you, honey," he said, handing her a skunk. "That will bring big money in Australia. Stuff it down the front of your pants."

She protested: "What about the smell?"

He shrugged his shoulders. "If it dies ... it dies."

* * *

A HUNTER had been tracking a huge bear and finally had him in his sights. He fired a shot and then bounded through the bush to where he expected to find the carcass. To his dismay there was no dead bear. To his horror he was tapped on the shoulder by a very live one.

"I am sick of being shot at by you darned hunters," said the bear. "I'm going to teach you a lesson. So get down on your knees and give me a blow job. Now!"

The terrified hunter did as he was told.

But next day the hunter returned with a bigger gun and spent hours waiting to ambush the bear. Finally he sighted him again, blasted away and dashed forward to where the dead bear should have been. Nothing.

Once more he received the terrifying tap on the shoulder. "You know the ritual," said the bear, "down you go."

The infuriated hunter returned the following day with yet a bigger and more accurate gun. This time he stalked closer and let go with both barrels.

He ran into the clearing only to find the very alive bear waiting for him once more.

"Okay, let's have the truth," said the bear, "you are not in this for the hunting are you?"

* * *

ARRIVING in New York for a political convention the candidate checked in to the swank hotel and was escorted by the porter to his room where he was surprised to find a naked blonde lying on his bed.

In a rage he turned on the porter and roared: "What's the meaning of this? Is this some cheap dirty trick to discredit my campaign, create a scandal which could eliminate my chance for election? I will sue this hotel for every cent it has got ..."

The porter cowered under this verbal barrage and was trying to explain he knew nothing about the young woman when the blonde got off the bed and reached for her clothes.

"Stay there young lady, stay where you are," said the candidate, "This doesn't concern you."

* * *

IN order to get the kids to study the teacher devised a plan. She would ask a questions early each Friday afternoon and those who could answer could go home.

"Can anyone tell me the square root of seven?" she said.

Nobody knew the answer so they remained at their desks.

Next week she said "Can anyone tell me the capital of Pakistan?" Again no answer so no escape.

Little Ronnie came up with a plan for the following Friday. He arrived with some black marbles and to the amusment of the other kids he rolled them with a clatter along the floor.

"Okay," said the teacher, "Who's the comedian with the black balls?"

"Bill Cosbie," shouted Ronnie, "See yer Monday."

* * *

A PUNTER approached Big Bessie in Harlem.

"Ah charges ten dollars," she said.

The punter said it was too much. He even refused it at five dollars.

"Okay. My last price," said Bessie. "Yo can have it fo three dollars, but at this price ah'm losing money."

* * *

DOWN in the Bronx the sign on the whorehouse door came straight to the point. It read: "Out to lunch. Go fuck yourself!"

Some of the customers complained to the managment that it was a bit crude so it was amended.

It now reads: "Out to lunch. Beat it."

* * *

WHEN there are clients more than a few
A cunning old madam called Lou
Will establish a line
By displaying a sign
That informs new arrivals: "Fuck Queue."

* * *

35

IT was peak hour on Saturday night and the sign on the brothel door said: "Last butt not leased."

* * *

ON the riverbank in Alabama he found some soft grass then took his trousers off and hung them on a tree.

"You must be from the north," said the wild southern belle.

"Right on, babe, but how could you tell?"

"A southern boy wouldn't hang up his clothes," she said, "because when we've finished we're gonna be miles from here."

* * *

RASTAS was giving evidence in a rape case but was reprimanded by the judge for openly using the magic word.

He began the second time. "Yes, yer Honour, on the night of the thirteenth I seen them on the beach and they was fucken..."

The judge was aghast at the frank language and rapped the bench with his gavel again.

"I will adjourn the case for five minutes to allow time for this witness to come up with a more palatable description," he announced.

After the break, Rastas resumed his evidence:
"Her pants were down
His arse was bare
His balls were flying in the air
His you-know-what
Was you-know-where
And if that ain't fucking
Then I wasn't there!"

* * *

IN the dock was a 13-year-old boy on a paternity charge.

To emphasise the ridiculousness of the case the defence counsel asked the boy to stand up then unzipped his fly and took out the alleged weapon.

Taking the limp tool in his hand he began: "Ladies and gentlemen of the jury, I ask you to study this undeveloped penis."

Emphasising his point by rattling the flaccid dick around he continued: "Ask yourself, is it possible he could have fathered a baby with this?"

The defendant tapped him on the shoulder and whispered, "If you don't stop waggling it around we're gonna lose this case."

* * *

AMERICAN yuppies take horoscopes seriously and live by the stars. It has got to the stage where people introduce themselves now add their birthsigns.

"Hi, I'm Bill Moloney, Sagittarius."

"Hi, I'm John Spriggs, Cancer."

"Hi, I'm Joe Bloggs, bladder infection."

And explaining why she was incompatible with her boyfriend she said: "I'm a Virgo and he's an arsehole."

While she said she was Libra on the cusp of Scorpio.

He replied that he was Taurus with penis rising.

* * *

BILL Clinton and Hilary were on a holiday cruise and playing deck quoits when they suddenly felt randy and went to their cabin.

It was a case of coitus interruptus.

* * *

BECAUSE the Viking voyage to America took so long Leif Ericson returned home only to find his name crossed off the list of village inhabitants.

He complained to the village chief who admitted he had made a mistake: "I must have taken Leif off my census," he said.

* * *

AS they were about to enter the baseball stadium they noticed a baseball groupie giving her idol a hand-job in the back of his car. A case of the Yankee and the Yanker.

* * *

THE waiter brought the cheque and the diner studied it, then sorted through his money. "By golly," he said, "Darned if I've got exactly that amount, but I'm afraid I haven't got enough for a tip."

"Let me add up that bill again, sir," said the waiter.

* * *

THEY'VE still got backwoodsmen in the States and when the census taker pulled up outside a lonely farmhouse on the prairie he approached an old geezer on the porch.

"What are ya selling, sonny?" asked the old man.

"I'm not selling anything. We are trying to find out how many people live in America."

"Well you've wasted your time coming out here," said the old man, "I haven't got the faintest idea."

* * *

JEROME Hearst Jnr. decided to quit the rat race. He sold up his business interests and picking a point on the map which looked isolated he went out into the backwoods and settled himself into a log cabin and a new life.

He was there a full week without seeing a soul and had to admit to himself that when a battered old car stopped by he was glad to see another person.

"I'm Jake," grinned the wild-looking backwoodsman. "I heard a stranger has moved in and I'm the welcoming committee in these here hills," he said.

Jerome was pleased.

"What about coming over to my place on Saturday night," said Jake. "We could have a welcoming party. We're a bit rough up here so there's likely to be plenty of drinking, a few fights, but plenty of sex, too."

Jerome was interested and offered to provide the grog. "How much will I bring. How many are coming?" he asked.

"Oh, just you and me," smiled Jake.

* * *

THE old hillbilly wanted to know why his son had suddenly cancelled his wedding when so much preparation for a wing-ding party had taken place.

"Well, Pa," drawled the son, "I got to feeling in Betsy-Lou's pants and I found out she's a virgin. That's why I decided not to marry her."

"Quite right, son," said the old man, "if she ain't good enough fer her kinfolks, then she ain't good enough for ours neither."

* * *

IN Yellowstone Park a jack rabbit was sitting on the park's ablution log. In American jargon he was "taking a crap," when an enormous Grizzly Bear squatted on the same log for the same purpose.

"Mornin'," grunted the bear to the terrified rabbit.

The pair continued their business for a few minutes until the bear said: "Say, does shit stick to your fur?"

"Nope," said the rabbit, "Never has."

With that the bear grabbed the rabbit and wiped his arse with him.

* * *

TO early Americans thrift was a virtue.

Many a squaw was a hit with the braves because she was tight with a buck.

* * *

A COLLEGE nymphomaniac in America is called a Go-go-go-go Girl!

* * *

DID you hear about the Harvard co-ed who finally got fed up with her boyfriend's shy and fumbling advances?

She finally put him in her place.

* * *

"DO you smoke after sex?" asked the burly grid-iron star.

"Don't know. I've never looked," she said.

* * *

THE pretty debutante was being driven back to college when the cab broke down. The driver soon had his head under the bonnet tampering with the engine.

"Do you want a screwdriver?" she said.

"Why not. It will help pass the time until road service arrives," he said.

* * *

A KINKY passenger on a Greyhound bus opened his coat and exposed himself to the stewardess.

"I'm sorry sir," she said, "you need to show me your ticket, not your stub."

* * *

THE pompous English colonel arrived in New York and hailed a cab. "Take me to Christ's Church," he said.

About ten minutes later the cab stopped outside St Patrick's Cathedral.

"That's not Christ's Church," protested the colonel.

"If He's in town He's in that one," said O'Flaherty.

* * *

IN the deep south Rastas was rambling along the road and almost stumbled over a $20 note. His sore feet prompted him to say: "Feet. At last I can buy you a comfy pair of shoes."

A little further, with the hot sun on his forehead he said. "And Head, we'll get a nice shady hat."

A bit further and the pangs of hunger prompted another promise. "Okay belly, "we'll get ourselves some tucker."

Then he looked down and noticed he had an erection.

"Okay Big Dick. Who told you we come into money?"

* * *

WITH his ten-gallon hat and his high heeled boots the big man leaning on the bar was obviously a Texan. And he soon had a woman by his side.

"Tell me," she said. "Is it true that everything is big in Texas?"

"Yes, Ma'am"

One thing led to another and they were soon back at her her apartment where he took off his big Texas hat, and his big Texas boots. He took off his Big Texas pants to reveal that indeed, everything was big in Texas.

They were having their post-bonk cigarette when he said: "By the way, Ma'am. What part of Texas do you come from?"

* * *

'THE truckie, the hitch-hiker and the monkey' is the intriguing title for this little yarn.

Ever since the hitch-hiker had climbed aboard he noticed the lack of conversation and that the truckie was the silent type. It eventually prompted him to ask the truckie if he had a radio.

"Nup," was the stern reply.

After another long silence the hiker said: "Well what do you do to help the time pass?"

There was yet another pause before the truckie finally answered: "Well I've got my little mate," and with that he snapped his fingers and a monkey jumped from behind the cabin and landed on the driver's lap.

It sat there for ten minutes or so until the hiker said: "Well you can't talk to a monkey. What's the use of that."

"Watch this," said the truckie. He gave the monkey a belt on the head and it opened the truckie's fly and gave him a head job.

Yet another poignant silence and the relieved driver said: "What do you think of that?"

"Not bad. I'm impressed," said the hiker.

"Would you like to try one yourself?" asked the truckie.

"Well I would, if you don't mind, provided you don't hit me on the head as hard as you hit the monkey."

* * *

THE truckie couldn't believe his eyes. There in the middle of the desert was a flashing neon sign: Mama's Desert Diner. He had crossed this desolate stretch many times and never seen it before.

"Yes, we're new here," said Mama. "What will ya have luv?"

"Two hamburgers and a hot dog," he ordered.

He saw Mama go the fridge, reach for two rissoles and whack them up under her armpits.

"What for?" roared the truckie.

"Everything is deep frozen out here luv," she explained, "that's the only way I can thaw them out."

"Well okay," said the reluctant diner, "but cancel the hot dog."

*   *   *

YOU can always tell when a woman in the Dallas jet-set loses her husband.

She's the one with the black tennis skirt.

ARABS

EGYPTIAN girls who forget to take the pill are called Mummies.

* * *

WHAT do Arabs do on Saturday nights?
  Sit beneath palm trees and eat their dates.

* * *

WHAT is gross stupidity?
  144 Iranians.

* * *

WHAT do you call an Iranian who practises birth control?
  A humanitarian.

* * *

SAID the Arab to the anthropologist:
  "A young boy for pleasure, a woman for sons, but for a good wife give me a camel every time."

* * *

A WHIMSICAL Arab from Aden
  His masculine member well laden
  Cried : "Nuptial joy
  When shared with a boy
  Is better than melon or maiden."

* * *

THE sexual urge of a camel
  Is stronger than anyone thinks
  He's lived for years on the desert
  And tried to seduce the Sphinx.

But the Sphinx's centre of pleasure
Lies buried deep in the Nile
Which accounts for the hump on the camel
And the Sphinx's inscrutable smile.

*　　*　　*

A QUEER Arab is one who speaks with tongue in sheik.

*　　*　　*

MOYSHE Isaacson was walking down a street in Belfast when he suddenly felt a pistol in his back.

"Catholic or Protestant?" demanded the voice behind him.

"Jewish," replied Moyshe.

"Well then. I am surely the luckiest Arab in the whole of Ireland."

*　　*　　*

IN Cairo the sailor was delighted to find himself a girl at the pub who appeared to be no drain on the pocket.

When he asked could he get her a glass of wine she said no, she didn't drink.

When he asked if she would like a cigarette she said no, she didn't smoke.

"What about a packet of crisps?"

"No, I'm not hungry," she said.

"A game of pool?"

"No, I don't play," she said.

"Then can I take you home?" said the sailor, who was delighted when she said yes.

When they arrived at her house she opened the front door, and there, lying in the hallway was a dead camel.

"Well," said the young woman, "I didn't say I was tidy, did I?"

45

BACK in Egyptian times when newspapers were carved on rock, two scribes were chiselling out news of the lusty young Pharaoh who had ascended to the throne. One tapped the other on the shoulder, "How do you spell macho, one testicle or two?"

* * *

A TOURIST in a Cairo market had been absorbed in watching a man grooming his camel with such care and devotion. In fact he had dallied too long and thought he might miss the rest of the party.

"Excuse me," he asked the camel man, "Can you tell me the time?"

The Arab knelt on one knee and gently lifted the camel's testicles. "Three minutes to four," he announced.

The tourist was amazed. He could hardly contain himself as he rushed off to the rest of the tourist party.

"Hold the bus a moment," he said. "You've got to come and see this fellow tell the time by holding a pair of camel's balls."

His incredulous friends followed him through the market until they came to the camel man.

"What's the time?" asked the tourist again.

The Arab knelt on one knee. Gently lifting the testicles and announced "Five past four."

Everyone was suitably amazed as they checked their watches.

"I'll give you ten dollars if you will teach me your secret," said the tourist.

The Arab pocketed the money and beckoned the tourist to kneel down beside him. He took the camel's balls gently in his hand and lifted them a little.

"Do you see the clock on top of the railway station over there?" he said.

* * *

AFTER micro-surgery, and with 303 stitches around his wrist Ali Ben Ali was recovering in hospital and was visited by a friend.

"I see you won your appeal, Ali," said the visitor.

* * *

YOU can't get a drink in Saudi Arabia, but you can get stoned anytime.

* * *

ELI Mustafa was in the Arab bazaar one day when he felt terrible stomach cramps. He couldn't control the thunderous fart which followed. Stall holders and customers alike were startled.

It was so embarrassing for Eli that he ran home, packed his bags on his trusty camel and wandered the Middle East for the rest of his business life.

At last, an old and weary man, he yearned to return to the town of his boyhood. He reasoned that most of those who witnessed his most shameful moment would be dead by now. He had grown a long white beard and he was so aged he was sure nobody would recognise him. His heart longed for the old familiar streets of his boyhood.

Once in town he headed for the bazaar and found that the power had been connected and there were bright lights.

He turned to a stallholder and asked when were such improvements carried out.

"Oh that," said the man, "That was done 15 years and five months to the day Eli Mustafa farted in the bazaar."

47

PILES are an occupational hazard for camel drivers and it was Bedouin folklore to treat the complaint by shoving a handful of cold tea leaves up where the sun doesn't shine.

Abdul did this ritual night and morning, but to no avail. So when the camel train eventually reached Cairo he took the opportunity to see an English doctor.

Dropping his dacks he bent over while the doctor spread his cheeks apart and began to mutter to himself: "Hmm, yes, hmmm."

"Something wrong?" asked Abdul.

"No, quite the contrary," said the doc, "You are going to take a long trip...you will meet a tall, dark romantic stranger ..."

CHINESE

CRITICAL about the lack of democracy in China the western reporter asked the Chinese General: "Then tell me, when did you have your last election?"

"Just before blekfast this morning," he replied.

* * *

CHARLIE ran a takeaway in the red light district. Indeed the girls would often eat there and relate stories about their trade and some of the tricks they got up to.

It got him so horny one night he closed the shop and went home early.

He tapped his wife on the bum and said: "What about a little 69?"

"Why the hell would I want chicken and almonds at this time of night?" she said.

* * *

ANGRY customer in a Chinese restaurant shouts to the manager:

"This chicken is bloody rubbery," to which the manager smilingly replies, "Thank you plerry much."

* * *

WHAT do you call a Shanghai woman who wins ten million dollars?

A Chinese fortunate cookie.

* * *

ACUPUNCTURE fees in China are so cheap it is called pin money.

* * *

WHEN visiting the local hospital Fred felt sorry for a Chinese patient who appeared to have no visitors. When he approached the bed in a friendly manner the Chinese mumbled something, went red in the face and then grasped his throat.

Fred asked if he could help, maybe get a doctor.

The Chinese frantically reached for pen and paper and scribbled some Chinese characters, then gave a last gasp and died.

A week later after ordering his usual Chinese takaway he produced the note for Charlie the Chow to interpret.

Charlie squinted at it and said: "Get off. You are standing on my fuk'n oxygen supply."

*　*　*

RON Sup was a Chinese funeral director.

On the front of his parlour was his business sign: "People Buried. R Sup".

*　*　*

THE estate agent said it was not the right location for a Chinese restaurant. He said, "They'd be flogging a dead horse."

*　*　*

SHE rushed into the police station. "I've just been sexually molested by a Chinese laundryman."

"Hang on," said the sergeant, "How did you know it was a Chinese laundryman?"

"Because he did the whole thing by hand."

*　*　*

THE car dealer was trying to flog a heap of junk parked outside the pub to a Chinese student.

"It's a reliable car," said Harry. "It is yours for five

hundred dollars, but if you have the cash I will take off 20%."

The student was too shrewd to admit he didn't understand the discount and said he would think it over.

When he got the chance he asked the barmaid quietly, "If I give you five hundred dollars, how much you take off?"

"Everything except my earrings, honey. No worries."

*   *   *

THERE is a Chinese-Jewish restaurant in our neighbourhood. It's called Ghengis Cohen.

*   *   *

MISTER Wong rushed his wife to the hospital where Mrs Wong gave birth to a bouncing baby boy. All white.

"It must have been the milkman," said Mr Wong sadly, "Two wongs don't make a white."

The doctor consoled him: "Occidents do happen," he said.

*   *   *

SAID the Chinese maid when she received her marriage licence: "It won't be wrong now."

*   *   *

THE Chinese cook had been teased unmercifully by the shearers who had put snakes in his bed and mice in his boots. Finally they relented and said enough was enough and assured him they would torment him no more.

"No more spiders under pillo?"

"No," they assured him.

"No more flighten me?"

"No, no more tricks," they said.

"Glood, then I stop pissee in the soup."

*   *   *

AFTER a week on board the new bosun asked "What do you do for sex on this ship?"

He was told "On Friday nights we fuck the Chinese cook for $23."

"Why does it cost so much?"

"Well the captain doesn't like it, so we slip him $10, the padre doesn't approve so we slip him $5 and the cook doesn't like it so we slip $2 each for four blokes to hold him down."

*   *   *

CHINESE Proverb: Man who goes to bed with sex problem on mind wakes up with solution in hand.

*   *   *

THE phone rang at the Chinese Laundry.

"Can I speak to Half-in?"

"No. Half-in's out."

"Is that Half-out?"

"No. Half-out's not in."

"Who's that?"

"I'm Half-up, the secretary."

"Sorry, I'll call back when you're not busy."

*   *   *

THE boss said the expedition was to set forth at dawn next morning. The Italian was to drive the truck, the German was to bring the tent and the Chinaman was put in charge of supplies.

Next morning the Italian and the German were punctual but there was no sign of the Chinaman. After waiting an hour the boss ordered the expedition to start. The truck had gone only a few hundred metres when the Chinaman jumped out from behind a tree yelling: "Surplise! Surplise!"

*   *   *

LEE Pung used to eat regularly at a Greek restaurant and always ordered fried rice as a side dish. Each night Con the Greek used to fall about laughing when Lee would order his "flied lice."

Sometimes Con would have two or three friends gather around to hear Lee say "flied lice."

Lee got sick and tired of the taunting and took a month off for an intensified course in Oxford English.

When he returned he ordered, loud and clear, "and a large serve of fried rice."

"What did you say?" said a very surprised Con.

"I said fried rice, you fluckin' Gleek."

*   *   *

ON business in Hong Kong he had been playing around too much and one day noticed his dick had turned yellow.

He went to an expatriate doctor who quickly diagnosed the trouble as Hong Kong Dong and told him that his dick would have to be amputated.

Shocked he sought a second opinion, only to receive the same advice on amputation.

As a last resort he went to a Chinese doctor who confirmed that the complaint was Hong Kong Dong, but there was no need for amputation.

"Oh, I'm so relieved," said the businessman.

"Yes, no need to cut off dick," said the Chinese medic, "in few days it fall off by itself."

*   *   *

CHARLIE Wong picked up a live duck at the market then found he had time to spare before going back to the restaurant so he decided to take in a movie.

The problem of the duck was easily solved. He stuck it down the front of his baggy trousers.

Unfortunately, half way through the movie the duck became fidgety through lack of air so Charlie opened his fly a little and let the duck stick its head out.

The woman seated next to him nudged her husband and whispered: "The bloke next to me has his thing sticking out."

Her husband, absorbed in the film, said not to worry about it.

"Don't worry about it?" she said, "The bloody thing is eating my popcorn."

DUTCH

THE brave Dutch lad stuck his finger in the dyke.
And she punched the bejeezus out of him.

* * *

AS a swimming instructor Hans would often feature a benign smile when his pupils would ask: "Will I really sink if you take your finger out?"

* * *

TWO Dutch beauties were having their picture taken and the photographer was taking some time getting the right angle.

"Vy ees he taking so long?" asked Inga.

"He's got to focus."

"No. You tell him picture first and maybe fokus after."

* * *

A YOUNG Dutch woman was thinking of buying a house. The estate agent was showing her the property and after they inspected the ground floor he said: "Come upstairs and I will show you the bedroom and den."

She looked at him sideways. "And den what?" she said.

* * *

A DUTCHMAN cleaning out his attic discovered an old violin and an oil painting. Thinking they might be valuable he took them to an art dealer.

"Well, that's a Stradivarius," mused the dealer, "and this here is a Rembrandt."

"Then, are they valuable?" he asked hopefully.

"Not really," said the dealer. "Stradivarius was a hopeless painter, and look at Rembrand's violin. You'd never get a tune out of it."

* * *

HANS came home late a little under the weather and carrying a duck under his arm and his wife Helga wanted an explanation for both.

"Well, it began as a competition at the pub," said Hans.

"What kind of a competition?"

"A manliness competition, you know," said Hans with a little embarrassment.

Helga got the awful message. "Oh Hans. You mean you exposed our love toy to the public?"

"Only enough to win the duck, Helga," he said.

* * *

HELGA was having a rare visit to the doctor.

"How often do you have a check up?" he asked.

"Never," said Helga. "A German and a few Frenchmen but never a Czech."

* * *

WE know a Dutch wanker who always wore clogs so that he could hear himself coming.

ENGLISH

YOU can tell a pommie, but you can't tell him much.

* * *

DID you know the population of London is denser than Ireland and Wales put together?

* * *

WHEN does a pommie become a Briton?
When he marries your daughter.

* * *

SIR FRANCIS Drake circumcised the world and did it with a hundred-foot clipper.

* * *

BRITONS have an infinite capacity for churning themselves up into a terrific calmness.

* * *

THERE is a certain style about the English as typified by this incident:

Winston Churchill sat in the first-class train compartment. Opposite sat an elderly gentleman with monocle and school tie reading The Times.

An hour passed in silence before the old gentleman, with a quizical eye on Winston eventually spoke.

"Name Churchill?" he enquired.

"Yes," replied the statesman.

"Winston?"

Churchill nodded.

Another long silence ensued as the gentleman, with

furrowed brow, continued to stare over the top of his paper.

Finally, he said: "Got it. Harrow, 88?"

"Yes," said Winston.

"Ay yes," said the gent, "Now I can place you."

*   *   *

THE colonel was sitting quietly in his club when Fonsonby approached. "Sorry to hear, old boy, that you buried your wife yesterday."

"Had to," replied the colonel, "Dead you know."

*   *   *

AN Englishman and his wife finally achieved sexual compatibility for the first time.

They both had a headache.

*   *   *

"ALGERNON, old boy, I think my wife had an orgasm last night."

"What makes you think that?"

"She dropped her nail file!"

*   *   *

THE Lord of the Manor asserts that a wife made-to-order can't hold a candle to one ready maid.

*   *   *

"WHY are you taking so long tonight?" asked her Ladyship.

"I'm trying, desperately dahling," he said, "but I just can't think of anyone."

*   *   *

"I'M afraid I can't make the lodge meeting tomorrow night, Smithers. I promised to take Thingummy out for our silver anniversary."

*   *   *

THE colonel was a rare drinker, but at the annual regimental dinner he ate too much food, drank too much wine and got the fright of his life when he was challenged to a duel.

His colleagues were quickly to the rescue and sent him home in a cab.

Next morning he had to explain to his batman why there was such a mess on his jacket. "Some bounder bumped into me and was sick all over my tunic. I'll give him a month's detention when I find him," he said.

The batman gathered up the clothes. "I'd make it two months, sir. The bastard has shit in your trousers, too,"

*   *   *

THE old timers were lamenting that the club had gone to the pack. "Noisy lot, all on the make," said one. "All corduroy trousers, thin moustaches and crew-cut hair.

And the women are just as bad."

*   *   *

"I SAY, old chap, who is Fonsonby talking to?"

"He is talking to himself."

"Then why is he shouting?"

"He's deaf!"

*   *   *

AS Paddy Murphy says: "Why do Englishmen wear bowler hats?"

"To protect their heads from woodpeckers."

*   *   *

WHY do British bulldogs have flat faces?

From chasing parked cars.

*   *   *

HOW do you save a pommie from drowning?
Shoot the bastard before he hits the water.

* * *

HOW do you get a pommie out of the bath?
Put water in it.

* * *

THE tombstone read: "Here lies John Brown, an Englishman and a gentleman."

"Never," said Paddy, "No gent would ever consent to be buried with an Englishman."

* * *

ONE Englishman said to the other: "I say, old chap, have you ever made love to a queer?"

"Certainly not!" said his chum, "but I once made love to a bloke who has."

* * *

CONNOISSEURS of coition aver
That the best British girls never stir
This condition in Persia
Is known as inertia
And is hardly the response you prefer.

* * *

LEGEND has is that there was once an English nymphomaniac who had to have it every six months.

* * *

LADY Muck finally confronted the Major and said it was about time their son Cecil was told about the birds and bees.

At the appropriate time that evening the Major did so.

"See here, Cecil," he said. "You remember that time I caught you rooting the maid? Well your mother wants you to know that the birds and bees do it too."

LADY Fonsonby received a letter from her son in boarding school which finished with the sentence, "last night I had my first naughty."

She was aghast and quickly wrote back berating him and instructing him not to have another one.

Eventually she got a reply. "No mother, I haven't had one since. The first one hurt too much."

* * *

HE was always writing home for more money. He needed money for football gear, for tennis, for excursions and for an extravagant social life.

Finally he wrote to say he had a part in the college's Gilbert & Sullivan show and he needed money for the costume. Father was annoyed, but mother sent the money.

A month later he wrote home to say thanks for the costume. "Everybody agreed I looked a proper count," he said.

"All that money," said the father "and he still can't spell."

* * *

THE annual university boat race resulted in an exciting finish, but there was a dramatic moment when a blonde rushed through the crowd and kissed the cox of the winning crew.

* * *

SIR Reginald Snodgrass was the epitome of British etiquette, so when he came home unexpectedly and found his young wife entertaining the young duke on the floor it was just too much.

"Sarah," he roared, "arch your back this instant and lift that gentleman's balls off the cold floor."

* * *

TWO Aussie tourists were motoring in England along one of those tight country lanes when the squire, in his Rolls, approached from the opposite direction.

As the cars drew close the squire wound down the window, looked the Aussies in the eye and shouted, "Pigs!"

Our lads were taken aback and were still getting over the shock when, right around the next bend, they ran into a herd of pigs.

* * *

THE English football team was examined by a medical panel and pronouced fit for FA.

* * *

"HAVE you got anything to say for yourself?" said the judge sternly after hearing the case.

"Fuck all," muttered the defendant.

"What did he say?" asked the judge learning forward to the clerk.

The clerk stood up, turned, and whispered quietly to the judge: "He said 'fuck all' your worship."

"That's funny," said the judge, "I'm sure I saw his lips move."

* * *

AND we mustn't forget the Royals.

Princess Di was given the option early in the piece:

"Which would you prefer, my dear, a crowned head or a royal shafting?"

* * *

WHERE did Prince Charles spend his honeymoon?
Indiana.

* * *

THE Prince of Wales looked resplendent in his naval uniform while delivering a stirring speech at the opening of the Oodnadatta Flower Show. But one astute reporter had noted he was wearing a fur hat with a tail hanging down his back.

Waiting for the right moment the journo siddled up to him and said: "Er, excuse me Yer Highness. The uniform looks great, but what's with the fur hat?"

"Oh that!" said the Prince. "I was tawking to Mommy last night. When I told her I was going to Oodnadatta she said 'wear the fok's 'at'!"

* * *

ONE day the Queen and the Princess Di were still on speaking terms and were driving through the Royal Estate in the regal landrover, a gang of IRA bandits jumped out from behind the trees.

"It's just yer jewels we want. Hand 'em over," said the gang leader.

It was a quick and audacious robbery and the gang soon made off with their loot.

"What a terrible loss," said the Queen. "How will we explain it?"

"Well, I saved all my jewels," said the princess, "I stuffed them up my you-know-what."

"Oh I wish I could think as quick," said the Queen, "I could have saved the crown."

* * *

THE king was wandering around the palace gardens when he saw the gardener's wife with seven kids.

"Are these all yours?" he asked.

"Yes, Your Majesty, and we have another seven at home."

"Good God, your husband deserves a knighthood,"

"He's got one sir, but he never uses it," she replied.

* * *

QUEEN Victoria lay in bed next to Prince Albert exhausted and delighted on their first night of love.

"Oh, Albert. That was wonderful," she said, "is there a name for it?"

"Yes," he murmured, "it is called intercourse."

She sighed: "Well it is far too good for the common people. Let's prohibit it."

* * *

HARRY and Alfie were two Cockney lads and while on a binge in a Soho pub Alfie could not stop looking at a matronly woman in the corner.

"It's the Queen," he said, squinting through the smoke.

"Getaway," said Harry.

But Alfie continued to squint and stare. "Ten pound says she's the Queen," he said.

"You're on, but how are we going to find out."

"I'll go over and ask her, straight up," said Alfie.

He gulped another pint and set off on his mission.

"I beg you pardon, Your Majesty, are you indeed the Queen?"

"Piss off you little runt," growled the woman, "before I kick your arse so hard you'll be wearing your ring for a collar."

Alf returned to the bar. "Well?" said Harry.

"Actually," said Alf, "she didn't say she was, and she didn't say she wasn't."

* * *

OF the Edwards tis thought that the First,

Although bad, was by no means the worst

The Third one is reckoned
Much worse than the Second
And the Third much worse than the First.

*   *   *

BEFORE riding off to the crusades King Arthur left his queen well strapped in her chastity belt, locked it and handed the key to the only knight he could trust, Sir Lancelot.

The King had just made camp after the first day's ride when his aid spotted a cloud of dust and a galloping horseman in the distance.

It was Sir Lancelot shouting "Wrong key, wrong key!"

*   *   *

KING Arthur prepared for his second crusade a year later and once again locked the chastity belt on his queen. This time, a little suspicious of Sir Lancelot, he not only took the key with him but devised a little scheme known only to himself. A little guillotine blade triggered by a spring would chop off anything that passed through the opening.

When King Arthur returned he summoned the knights of the Round Table to drop their drawers. All had suffered a terrible fate. Not a dick in sight, except Sir Lancelot's.

"My faith in you is restored," said the king, "Name any request and its yours."

The good knight didn't respond.

"Come, speak up Sir Lancelot, have you lost your tongue?"

*   *   *

THERE was a young stud called Sir Lancelot
Women would glance him askance a lot.

For whenever he'd pass
A presentable arse
The front of his pants would advance a lot.

*   *   *

SIR Lancelot led his war weary troop back in to Camelot and reported to King Arthur: "I have raped and pillaged all the Saxons to the south."

"You idiot," exclaimed the king, "I told you to rape and pillage the Saxons in the north. I don't have any enemies in the south."

"You do now," said Sir Lancelot.

*   *   *

THE king fell madly in love with the court jester. More often than not the monarch could be found at his wits end.

*   *   *

A KNIGHT of the realm asked the royal alchemist if he had discovered something to allieviate the knight's constant erection.

"No, M'Lord," said the alchemist, "But I mentioned it to the king and he has a new post for you."

"What's that?"

"You have been named His Majesty's sundial."

*   *   *

NAPOLEON asked Lord Nelson why the British Navy was always successful at sea.

"That's easy," replied Nelson, "it's because we pray before battle."

"But so do we," complained Napoleon.

"No doubt you do," said Nelson, "but we pray in English."

*   *   *

NAPOLEON was making his regular call on Josephine and asked her why a pair of long rubber boots were on her front porch.

"They are not rubber boots, silly," she said. "They're Wellington's."

*   *   *

FONSONBY from the War Office finally got invited to the diplomatic corps dinner where he intended to make some valuable contacts. However the pre-dinner cocktails had the effect of getting him in a randy mood and he made sure he sat next to the long-legged blonde.

When his hand wandered under the table and came to rest on her knee he was encouraged by the lack of resistence. He moved a little further up her thigh. Again no rejection. He moved further, to her stocking tops.

His heart quickened as he saw her write a note and pass it to him.

It read: "Don't give the show away when you reach my balls. Smithers from MI5."

*   *   *

WHEN Lord Ponsonby announced that he was to get married Jeeves was alarmed about his future at the manor. And although the squire assured him that his position was safe, Jeeves still worried while they were away on their honeymoon.

"Jeeves, how many times do I have to tell you it's business as usual," said the squire on his return.

Sure enough, next morning, the squire was up at dawn for his breakfast, promptly at 6.30 his horse was ready, and at seven Jeeves went into the bedroom, slapped the bride on the bum and said: "Okay, back to the village my lass!"

* * *

LORD Ponsonby awoke one morning with a roaring morning glory. "Jeeves," he called.

When the butler spotted the rampant member he said. "Ah, shall I summon her ladyship?"

"No," said his lordship, "Bring me my baggy trousers and we'll try to smuggle this one down to the village!"

* * *

THE lady of the manor was becoming increasingly alarmed at Jeeves' practice of walking in to her bedroom without knocking. Finally she took him to task.

"It could be very embarrassing if I was in a state of undress," she admonished.

"No need to worry about that, m'lady," said Jeeves. "I always take a peek through the keyhole first!"

* * *

ON their wedding night Algernon dropped his trousers and climbed in beside her.

"Oh, what a nice pee-wee," she said.

"My dear," he said with the authority of a new husband. "The first thing you must learn dahling, is that it isn't called a pee-wee. It's, it's called ... a cock."

"Oh, no," she said. "A cock is long, black and fat. That's a pee-wee."

* * *

THE pompous English colonel settled into his New York hotel room and was soon jiggling the telephone receiver.

"I say operator," he said in his cultured Etonian

voice, "I jolly well want to speak with Brigadier Barrington. He's a guest in this establishment."

"I can't understand you sir," said the operator, "I guess you are English?"

"My dear madam," said the colonel, "If I was any more English I couldn't talk at all."

* * *

A TOURIST asked an Englishman at a bus stop if he knew the way to Albert Hall.

"Yes, I do," replied the Englishman, and calmly boarded the bus.

* * *

"WITH all due respect, my dear chap, I really think our English custom on the telephone is far more practical than merely saying Hello," said the colonel.

"Why, what's the procedure in England," asked the American.

"Why, we simply say 'Are you there'? And of course, if there is nobody there then there is no point in going on with the conversation."

* * *

"THE trouble with you British," ranted the American, "is that your nation has been too isolated. There should be more mingling. In my blood there is Greek, Italian, Russian and Portugese."

"My word," said the Englishman, "that was very sporting of your mother."

* * *

THE Lady of the Manor called Jeeves into her bedroom. "Jeeves, please unzip my dress."

With a great deal of embarrassment he did so.

"Now Jeeves," she said. "Take off my stockings."

Jeeves was now in a sweat.

"Now take off my underwear ... and if I ever catch you wearing them again you will be instantly dismissed."

*   *   *

A WELSHMAN and a pom were arguing politics in the pub.

The left-wing pommie said: "I think Margaret Thatcher has a face like a sheep's arse."

The Welshman swung his fist and punched him on the nose.

"I didn't know you were a conservative?" said the wounded pom.

"I'm not," said the Taffy, "I'm a shepherd."

*   *   *

AN old woodsman was giving a lecture on the technical details of shoring up tunnels and trenches to a bunch of army officers and was being continually interrupted by a la-di-dah lieutenant who corrected "helm" tree as elm, "hash" as ash, etc.

When the carpenter said, "and now we have some hoak," the officer broke in, "you mean oak of course."

"O,coars. Aye, the very finest timber for pounding piles into piers, and for the benefit of our young friend 'ere I don't mean pushing 'emmeroids hup harses or hanuses of the haristocracy!"

*   *   *

HE said he came from a big family where all the names began with haitch.

"There's 'Arold, 'Orace, 'Erbert, 'Enry, 'Ubert, 'Ugh, 'Etty and 'Ariet," he said, "all except the baby, Halice!"

*   *   *

LORD Ponsonby called his butler to ride down to the village to fetch a bottle of whisky, a box of cigars and a few ounces of snuff. "That free-loading bishop will be calling in this afternoon."

Jeeves mounted his trusty bicycle and was off on his errand. It was not until returning home and after peddling up the long hill to the manor gates that he realised he had forgotten the snuff.

What to do? It was too hot and too far to ride back down to the village. By chance the problem was solved, right there on the nature strip was a barker's nest with three of those white eggs dogs leave in neat little clumps. When dried in the sun and ground back to powder it looks for all the world like snuff.

Did he dare take the chance?

Jeeves quickly bent down, snatched up three portions and put them in his pocket.

"Did you get the whisky, Jeeves?"

"Yes, M'lord."

"And the cigars, and the snuff?"

"Yes M'lord," said Jeeves as he prepared to leave the room.

"I say, Jeeves," said Lord Ponsonby sniffing the air. "You didn't by any chance stand in something down in the village?"

"No M'lord."

The bishop arrived soon after and headed for the Scotch. "You don't mind if I have a drink, Ponsonby old boy?"

"Not at all, Bishop, go for your life," but Ponsonby was preoccupied with the pervading odour.

"I say bishop, can you smell dog's doings in here?"

"Can't say as I can dear boy," said the bishop. "I happen to have a heavy head cold."

"In that case, take a pinch of snuff," said Ponsonby.

The bishop responded by taking two pinches and sniffing it up both nostrils.

"My Gawd," he said. "You always get the best snuff. Cleared my head completely. I can sure smell that dog's stuff now!"

* * *

AN UPPER-class pom went into a butcher shop in Dublin and with a haughty accent said: "I'd like a sheep's head, my man. And make sure it is an English sheep."

So the butcher shouted to his apprentice: "One sheep's head, O'Reilly, and take the brains out."

* * *

THERE are two races which have dominated England since the early invasion of the Romans.

They are the Grand National and the Derby.

* * *

THE lady of the manor decided to dismiss the parlour maid and dressed her down with some sarcastic remarks about her unsatisfactory service as a cook and general housekeeper.

But the fiery parlour maid took the opportunity for a parting shot. "Your husband happens to think I am a better cook and a better housekeeper than you are," she retorted. "And what's more I am a damn sight better in bed than you are."

"Oh, and my husband told you that too?"

"No, Jeeves told me that!"

* * *

LADY Montague-Smythe took more than the usual care of her staff. So when her butler was hurt in an accident she was quick to attend the hospital.

"Sorry," said the nurse, "No visitors except family. Are you his wife?"

"Indeed not," said her ladyship, "I'm his mistress."

* * *

EVERY time her ladyship swoons
Her boobs would pop out like balloons
With nary a stare
Jeeves would always be there
To lift them back in with warm spoons.

* * *

WHY is British beer like making love in a canoe?
They are both fucking close to water.

* * *

DOCTOR Watson was amazed to be told by Sherlock Holmes that the three women eating bananas in the park were a spinster, a hooker and a newly-wed.

"Amazing," said Watson, "But how can you tell?"

"Elementary, my dear Watson," replied Holmes, "You see how the spinster breaks the banana into little pieces before delicately popping them into her mouth, while the prostitute, the one in the middle, holds the banana in both hands."

"Yes, Holmes, but how can you tell the third is a bride?"

"See how she holds the banana in one hand and thumps herself on the back of the head with the other?" explained the detective.

* * *

SHERLOCK Holmes was not all he was made out to be.

The great detective had a sinister trait to his character as revealed when Dr Watson came around to 221b Baker Street one afternoon and was told by the housekeeper that a schoolgirl was visiting his famous friend.

Watson heard muffled sounds coming from the study and fearing that Holmes was in some kind of danger he broke open the door only to find his friend and the girl engaged in a rather shocking form of play.

"Good gracious, Holmes," said the good doctor, "What kind of a schoolgirl is this?"

"Elementary, my dear Watson, Elementary."

* * *

AT one of the recent palace tea parties a young man was presented to the Queen.

"What do you do for a living?" she enquired.

"I am a photographer, Ma'am," he replied.

"Isn't that remarkable," said the Queen, "My brother-in-law is a photographer."

"Indeed it is remarkable," said the photographer, "My brother-in-law is a queen."

* * *

FORMER big game hunters Sir Algernon Fonsonby and Lord Fotheringham were having lunch at the club.

"I say old man," said Sir Algernon, "I do believe the word is spelled w-o-o-m-b."

"No, no, Algie old bean. It is spelt w-o-m-m-b."

"Begging your pardon gentlemen," said the waiter who happened to overhear, "I believe the word is spelled w-o-m-b."

"Well, old chap," said Sir Algernon, "It is quite clear this chappie has never been to Africa and heard an elephant fart under water."

* * *

A COUPLE of pommies were in a train compartment when a Catholic priest hobbled in on crutches.

"Been in the wars, eh' Father?" said one as a matter of small talk.

"Yes," replied the priest, "I'm afraid I slipped while getting into the bath."

There was silence until the priest finally got out at his station, and when he was gone one pommie said: "What's a bath?"

"I dunno," said the other, "I'm not a Catholic."

* * *

WHEN Britain was an empire it was ruled by an emperor.

When it was a kingdom it was ruled by a king.

When it became a country it was ruled by Maggie Thatcher.

FRENCH

ON the question why Frenchmen liked girls' legs, 19% said they liked fat legs, 27% said they liked slender legs and the rest said they liked something in between.

* * *

FRENCH girls are good at holding their liquor.
  "First, get ze good grip on 'ees ears," said Fifi.

* * *

THE best time to visit Paris is between your 18th and 25th birthdays.

* * *

A FRENCHMAN is a man who kisses other men on cheeks, and girls on all fours.

* * *

FRENCH kissing is like a toothpick.
  It's good either end.

* * *

A FRENCH Square Dance is a Go Down Hoedown.

* * *

THERE will never be a French astronaut.
  Who ever heard of a Frenchman going up?

* * *

THE French groom was so exhausted by the wedding celebrations he fell asleep the moment his feet hit the pillow.

* * *

PIERRE says the French are wise in the ways of love and every man should have a girl for love, companionship and sympathy, "and preferably at three different addresses," he added.

*   *   *

A FRENCH politician was pleading for legislation giving more equality to women.

"After all," he told the House, "there was very little difference between men and women."

The chamber rose as a body and shouted: "Vive la difference!"

*   *   *

THE difference between a madam and a mademoiselle, is a monsieur.

*   *   *

THE new French consul was being shown around the city.

"And that is our tallest building," said his guide, "What do you think of it?"

"It reminds me of sex," said the French dignatory.

"That's strange," said his guide, "How can a building remind you of sex?"

"Everything does," replied the Frenchman.

*   *   *

THE restaurant was not doing so well so the proprietor decided to hire a French chef to stimulate business. But the Frenchman proved to be a hopeless cook, and worse, the proprietor discovered him performing cunnilingus on his wife.

"Look at that," he said, "First he screws up my eating, and now he's eating up my screwing."

*   *   *

CUSTOMER in a French restaurant. "Waiter, do you have frogs legs?"

"Oui Monsieur"

"Then hop across the road and get me a packet of cigarettes."

* * *

ON their first date he decided to impress her.

He took her to a posh restaurant and ordered the whole meal in French.

Even the waiter was surprised. It was a Chinese restaurant.

* * *

WHEN Maurice the *maitre'd* saw Monsieur Pettard arrive and seat himself at the corner table he expected another troublesome night. Pettard was the restaurant's most finnicky customer, always complaining.

Sure enough, when Pettard found a hair in his spaghetti he held it high and protested loudly.

"What's this? What kind of a restaurant is this? I want to complain to the management."

Maurice promptly sent Fifi the waitress across with another plate of spaghetti to placate Pettard as quickly as possible, but Pettard suddenly became more interested in Fifi than the pasta dish.

Maurice was surprised when he noticed they had both disapeared. When he found them under the table with Pettard's head between Fifi's legs Maurice could not contain himself. "You hypocrite," he said. "You complain about hair in your spaghetti and here you are having muff pie for dessert!"

"Oui, Monsieur," said Pettard, lifting his head momentarily, "and if I find a bit of spaghetti in it I will certainly lodge a complaint with the management."

CLAUDE and Rene could not understand it. They considered themselves clean cut and presentable, yet all the girls seemed to be going for the gormless guy in the ill-fitting suit at the end of the bar.

"I don't understand it," grumbled Claude, watching the girls practically flaunting themselves before him.

"Me either," said Rene. "He certainly ain't handsome. Just sits there licking his eyebrows."

*   *   *

THE difference between French women and those in the rest of the world is simple: All women know what men like, but the French girl doesn't mind.

*   *   *

IN fact, a French girl went to live in London for a time, but she missed her native tongue.

*   *   *

PIERRE was sipping coffee at a side-walk cafe when his friend Maurice rushed up to sit beside him and relate the news.

"I just saw a man going in to your house," said Maurice.

"Who is this man, Maurice, what did he look like?"

Maurice said he was tall, dark and had a thin, black moustache, and he was carrying a bottle of champagne.

"And did he wear a red cravat and checked shirt with a black beret?"

"Yes, indeed he did," said Maurice.

"That was only Rene," said Pierre, "he will make love to anybody!"

*   *   *

THE French salesman was suave and with his foot in the door had been observing the curvacious shape of the housewife.

"I can arrange ze easy credit terms, Madam," he said.

"How easy?" she asked.

"Nothing down but your pants," he said.

* * *

A FARMER from Provence was on trial for shooting his wife when he found her in bed with a neighbour. He was asked why he didn't follow the usual French tradition and shoot the lover instead of his wife.

With rural logic he replied: "Tis better to shoot a woman once than a different man every week."

* * *

IT was a nasty accident that could only happen in France. A woman who swallowed a razor blade was rushed to the emergency ward. After an X-ray the doctors decided to let it take its natural course.

A few months later she eventually passed the razor blade, but in the meantime she had not only given herself a tonsillectomy, an appendicetomy and a hysterectomy but had also castrated her husband, circumcised his best friend, given the vicar a hare lip, and cut the finger of a passing acquaintance.

* * *

THREE young French boys from Paris were spending their summer on a farm in Normandy. While walking across a field they saw a milk maid and a farm hand in amorous contortions in a haystack.

They stopped to watch.

"Look at the grown-ups fighting," said the seven-year-old.

"They're are not fighting," said the wiser eight-year-old, "They are having sex."

"Yes," said the nine-year-old, "and they are not very good at it."

* * *

THEY were adjusting their clothes after a quickie in the back seat of the Citroen. "Fifi, my cherie," he said. "If I knew you were a virgin I would have taken more time."

"Pierre, if I knew you had more time," she said, "I would have taken off ze panty hose."

* * *

FIFI and Claudette sat in the vet's waiting room together. Claudette confided that the cheeky poodle on her lap, Little Pierre, had the embarrassing habit of humping her ankle, her visitor's ankle, in fact it would hump anything in sight.

"What a coincidence," said the shapely Fifi, "my Great Dane, Roger, has the same behavioural pattern."

"So you are here to have your dog de-sexed too?" said Claudette.

"No. I'm getting his nails clipped," said Fifi.

* * *

AN angry young man who discovered Pierre had been screwing his fiancee sent a letter challenging Pierre to a duel at an appointed place and time.

Pierre wrote back: "I have received your circular letter. I will be present at the gathering."

* * *

PIERRE passed away at 69
  And we all miss him so
  Pierre passed away at 69
  Boy, what a way to go!

A WOMAN in high Parisian society was interviewed after the birth of her fourth son and lamented the fact she didn't have a daughter. She appealed to the newspaper readers for suggestions on how to have a baby girl.

Letters soon arrived from all over the world. "If at first you don't succeed, try, try again," wrote an Englishman.

An Irishman sent a bottle of Irish Whiskey.

A Dutchman sent a package of cheese with instructions to place it beneath her pillow.

A German sent a parcel of whips.

An Indian suggested Yoga exercises.

A Frenchman turned up on her front porch, rang the bell and said "Can I be of service?"

* * *

THE Frenchman was listening to an American and an Englishman arguing the meaning of *savoir faire*.

The American said, "It means that if you came home and found your wife in bed with another man and you refrained from killing the son of a bitch, that's *savoir faire*."

The Englishman said: "Hardly old chap. If you found your wife in bed with another man and excused yourself for interrupting and invited them to carry on, well that's *savoir faire*."

The Frenchman had a different view: "If you came home and found your wife in bed with another man and you said 'Please continue, Monsieur' and he was able to, then HE'S got *savoir faire*."

GERMANS

HITLER was depressed and consulted his clairvoyant about his future. The mystic studied her crystal ball for some time without a word, for all the prospects were grim.

Finally, she said: "At least you will die on a Jewish holiday."

"Which Jewish holiday?"

"No matter. Any day you die will be a Jewish holiday."

* * *

THE German was so naive he thought Einstein was a single glass of beer.

* * *

A LAZY German lives by the sweat of his frau.

* * *

THE pretty fraulein approached the Aussie tourist in the Munich beer hall and invited him home. She gave him a nice meal and took him to bed.

In the morning, after breakfast, he prepared to take his leave and was making a little speech in appreciation of such outstanding German hospitality.

"Ya, the speech is nice," she said, "but what about marks?"

"Bloody oath. Nine out of ten I reckon," he said.

* * *

NEAR the conclusion of Wold War 2 Hitler's valet told him that the gossip around the ranks was that he should make an appearance at the front line.

"I have laid out your red tunic," said the valet, "because Napoleon used to wear red in battle so that nobody knew if he was wounded and bleeding."

"Indeed," said Hitler, "In that case get my brown trousers."

*   *   *

ONE day the Devil was doing his rounds in Hell to ensure all the sinners were really being punished. He was surprised to see Hitler in a cesspool, smiling.

"You are up to your neck in shit, why are you smiling?" asked the Devil.

"I'm standing on Mussolini's shoulders," said Adolph.

*   *   *

IT is odd that the German police have been unable to catch the Nazis, particularly when they were so efficient when they were the Nazis.

*   *   *

IF the answer was "Nine-W" what was the question?

The question was: "Hey Fritz. Do you spell Wagner with a V?"

*   *   *

THE Lufthansa flight was about to take off and the captain's voice was heard:

"You vill now fasten your safety belts. And I vant to hear just vun click. Not clickety-clickety click."

*   *   *

IT had been an all-night flight and as the sun began to rise the crew switched on the cabin lights for breakfast.

"Who switched on those fucking lights?" said a

male passenger who had made a constant nuisance of himself.

The hostess had had enough.

"These are the breakfast lights, sir," she said, "The fucking lights are much dimmer and you snored right through them."

* * *

A YOUNG man was enjoying his first night in a Munich beer house when a pretty young fraulein sat beside him.

"Hello," he said. "Do you understand English?"

"Only a little," she answered.

"How much?" he asked.

"Fifty dollars," she replied.

* * *

AFTER a slight collision two Volkswagen beetles had their bumpers locked together. The owners were having difficulty disengaging them when a passing dachshund threw a bucket of water over the cars.

* * *

THE German tourist dived into the river, dragged the apparently drowned dog ashore and revived it.

"Are you a vet?" asked an impressed bystander.

"Ya, I'm bloody soaking," he replied.

* * *

JERRY the Juggler did so well on the theatre circuit he was considered ready for a tour of the Continent.

"My first gig is in Germany," he told a colleague.

"Oh, that's bad news," said his friend. "You will find the German audiences very unresponsive, very cold. You will find it hard work."

Refusing to be dissuaded Jerry set off and faced his first audience in Munich only to find that his friend had spoken the truth. Nothing but stony silence after his first routine.

Right, he thought, he'd fix these bloody huns and he stepped up the pace with some fantastic juggling.

Again not a murmur nor a single hand-clap.

Undaunted he pulled out all stops, stood on his head, blew whistles and rang bells while juggling 30 oranges and a pumpkin.

Still no applause.

He stepped forward and announced: "Is there anybody here who speaks English?"

A hand went up in the back row, "Yes, I do," said a voice.

Pointing directly at the man Jerry said: "Well, you can get fucked for a start."

GREEKS

THE Greek treasurer was addressing parliament. "When I took over the economy the nation was poised on the edge of an abyss. Well, I am proud to announce that since then we have taken a great leap forward."

* * *

IN a highly intellectual discussion on physiology a German, a Frenchman and a Greek were wondering why there was a knob on a man's penis.

"It is there," said the German, "to give the man more pleasure."

"Rubbish," said the Frenchman, "It is there to provide more sensitivity for the woman."

"Both wrong," said Yorgos, "It is there to keep your hand from slipping off."

* * *

FOLLOWING a session of love-making Toula gave Panos a shove and gave him the cold shoulder.

"What for?" asked Panos.

"For being a lousy lover," she said.

He gave her a thump on the bum.

"What for?" she said.

"For knowing the difference," he said.

* * *

THE Greek businessman went to his favourite taverna and was surprised to be served by a Vietnamese waiter who spoke perfect Greek.

When paying his bill he raised the point. "How come the waiter speaks perfect Greek?"

Con the proprietor replied: "Ssh! Don't mention it. He thinks it's English."

* * *

THE health inspector made one of his surprise visits to the Greek taverna kitchen to find Nick the pastry-cook crimping the edge of the apple pies with a set of false teeth.

"Haven't you got a tool for that?"

"Yes, but I save it for putting holes in the dough-nuts!"

* * *

SIGN in a Greek restaurant window: "Kitchen hand wanted, to wash dishes, and two waitresses."

* * *

THE Greek taverna and the Chinese take-away were side by side and each Friday morning the two owners would sweep the pavement.

Con the Greek would take the opportunity to have his little joke: "What day is it today, Charlie?"

"It's Fliday," the Chinaman would reply, and Con would roll about laughing.

Each week it was the same and Con would even get some friends to come along and listen to Charlie say "Fliday."

It got on Charlie's wick. So he took time off for elocution lessons and concentrated on "Friday, Friday, Friday."

Next morning he was waiting for the big show-down, sweeping a clean pavement for ten minutes before Con appeared.

"What day is it today, Charlie," grinned Con.

"It's Friday ... you Gleek plick!"

* * *

WHEN near-sighted Doreen saw Papadopoulos she thought he was a Greek God.

Now that she's had her eyes fixed he lookes like a Goddamned Greek.

* * *

A GREEK truck-driver had just carried a large sack of potatoes up six flights of stairs.

"That will be seven bucks lady," he said.

Smiling, the woman let her robe slip open. "Wouldn't you like some of this instead?" she said.

"I'll have to see my partner," said the driver, "already this morning we have screwed away ten cases of bananas, 20 kilograms of tomatoes and seven sacks of potatoes."

* * *

IT was Friday evening and Con went out on his rounds to collect some bad debts.

Miss Lottsabazooma had owed $7.50 for some time and he meant to collect it. She opened the door wearing a short flimsy nightie and invited him in.

She apologised for not having the money, claiming she hadn't been able to get to the bank. "Maybe there is some other way I can square the account?" she said suggestively.

"Okay, then, but can I borrow some string?"

She found some twine and watched with a puzzled frown as he tied it around his donger, halfway down the shaft.

"It's a marker," Con explained. "you're not getting all this for $7.50," he said.

* * *

THE little old lady was short sighted.

"Can I help you?" said Con the butcher.

"Yes," she said, "I will have a kilo of those pissoles."

"My dear lady," said the butcher pointing to the appropriate label, "that's an "R" not a "P.""

"Right then," she said, "then give me a kilo of them arseholes."

*   *   *

SPIRO the soccer star was a costly import, yet he wasn't living up to his reputation.

The runner was sent out with a message. "The coach says he will pull you off at half time."

"That's great," replied Spiro, "We only got a cool drink at Hellinas."

*   *   *

CON told Parnos that to get the best excitement out of sex he should make love to his wife 'rodeo style'.

"What's that?" asked Parnos.

He said that's when you mount her from behind and whisper in her ear: "This is how I do it with your sister."

Then try to stay on for ten seconds.

*   *   *

THERE was a drum roll and the spotlight hit Spiro, the Great Greek Lion Tamer as he approached the growling cat. He cracked the whip and the lion opened its jaws wide. Spiro the Great stepped closer, unzipped his fly and to the amazement of the audience, flopped his donger between the gaping jaws and rapped the lion on the head with the butt of his whip.

When he stepped back after a terrifying ten seconds

there was resounding applause and the ringmaster proclaimed it the bravest act in circus history.

"Indeed, anyone who can emulate that feat right here and now will readily receive the sum of one hundred thousand dollars." roared the ringmaster. "Do we have a volunteer?"

There was a timid voice of acceptance in the back row and the spotlight picked out a reluctant hero being pushed to the front of the crowd.

He finally reached the ringmaster and said: "I'm willing to give it a try, provided Spiro doesn't hit me on the head like he hit the lion."

GYPSIES

GYPSIES are good at predicting the future because their fathers had crystal balls.

* * *

IN court last week the gypsie clairvoyant sued for divorce on the grounds of her husband's adultery next week.

* * *

RODAN the Gypsy pharmacy clerk had earned himself quite a reputation for predicting clients' ailments as they came through the door.

He would have aspirin ready for those he knew had a headache. For the chap looking embarrassed he would have the condoms ready in a brown paper bag. He would study facial expressions as customers came in and accurately predict their needs.

"Wait," he said to the blonde before she could say a word. "I know what you want."

He handed her a packet of tampons.

"No," she replied. "I want a roll of toilet paper."

"Darn," said Rodan, "Missed it by a whisker."

* * *

WHEN a midget fortune teller escaped from jail the newspaper headline read: "Small Medium at Large."

* * *

HE asked Madame Celeste to look into her crystal ball.

"I fear I am going to die," he said.

"Rubbish," she said confidently, "That's the last thing you'll do."

* * *

She took his palm, gazed in to it for some time and said: "You will live to be ninety."

"But I am ninety."

"Well there you are then, what did I bloody-well tell you!"

* * *

A MAN visited the gypsy fortune teller at the circus and sat down in front of her crystal ball. He was a sceptic.

"I see you are the father of two children," she began.

"Ha! That's what you think," replied the man, "I'm the father of three children."

"That's what you think," smiled the fortune teller.

* * *

THE sceptic sat silently while she looked into the crystal ball. Suddenly she threw her head back and began roaring with laughter. She shook with mirth until he leaned across and punched her in the nose.

It was the first time he had struck a happy medium.

* * *

THE annual general meeting of the Clairvoyants' Society is postponed, due to unforseen circumstances?

INDIANS

AS soon as Kumar got settled in Australia he set up an Indian restaurant. Anxious to have everything done by the rules and regulations he was ready for the first inspection from the health department.

The inspector looked around for a while and finally said: "You've got too many flies in here."

"Is that so?" replied Kumar, "how many should I have?"

*   *   *

AN Indian went into the grocery store for the week's supplies and asked if there was any toilet paper.

"Sure thing," said the proprietor, "We've got Sorbent, Double Soft, Smooth Edge, Crinkle Cut, Non-Slip and No-Name."

"What's this No-Name?" asked the Indian.

"Just no brand name, but half the price of the rest."

"I'll take ten rolls," said the Indian.

A week later he was back in the store. "Remember me?" he said.

"Sure. You are the bloke who bought the toilet paper."

"Yes," said the Indian, "And I've got a name for it now. You should call it the John Wayne Toilet Paper."

"How's that?" asked the proprietor.

"Because it's tough, it's rough, and it sure takes no shit from Indians."

*   *   *

WHEN the Australian Minister for Foreign Affairs paid an official visit to India he was alarmed to see so many people squatting in the fields to relieve themselves.

The experience moved him to make an immediate donation to the Indian government's plan to build more toilets.

It seriously embarrassed his host who rankled under this imposition, until he finally made a reciprocal visit to Canberra. And as luck would have it he saw a chap having a shit behind a tree in the park.

"Here," said the Indian official, "I would like to make a contribution towards the construction of toilets in Australia," he said.

"No need to," said his host. "That bloke always shits behind that tree. He's the Indian ambassador."

*　　*　　*

THERE was a young maid from Madras
　Who had a magnificent ass
　Not pretty and pink
　As you probably think
　It was grey, had long ears, and ate grass.

*　　*　　*

ONE of the toughest Ghurkas in the regiment ended up in hospital with his head so swathed in bandages he could only be fed rectally through a tube.

The orderly had just served his morning coffee when he began waving his arms around.

"What's up?" he said, "too hot?"

He bent down to hear his muffled response: "Too much sugar."

*　　*　　*

NEXT day the Ghurka's wife called to see how he was recovering.

"How is his appetite?" she asked.

"Terrific," said the orderly, "It would have done your heart good, Ma'am, to see his arse snap at a piece of toast this morning."

* * *

THE young officer arrived at the India regiment and reported that he was eager for active service to defend the empire.

"Oh no, all that skirmishing stuff is over," said the colonel, "we have a different program now, old chap. Tomorrow is Tuesday, which means we play tennis."

"Oh, I don't play tennis," said the officer.

"Well then, Wednesday we play polo. You do play polo?"

"No sir."

"Hmmm," said the colonel, "Then Thursday we enjoy the regimental dance."

"I'm afraid I don't dance at all, sir."

"Then you will enjoy Fridays," said the colonel, "That's wife-swapping night. Lot's of sex and fun."

"Sir, I'm, afraid I couldn't be part of anything like that," said the officer.

"Good gracious man," said the colonel, "You must be some kind of homosexual?"

"No, I certainly am not," replied the officer.

"Then you probably won't like Saturday nights either," said the colonel.

* * *

IN Bengal on safari the hunter and his Indian guide pulled on their heavy boots for trekking through the jungle. But there came a day when Sabu the guide pulled on a pair of running shoes.

"What for?" asked the big white hunter lacing up his heavy boots.

"There is a man-eating tiger in these parts, sahib."

"But you won't out run a tiger in those."

"Don't have to," said Sabu. "I just have to be faster than you."

* * *

THE Maharaja of an Indian province once decreed that no wild animals were to be killed. Soon his realm was overrun with tigers. When the people could stand it no longer they gave the Maharaja the heave-ho.

It was the first time on record where the reign was cancelled because of the game.

* * *

A VAST crowd had assembled in the city square in New Dehli for the drawing of the State Lottery.

"And the third prize is," roared the compere, "Number 582,677,553,901."

It takes 20 minutes for the ticket holder to make his way to the stage where the compere congratulates him and announces: "You and your family have won a year's cruise around the world."

"And the second prize is," he roars, "Number 774,883,595."

A shout goes up and a little bloke waving his ticket eventually reaches the stage.

"And you have won a three-tiered tinsel wrapped fruit cake."

"What?" roars the little bloke in disgust. "The geezer who won third prize gets a trip around the world and I get a bloody fruit cake?"

"Yes, but it was baked by Mrs Ghandi."
"Fuck Mrs Ghandi."
"No. That's the first prize!"

IRISH

THE reason there are so many Irish jokes is because the Irish have a quaint way with words. Like the Irish patient who hobbled into the surgery's waiting room: "I hope to God the doctor finds something wrong with me because I'd hate to feel like this if I was well."

*   *   *

ANOTHER example of Irish logic: "Hey Paddy, here's the five dollars I borrowed last week."

"Thanks, Mick, I had forgotten all about it."

"Then why the bloody hell didn't yer say so?"

*   *   *

THE priest was in the pub having his evening ale when he heard the local joker telling a yarn that was both dirty and Irish.

"Don't you know that I'm a priest and that I'm Irish?" protested the cleric.

"No. I'm sorry. I'll start again and talk slower."

*   *   *

ACCORDING to the Bible Adam and Eve were Irish.

He looked at her and said: "Oh, Hair!"

She looked at him and said: "Oh Tool!"

*   *   *

MURPHY hates daylight saving.

He gets his early morning erection on the 8.30 train to the office.

HOW do you confuse an Irish road worker?

Give him two shovels and tell him to take his pick.

* * *

HOW do the Irish count bank notes?

"One, two, tri, four, foive, another, another, another ....!"

* * *

THE Irish call their basic currency the punt, because it rhymes with bank manager.

* * *

IRISH loan sharks lend money at ridiculous rates, then skip town.

* * *

TERESA Mulligan walked into the bank and placed a $100 note on the counter. The teller examined it closely and said: "I'm sorry Miss. This is a forgery."

"Begorrah," cried Teresa, "I've been raped again."

* * *

THE three Murphy sisters, Sandy, Mandy and Fanny were the prettiest, and tallest girls in town. They also had the largest feet in town.

One night Sandy and Mandy met two fellows at the local dance and when one noticed the size of the girls' shoes he said: "Crickey, you girls have sure got big feet."

"That's nothing," said Mandy, "You should see our Fanny's."

* * *

PADDY thought oral sex was just talking about it.

* * *

NEWS Flash! A helicopter crashed into the cemetery of an Irish village this afternoon. At last count 705 bodies had been recovered.

* * *

WHEN the Mercedes roared away from the curb Paddy was first to dash inside with the news.

"Hey boss, they've just stolen your car."

"Oh, Christ, no," lamented his boss.

"Not to worry," said Paddy, "I took down the licence number."

*　*　*

WHY is semen white and urine yellow?

So that an Irishman can tell if he is coming or going.

*　*　*

MURPHY was a suspect in an indecent assault case and was asked by the police if he would mind being part of an identification line-up.

He agreed. But when the woman came in he jumped out of the line and said: "That's her!"

*　*　*

THE police had been told to clean up the neighbourhood so it was dead easy when the drunk staggered towards the constable and said: "Excuse me offisher, what time is it?"

The cop replied, "It's one o'clock," and bonked him on the head with his baton.

"Jeez," said Paddy. "I'm glad I didn't ask you an hour ago!"

*　*　*

WHEN Flannigan entered the pub it prompted a snigger among his mates. "Boy, the joke was on you last night," explained Murphy. "You left your bedroom light on and the blind up. You and your wife put on a great performance."

Flannigan took a sip of his beer. "Well the joke's on you lot," he said, "cos I wasn't home last night."

*　*　*

WHEN Flannigan came home fairly late from the pub he found his wife Teresa waiting for him at the front door. She looked a little distressed.

"Oh Flannigan," she said, "we had a burglar."

"Did he get anything?"

"Yes," she said, "I thought it was you."

* * *

ALTHOUGH Pat and Mick staggered out of the pub together they soon got lost in the crowded street.

Pat approached a policeman, "Excuse me offisher," he said. "Have you seen a fellow wandering about without me?"

* * *

IRISH Publican: "Sorry gents, the pub won't be open for an hour. But would you like a drink while you're waiting?"

* * *

FEELING peckish a bloke goes into Paddy's sandwich shop and says: "I'll have a salad sandwich, but with no cucumber thanks."

Paddy scratches his head. "Sorry, we are clean out of cucumber. Will you have it without tomato?"

* * *

PADDY fronted the bar and said: "Drinks all round, barman, and have one yourself."

Paddy was immediately the toast of the pub and after all pots were quaffed the barman gave him the bill.

"But I haven't got a cent," he said.

The angry barman grabbed him by the scruff of the neck and hurled him straight through the swinging doors onto the pavement outside.

It was a few moments before Paddy managed to

stand himself up and dust himself down. He staggered back into the pub.

"Drinks all round," he proudly declared for a second time, "but not you, barman. One drink and you go bloody mad."

*　*　*

ON his way home from the pub Paddy climbed on the bus and stumbled down the aisle knocking over brief cases and bags. He finally collapsed in an untidy heap beside a prim old woman.

She glared at him and said: "I hate to say it but you are going straight to hell."

Paddy leapt to his feet. "Christ, I'm not on the wrong bus again am I?"

*　*　*

AT Alcoholics Synonymous it came Paddy's turn to declare his troubles with the grog.

"I'll never forget the first time I turned to the bottle as a substitute for women," he said.

"Tell us all what happened?" encouraged the counsellor.

"I got got my dong stuck in the top," said Paddy.

*　*　*

CLEANLINESS is next to Godliness.

But only in the Irish dictionary.

*　*　*

PADDY and Shamus were walking along the pavement when Paddy suddenly grabbed Shamus by the arm.

"Look out, mind where you are stepping, it looks like dog shit."

Paddy bent down and pushed it with his finger. "It feels like dog shit," he said.

He put his finger to his lips. "It tastes like dog shit."
"Shamus my friend I think it is definitely dog shit.
Lucky we didn't step in it!"

* * *

PADDY entered the bar and approached his mates
with a handful of dog shit.

"Look what we nearly trod in," he said.

* * *

PROFESSOR Flannigan made his mark as Ireland's
most prolific inventor. Most notable were:
Water-proof tea bags.
Peddle wheelchairs.
Parachutes which open on impact.
L-shaped mobile homes.
The one-piece jigsaw puzzle.
An inflatable dartboard for campers.
An index for a dictionary.
Beer glasses with square bases that don't leave rings
on the bar or tables.

* * *

MUCH less successful was his invention of the pencil.
He used it for a few minutes before the lead snapped.
He decided his invention was pointless.

* * *

WHEN he told his banker he had invented a new
female deodorant which, when brushed lightly over a
women's pubic hair gave it a delicate aroma of fresh
oranges the banker said he wasn't interested.

"But if you can invent a cosmetic to brush over
oranges that will give them a delicate fanny flavour
you can have your loan on the spot and I will take
shares."

* * *

HOW do you sink an Irish submarine?

Knock on the hatch.

* * *

MURPHY had been at sea for five weeks and after settling into his room at his usual waterfront pub he picked up the phone and asked reception to send up a whore.

The publican had married since Murphy was last there and the new landlady was shocked to hear Murphy's request.

She demanded that her husband go up and throw Murphy out. He tried to explain that Murphy was a regular guest but to no avail. "If you are too frightened to throw him out then I'll do it myself," she said.

She was a formidable woman and when she marched up the stairs the publican could hear the sound of furniture being thrown around, thumps, bangs and curses.

Finally Murphy came down, red-faced, puffing, face scratched and shirt torn.

"That was a rugged old bitch you sent up," he said to the publican, "it was more like a wrestle than a screw."

* * *

SHAMUS the Irish gourmet said, contrary to the usual culinary practice, one shouldn't drink wine with fish.

"Eventually I find the fish tend to become abusive," he said.

* * *

SIGN on an Irish pub door: "Gone to lunch, back in an hour. PS: Already gone 15 minutes!"

* * *

TERESA Flannigan, down from the country called at the hospital.

"I'd like to see an out-turn, please," she said.

"You mean an intern," said the nurse.

"Whatever you call him, I want a contamination," she insisted.

"You mean an examination," said the nurse.

"Yes, I need to see the fraternity ward."

"You mean the maternity ward."

"Call it what you will," said the girl with annoyance, "But I certainly know I haven't demonstrated for two months and I think I'm stagnant."

* * *

AN ENGLISHMAN, a Frenchman and an Irishman were caught smuggling in Mexico. "We'll give you gringos a fair trial and shoot you tomorrow," said the 'capitan' of the guard.

"It's not such a worry, old chaps," said the Englishman, "I shall invoke the natural disaster plan. These Mexicans are terrified of natural disasters. I'll go first and just watch my form."

Next morning the pom was placed against the wall and the sergeant started to give the orders: "Take aim, ready ..."

And the Englishman shouted: "Earthquake!"

The Mexicans panicked and ran for cover in all directions while the Englishman, in the confusion, got clean away.

The Frenchman decided to follow suit and when the firing squad had been regrouped he was stood against the wall.

"Take aim, ...ready ..."

"Flood!" roared the Frenchman, and again the

squad scrambled for cover while the Frenchie escaped.

This cunning procedure wasn't lost on Paddy who had watched it all from his cell.

When he was led out and placed against the wall the plan was set in his mind.

"Take aim,...ready...

"Fire!" hollered Paddy.

*   *   *

WHEN Paddy spotted Mick with a bag on his shoulder he asked what was in it.

"Chickens," replied Mick.

"How about a wager," said Paddy, "if I guess how many chickens you've got will you give me one?"

"Tell ya what," said Mick who was always a sport, "If you can guess how many are in the bag you can have them both."

*   *   *

THE reporter called at the Shamrock Twilight Home and wanted to interview the oldest resident.

"Too late," said Paddy, "We had one but he died last week."

*   *   *

IRISH cop stopped a motorist. "Would you be having a driver's licence?" he asked.

"Indeed I have," said the driver.

"Well that's good. Because if you didn't I'd have to see it."

*   *   *

AN Irish alcoholic believes a teetotaller is someone who practises moderation to excess, and abstinence is okay provided you do it in moderation.

*   *   *

FLANNIGAN joined Alcoholics Unanimous. "There are no arguments," he explained.

* * *

PATRICK asked a passer-by if he knew the way to Alcoholics Anonymous.

"Why," he said, "do you want to join?"

"No, I want to resign."

* * *

HE stumbled into the AA meeting and knocked over a few chairs.

The secretary frowned: "Oh, we were so happy last night when you turned up sober."

"Well, tonight it's my turn to be happy," said Patrick.

* * *

TERESA answered a knock on the door. "I am collecting for the Home for Alcoholics," said the caller.

"Well come back around nine o'clock," she said. "My husband will be home then, and you can have him."

* * *

PADDY got into a fight at the pub and was knocked down five times.

"Well, have you had enough?" said his much bigger opponent.

"Don't know," said Paddy. "This is my foirst foiht."

* * *

AS luck would have it the first time Paddy went hunting he was killed by his prey. He was following some tracks when all of a sudden the train hit him from behind.

* * *

VISITING an orchard Paddy asked the farmer how much he charged for the apples.

"All you can pick for a five dollars."

"Good," said Paddy, "I'll take ten dollars worth."

* * *

THE barman called to Paddy: "What time is it?"

Paddy replied, "Don't know, but it is certainly not three o'clock."

"What makes you so sure?"

"Because I told the wife I'd be home by three and I'm still here."

* * *

PADDY the Punter cleaned out the bookies at Flemington and his friends were soon pressing him to divulge his system.

"I'm superstitious, and I watch for omens," said Paddy. "On my way to the races I took a Number 5 tram. It made five stops on the way and it cost me $5 to get into the track.

It was three fives telling me something. So I added them up, three fives are 16 so I backed Number 16 and it won by a street."

* * *

FLAHERTY says women have only themselves to blame for all the lying men do.

"They ask so many damned questions," he said.

* * *

MRS Murphy said: "Oi don't t'hink my husband has been completely fait'ful t me."

"Why, what makes you so suspicious?"

"My last child doesn't resemble him in the least.

* * *

WHEN the cop asked the Irish busker if he had a permit to play the mouth organ in the street Paddy admitted he didn't have one.

"In that case you will have to accompany me."

"Great. What numbers d'yer know?"

* * *

PADDY was a builders' labourer and found he had been overpaid a fiver. He didn't say anything about it.

However, the following week he was underpaid a fiver and he went straight to the boss to complain about being short-changed.

"But you didn't complain last week when you were overpaid," said the boss.

"One mistake is one thing," said Paddy, "but to make two mistakes in successive weeks is very sloppy administration."

* * *

UNBEKNOWN to Paddy the zip on his fly was broken. The woman sitting opposite on the train could stand it no longer.

"My man," she protested, "your member is sticking out."

Paddy looked down: "Don't flatter yourself. It's only hanging out."

* * *

WHEN Murphy's somewhat plain daughter came home pregnant he reached for his shotgun. "But father," she said, "it was the squire of the manor."

With his shotgun cocked he headed for the manor in a rage.

"Hold on Murphy," said the squire, "I'll do the right thing by your daughter. If it's a boy I will settle $5000 for you. If it's a girl, then $3000."

"And what if it's twins?" snarled Murphy.

"Double of course," said the squire.

Murphy pondered for a moment. "And if she has a miscarriage, can she have another go?"

* * *

AT the clinic the nurse asked Teresa, "When did you have your last check-up?"

"Never have," said Teresa, "A Pole and a Ukranian, but never a Czech."

* * *

PADDY O'Leary boarded a train and found himself sharing a compartment with a snobby Englishman and his large dog.

"And what koind o' dog be that?" he asked the pommie.

"It's a cross between an ape and an Irishman," was the surly reply.

"You mean it's related to both of us," said Paddy.

* * *

PADDY said his wife was obsessed with shopping.

"She is shopping crazy," he told Shamus. "She will buy absolutely anything marked down.

"Yesterday she came home with an escalator," he said.

* * *

"THAT'S nothing," said Shamus, "My wife is a kleptomaniac, but her sister is worse. She walks into stores backwards and leaves things on the counter."

* * *

THE advertisement for a kitchen gadget said it was so marvellous it would cut the housework in half.

So she bought two.

* * *

SHOPKEEPER Flannigan was giving his female assistant a knee-trembler against the counter. He was right on the gravy stroke when the front door clanger signalled a customer coming in.

Panic! Where to hide?

She dived under the counter and he stuck his donger in the till.

The customer said: "You look pleased with yourself today, Mr Flannigan."

"Yes," he said. "I've just come in to money."

* * *

PADDY was delighted to tell his mates at the pub that he had just got an exemption from the Penis Tax.

How did you do that?" asked Flaherty.

"Because it is usually hanging around unemployed. The rest of the time it is either hard up, pissed off or in a hole. It also has two dependants and they are both nuts."

* * *

THE Irish ventriloquist was so bad his lips were moving when he wasn't saying anything.

* * *

IT was talent time at the pub and Paddy gave his rendition of 'When Irish Eyes are Smiling' everything he had. When he finished he noticed a woman with a hankie to her eyes wiping away a tear.

Thinking she was moved with emotion he said, "You must be Irish?"

"No," she sobbed. "I'm a music teacher."

* * *

THE passenger got a hell of a shock when Shamus the cabbie accelerated and raced through an intersection against the red lights.

"Hey, go easy, where the heck did you get your licence?"

"Relax," said the Shamus. "My brother taught me to drive and he taught me how to run red lights."

The lights were red at the next intersection and to the passenger's horror he raced through again.

It was not until he approached the fifth set of lights that they suddenly turned green and the Shamus nearly stood the taxi on end as it screeched to a stop.

"I don't understand, that's a green light," said the passenger.

"I know that, mate," said the cabbie looking both ways, "but my brother drives around this neighbour-hood."

*   *   *

MURPHY was a keen one for conundrums, so when the barman presented one he listened intently.

The barman said: "My mother had a child. It wasn't my brother and it wasn't my sister. Who was it?"

Murphy scratched his head and admitted he was beat.

"It was me," declared the barman triumphantly.

Murphy thought it was a good one and couldn't wait to relate it to his wife. In fact he woke her up to tell it.

"My mother had a child. It wasn't my brother and it wasn't my sister. Who was it?"

His sleepy wife said she didn't have a clue.

"Easy," said Murphy. "It was Harry the barman down at the pub."

*   *   *

TERESA was washing her hair when the phone rang. Her roommate answered then called out: "Teresa, it's an obscene phone call for you."

"Get his number. I'll call back," she replied.

* * *

PADDY dragged a shaggy mongrel into the talent scout's office and announced, "This is the best dog act you're ever likely t' see. This dog can count, and I trained him m'self."

The agent gave the pair a dubious stare.

"Okay, I'll prove it," said Paddy, and holding a commanding finger to the dog said, "Right Nigel, what's two and two?"

The dog went "woof, woof." Then there was a pause until Paddy said, "C'mon Nigel, you can do it."

There was another "woof" then a long pause and another "woof."

"C'mon Nigel," said Paddy. "Just one more."

* * *

THERE was a 10pm curfew in Belfast so the sergeant in charge of the patrol got a surprise when he heard a shot ring out at 9.30pm. He was alarmed when he discovered that Private Murphy had shot a man.

"Why did you do that?" demanded the sergeant.

"But that's O'Flannagan," said Murphy, "I know where he lives. He would never get home by 10pm."

* * *

AFTER years in a high security jail Pat devised a way of communicating with his mate Mick. It was an ingenious ploy using a secret code to tap out messages on pipes.

However the scheme was eventually thwarted when they were transferred to separate cells.

WHEN the little man came home, his rather formidable wife gave him such a wallop on the head with a rolling pin that his knees buckled and he fell to the floor.

Shaking his head groggily he said: "Was that a joke, or did you mean it?"

"I bloody-well meant it," she said.

"That's okay then. Because I don't appreciate jokes like that."

*　　*　　*

RED Adair's fame in quelling oil-rig fires stretches around the globe so when a well in the middle of the Sahara Desert spewed smoke and flame the alert went out, "Get Red Adair!"

But Red had his hands full with a fire crisis elsewhere and nobody can be in two places at the same time.

The Exon magnates were frantic. Without the famous Red Adair they were in heaps of trouble.

"Why not try Green Adair," suggested a lackey.

"Who?" But as the flames roared higher in the sky why not try Green Adair indeed.

Green Adair was contacted in the Limerick Arms in Belfast and offered one million dollars to do the job.

Within a few hours the oil engineers were amazed to see an air transport land in the desert. They gasped as the nose of the aircraft opened and a truck bearing Green Adair and his crew sped towards the fire.

They watched in awe as the truck approached the wall of flames and disappeared straight into the very heart of the fire.

The could see Green Adair and his men leaping about, jumping and stamping out the flames.

Finally, all charred, singed and blackened, they emerged from the smoke to the cheers of their incredulous admirers.

"What will you do with the million dollars?" asked a reporter quickly on the scene.

"The foist thing I'll be doing will be to get some brakes for that bloody truck!"

* * *

PADDY was staggering home as usual when he was stopped by the priest.

"What makes you drink so much?" asked the cleric.

"Nothing makes me," said Paddy. "I'm a volunteer."

* * *

THE O'Flaherty family were small. They were all small. Even the smallest was no bigger than the rest, and what's more they never went anywhere alone unless they were together.

* * *

MURPHY dropped dead the day he arrived back from a vacation in the tropics. He was laid out in the coffin for friends and neighbours to pay their last respects.

"He's got a great tan," mused Mrs Doolan from next door. "The holiday did him the world of good."

"And he looks so calm and serene," said Mrs McGinty.

"That's because he died in his sleep," explained Mrs Murphy, "and he doesn't know he's dead yet. But when he wakes up and finds out, the shock will kill him."

* * *

THERE was a power failure in a Dublin department store. Thousands of shoppers were stranded on the escalators for hours.

* * *

THEY were two of the IRA's top men and they lay in ambush for the Chief Provost of the Ulster Brigade. "Okay," says Paddy, "let's go through the schedule once more. At 4.45 he leaves his office. At 4.50 his car leaves police headquarters with an escort through peak hour traffic. At 5 pm the first of his bodyguard turn this corner and we keep low and let them pass. At 5.10 the provost himself comes by in his disguised car and we let him have it. Is that all clear?"

"Clear as a bell," says Shaun looking at his watch. "But it is 5.15 now. I hope nothing terrible has happened to him."

* * *

MURPHY arrived home late from the pub, well oiled and ready for trouble. As he stumbled up the stairs his wife called out: "Is that you, Murphy?"

"Be Jeezus, it had better be!"

* * *

D'YER think if I pour you some gin again,
Said Finnegan, you might care to sin again.
Said she with a grin
If you want it back in
You must pay me a fin a'gin, Finnegan.

* * *

THERE was a young colleen named Flynn
Who knew fornication was sin
But when she was tight
It seemed quite alright
So everyone filled her with gin.

117

McTAVISH knew he was in an Irish pub, but never-theless, when he had a few under his belt it always made him feel boisterous.

"Down with the Pope" he roared for his fifth toast. And Paddy O'Reilly stepped forward and flattened him.

When he came to his friends asked McTavish. "Didn't ya know O'Reilly was a Catholic?"

"Of course I did," he said. "But why didn't some-body tell me the Pope was?"

*   *   *

TWO tough labourers were working on a building site when Murphy fell from the second floor scaffolding.

"Are ya dead?" cried Gallagher calling from above.

"To be sure I am," replied Murphy.

"You are such a liar Murphy that I don't know whether to believe you or not," called Gallagher.

"That proves I'm dead," said Murphy's voice from the rubble below, "because if I was alive you wouldn't be game to call me a liar!"

*   *   *

MRS O'Flannigan went to the hardware shop and bought a few household items.

"I suppose you'll want a screw for that door?" said the shopkeeper.

"No, but I'll give you a blow job for that toaster," she quickly replied.

*   *   *

PADDY had just become the proud father of twins and he was asked if they were identical.

"The boy is but the girl's not," he said.

*   *   *

THE tourist was booking in to an Irish pub when he was asked if he wanted a room with a shower or a bath.

Thinking of his budget he replied, "What's the difference?"

"You stand up in the shower," said the landlord.

* * *

YOUNG Teresa came home and related the awesome news to her parents. She was pregnant.

"How do you know it's yours?" asked her Dad.

* * *

"TERESA has just had twins," roared Murphy angrily. "Wait till I get my hands on the other fellow."

* * *

PADDY: "Hey Shaun, what's Mick's surname?"

Shaun: "Mick who?"

* * *

ON his way home one night Paddy dropped in to the pub. The barman poured him a beer and asked if he wanted to be in a raffle.

"What's it for?" asked Paddy.

"It's for a poor widow with 13 kids," said the barman.

Paddy shook his head. "No good to me. I'd never be able to keep them."

* * *

DUBLIN'S contestant in the international quiz was waiting for his first question.

"First, what's your name and occupation?" the compere asked.

"Pass" responded the contestant.

* * *

PADDY had been stranded on the deserted island for two years. Then one afternoon a lifeboat drifted close enough for him to swim to it and drag it to the beach, where he knocked it to bits and made himself a raft.

*   *   *

IT was lunch time on the building site and Mick opened his brown paper parcel of sandwiches.

"Aw, shit," he said, "Not bloody jam sandwiches again."

His mate said: "Why don't you have a word with your wife?"

"I can't," said Mick, "she's away seeing her mother. I've had to cut my own lunch."

*   *   *

SHAMUS asked Paddy how he got his black eye.

"You'd never believe it," said Paddy, "but I got it in church."

He said he had been sitting behind a fat lady and when they all stood for a hymn he noticed her dress was creased into the cheeks of her bum.

"All I did was lean forward and pull it out and she turned round and hit me," said Paddy.

It was a week later and Shamus was surprised to see Paddy had another black eye. "I got it in church," he began to explain.

He said he found himself behind the same fat woman and when they stood for the hymn her dress was once again creased into the cheeks of her bum.

"My little nephew reached forward and pulled it out. But I knew she didn't like that, so I leaned over and tucked it back!"

*   *   *

MURPHY and his bride sat up all night waiting for their sexual relations to arrive.

* * *

"I WOULDN'T go to America if you paid me," said Fred.

"Why?"

"Cos they drive on the wrong side of the road."

"What's wrong with that?"

"I tried it the other night," said Fred. "It's bloody dangerous!"

* * *

PADDY was ever fearful of the boss and would work tirelessly, even with a head cold.

"Why don't you take the day off?" said his more forthright workmate.

"The boss wouldn't like it," snuffled Paddy.

"Go on, you won't get caught. He is never here on Wednesdays anyway."

Paddy reluctantly took the advice and went home. But as he passed his bedroom window he saw his boss in bed with his wife.

He rushed back to the office. "You and your advice," he said to his mate, "I nearly got caught."

* * *

"DO you know a bloke with one leg called Moloney?"

"No. What's the name of his other leg?"

* * *

THERE was an almighty row when Flaherty discovered his best friend, Paddy, was having an affair with his wife.

"But you mustn't blame her," said Paddy. "It is all my fault. I was the one who answered her advert in the personal columns."

TERESA the barmaid complained that she had been only working an hour and two improper suggestions had been made to her.

She was quite upset about it. Normally she has nine or ten.

* * *

LETTER FROM AN IRISH MOTHER

DEAR Son. Just a few lines to let you know I'm still alive. I'm writing this letter slowly because I know you can't read fast. You won't know the house when you get home because we have moved.

About your father. He has a lovely new job. He has 500 men under him; he cuts grass at the cemetery. There was a washing machine in the new house when we moved in but it hasn't been working too good. Last week I put Dad's shirt in, pulled the chain and haven't seen it since.

Your sister Mary had a baby this morning but I haven't found out if it is a boy or a girl yet, so I don't know if you are an auntie or an uncle.

Your Uncle Patrick drowned last week in a vat of whisky at the Dublin Brewery. Some of his workmates tried to save him but he fought them off bravely. They cremated him and it took five days to put out the fire.

I went to the doctor last Thursday and your father came with me. The doctor put a small glass tube in my mouth and told me not to talk for ten minutes. Your father offered to buy it off him.

It only rained twice this week, first for three days and then for four.

We had a letter from the undertaker. He said if the

last payment on your grandfather's plot isn't paid within seven days, up he comes.

Your loving Mother.

PS: I was going to send you $10 but I had already sealed up the envelope.

ITALIANS

LUIGI considered himself a charmer and had no qualms about heading for the prettiest blonde at the bar.

"Hello darling," he said, "are you Italian?"

"No," she relied.

"You look Italian," he said.

"Well I'm not."

"Surely you have a bit of Italian in you?"

"No I don't," she insisted.

"Would you like some?"

Is an IQ of 105 considered high?

Yes.

For ten Italians?

*   *   *

IT was Luigi's first day on the job, high on the scaffolding of the 51st level of a Collins St sky-scraper when the hook of a crane knocked him off balance.

He fell into the rubbish shoot, and for the next five minutes he crashed, banged and walloped his way to the ground until he was discharged in a cloud of dust on the footpath.

"Where the hell did you come from?" asked the surprised foreman.

"Italy," said Luigi.

*   *   *

THE sign in the factory read: "Any Italian who wishes to attend the funeral of a relative must tell the foreman on the day of the game."

* * *

LUIGI said he was damn lucky. He's got a wife and a transistor, and they both work.

Why does an Italian have a hole in his pocket?
So he can count to six.

* * *

THE Mafia moll dumped her boyfriend when she learned he was just a finger man.

* * *

RECTAL thermometers are banned in Italy.
They found they cause too much brain damage.

* * *

When the Italian girl told her brother the astounding news that she was going to have a baby he replied: "Well, I'll be a monkey's uncle."

* * *

HOW do Italian men propose to their girlfriends?
"You're gonna have a what?"

* * *

LUIGI has a problem about the future. He's getting married in a month and he hasn't found a job for his wife.

* * *

MARIA was being let out on her first date and Gino, her stern father, was intent on having the last word: "Young man, I want Maria to be home early tonight."

"Donjoo worry, Papa," said the young suitor, "I'll have her in bed by ten."

* * *

THEY were cuddled up in the back seat of the car when Bruno proffered it to her.

"But if I do perform oral sex on you," she said squinting at the monster in front of her, "won't you lose respect for me in the morning?"

"Of course not," he said, "provided you are good at it."

* * *

THE doctor was examining Luigi.

"Have you ever committed sodomy?" he asked.

"No way. One wife is enough for me."

* * *

DID you here about the Italian who stayed up all night studying for his urine test?

* * *

ITALIAN is an easy language to learn. All you need to know is one word, Atsa.

Then you can speak fluently: "Atsa car, Atsa church, Atsa woman, Atsa everything."

* * *

WHEN the Italian girl had sex in the back seat of a hire car she said: "Itsa Herts."

* * *

WHAT'S the difference between an Italian hooker and a big cuddly bear?

One lies on its back for peanuts. The other lives at the zoo.

* * *

IT was a strange invitation from the Italian family next door.

It said "Gina Mr. U,2 wedding!"

After studying it for a while the husband said:

"Looks like we are going to an Italian wedding. It says Gina mister period, you comma to wedding!"

* * *

SIGN on Luigi's new house: "Costa Plenti."

* * *

WHEN the Italian girl discovered she didn't have enough money to pay for the taxi fare she alerted the driver: "You gotta stop. I can notta pay you."

"That'sa alright," said Luigi checking her out in the rear vision mirror, "I'll stop down the lane and you can take your panties off."

"You'll be robbing yourself," she said, "My panties costa only ninety cents."

* * *

WHAT is a specimen?

An Italian astronaut.

* * *

BRUNO was a recent migrant to the country and they asked him how he was settling in.

"I dunno understand," he said. "They call a bald man Curly, they call a man with red hair Bluey, they call a big man Tiny, and me who has been here for a year with no girlfriend they call a Fucking Wog."

* * *

THE Italian don was returning to Italy for a visit and had arranged two appointments, one with the Pope, the other with the Mafia boss.

Who should I see first, he asked his lieutenant.

"The Pope first," said his adviser, "you've only got to kiss his hand."

* * *

BEFORE the Mafia case started the judge called the opposing lawyers together on a serious matter.

"I have been told by my clerk that both of you have lodged a bribe in an attempt to sway my decision."

They squirmed under his gaze.

"You, Attorney Salami, gave me $15,000. And you Attorney Petroni gave me $10,000," growled the judge.

He then pulled out his pen and wrote a cheque and handed it to Attorney Salami. "I am returning $5000 and we're going to decide this case on its merits."

* * *

SMARTING under accusations that they had been responsible for an assassination attempt on the Pope, the Mafia launched its own investigation into the matter.

After extensive interviews with the suspect and repeated viewings of the videotapes they came to the conclusion that the Pope opened fire first.

* * *

LUIGI was in the dock and protesting loudly: "How can I be charged with forgery when I can't even write my own name?"

"Ah," said the judge, "but you are not charged with writing your own name."

* * *

ST PETER was checking in new arrivals at the gates.

"Name?" he said.

"Lulu Bell," she replied.

"Cause of death?"

"The clap," she said.

"Couldn't be," said Pete, "nobody dies of the clap."

"You do when you give it to the Mafia boss."

* * *

THE sociologist was taking a survey in the Italian Quarter and approached a gentleman in a black suit.

The survey eventually got to sex.

"How many times do you do it, sir?"

"Oh, about seven or eight times a year," said the gent.

"But you are Italian," said the sociologist, "Italians are supposed to be great lovers."

"Well, I'm not doing too badly for a 65-year-old priest without a car."

* * *

THREE Italians appeared to be having trouble with the English language.

One was lamenting the fact that he and his wife had no children. "She is unbearable," he explained.

"No, you mean she is inconceivable," said the second.

"You are both wrong," said the third. "He means his wife is impregnable."

* * *

THE first lesson you receive at an Italian driving school is how to open a locked car with a wire coat hanger.

* * *

WHAT'S the national bird of Italy?

The stool pigeon.

* * *

IN Sicily a tourist was arrested for failing to bribe a police officer.

* * *

WHAT do you call Sophia Loren?

A pizza of arse.

* * *

BIGOTRY is a tall redwood, while a bigamist is a thick fog over Rome.

And an innuendo is an Italian suppository.

* * *

LUIGI had migrated to Australia and after a few years eventually stood before the magistrate to be tested for his citizenship papers.

"You Honour," he began tentatively, "I no speeka da good Eengleesh because I no been ina dis country for long time and since I talka like dis you think I no getta da papers?"

The magistrate said: "Thassa okay, no worries you'll getta your papers, no problem, mate."

* * *

BRUNO told the doctor he felt weak and run-down.

When questioned about his sex life Bruno admitted he had sex with five, sometimes six different girls every night.

"Well," said the medic, "that's obviously the cause of your trouble."

"I'm glad to hear that, Doc," said the hot blooded youth, "I was afraid it might be the masturbation."

* * *

EXAMINING Luigi for constipation the doctor gave him three suppositories. "You put them up the back passage, do you understand what I mean?" said the doc.

"No worries," said Luigi.

A week later Luigi was back, to complain he still had the constipation. "The pills were useless," he said. "I did what you told me, but for all the good they were I might as well have stuck them up my arse!"

* * *

HOW can you spot the Italians at a cock fight?

They are the ones betting on the duck. -

And how do you if the Mafia is involved?

The duck wins.

*   *   *

A BLOKE went into a pub, pulled a mouse out of his pocket and dropped it into a beer glass. The tiny creature immediately stood on its back legs and broke into an aria from La Traviata.

Another drinker nearby was amazed. "How much do you want for that mouse, mate?" he asked.

"You can have it for ten bucks," the bloke replied.

The deal was struck and the new owner left with the little performer.

The barman had witnessed all this. "You must be crazy," he told the bloke, "how come you parted with the mouse so cheaply?"

"It wasn't that good," shrugged the bloke, "it could only sing in Italian."

*   *   *

LUIGI the barber was giving his usual advice on all and sundry while Tony was getting a haircut.

"You going on holiday this year?" asked Luigi.

"Yes, my wife and I are flying to Rome for a few weeks."

"Which airline?" asked the barber.

"United," replied Tony.

"No good," said Luigi, "the food is lousy and the hostesses are rude. Where you stay in Roma?"

"At the Sheraton," said Tony.

"Donna stay there. The food is terrible and the rooms are too small. What you gonna do in Roma?"

Tony said he and his wife would visit the Vatican and seek an audience with the Pope.

"Donna waste your time. It will be too crowded. You will never get near him," advised the barber.

Tony paid his bill and left. A month later he was back in the same chair.

"Did ya go to Roma?" said Luigi.

"Yes," said Tony.

"I betcha you found it as I said."

"No. Actually we flew United and found the service excellent and the staff courteous," said Tony. "And we stayed at the Sheraton where the rooms, service and food were excellent. And we visited the Vatican to find it wasn't crowded."

"But you didn't see the Pope."

"Yes. Indeed we did, and he came over to speak to us," said Tony.

Luigi was impressed. "What did he say?"

"As I knelt before him to receive his blessing he said, 'For Chris' sake, where did you get that haircut?"

* * *

LUIGI later broke his leg in a skiing accident.

Now he can only cut hair on crutches.

* * *

THE sign on the barber shop read: Haircuts while you wait!

* * *

WHEN Gino brought Gina into the clinic to tell the doctor that she was once more in the family way the doctor exploded. "Didn't you use the condom as I instructed?"

"Si, Doc," said Gino, "But we haven't got an organ

so I stuck it over the tamborine. It's the only musical instrument I've got."

*　*　*

GUISEPPE proudly announced that his brother in Italy had just become the father of twins, a boy and a girl.

"That's nice," said his mate. "What did they call the girl?"

"Denise," he said.

"And what did they call the boy?"

"De Nephew," said Guiseppe proudly.

*　*　*

THE priest stood before the crowd in the village hall.

"You must not use the pill," he declared.

An attractive signorina stepped forward and said: "You no play-a da game. You no maka-a da rules."

*　*　*

TWO old dons were lamenting human nature and the idiosyncracies of life. "I was the town planner in this village," said one. "Look at all those fine buildings. I was responsible for all that architecture, but do I get any recognition? Eh? No."

"I donated money to the church all my life, but do I get any acknowledgement, eh? No. But fuck one single goat ..."

*　*　*

AT an Italian wedding you can always tell the Mafia from the musicians.

The musicians are the ones without the violin cases.

*　*　*

THE Italian opera singer declared he never had sex in the morning. "It is bad for the voice, it's bad for the health, and besides, you never know who you might meet in the afternoon."

* * *

THE restaurant manager spotted Luigi the waiter pocketing $25 which had been left on the table by the customer.

"What do you think you are doing?" he demanded.

Luigi pretended to be equally surprised: "Some people are odd," he said, "that bloke doesn't pay his bill yet leaves a sizeable tip."

* * *

A WOMAN who had dined at an Italian restaurant took the opportunity to visit the ladies' room before she left.

On the way out she said to a waiter: "You can tell the proprietor that I found your graffiti in very bad taste."

"Sorry," he said. "But if you had told me earlier I would have swapped it for spaghetti."

* * *

WHEN Fred asked for two pies and some dim sims at Luigi's takeaway he was impressed to see Luigi using tongs to place the food in the bag.

"Yes, sir," said Luigi, responding to Fred's comments, "we are very clean here. Always use tongs. No hands ever touch the food."

As Fred turned to leave he noticed a piece of string hanging from Luigi's fly and asked its purpose.

"All part of the hygiene program," said Luigi. "When I go to the toilet I simply pull donger with this string. Not touched with human hands."

Fred was about to leave when the obvious question prompted him. "How do you get it back?"

"With the tongs," said Luigi.

* * *

"I'LL have some Spinoti Vertimicelli," she said.

"Where did you see that?" said the waiter.

"On the menu."

"Oh, that's the name of the proprietor."

* * *

IT was one of the elite chapters in the Mafiosa. Why the membership of the committee alone represents a hundred years off for good behaviour.

Half the membership couldn't attend because they didn't have the time. The other half was doing time.

Big Luigi was leader of the Mob. He speaks to God and nobody else. He is so big he wears a cross with nobody on it. He calls dial-a-prayer to see if there are any messages.

* * *

GUISEPPE was complaining to Luigi the barber about the price of his haircuts.

"I just come back from New York," said Guiseppe, "Over there you can get a good haircut for about five bucks."

"As maybe," said Luigi, "But what about the fare?"

* * *

AT The Greasy Spoon Cafe the impatient customer grabbed the sleeve of Luigi the waiter as he passed the table.

"I only have an hour for lunch," he said.

"I ain't gotta da time to talk about your industrial problems," replied Luigi.

* * *

IN the swank department store Signora Lottzaba-zooma approached the information desk.

"Scusa, canna you tell me where the ladies' room?"

"Escalator."

"No, I musta go now," she said.

*   *   *

IN America an Italian is really a Mexican with a job.

*   *   *

THE Mafia boss in Sicily learns from his accountant that someone in the Chicago family has been stealing money so he tells Mario, his interpreter, to join him on the next flight to the States.

He brings the suspects in one at a time and has Mario accuse them of the crime. Whenever they deny it he puts a gun to their head. If they still say no he lets them go.

The last to be interrogated is Luigi and he is sweating with fear.

"So," said the don, through his translator, "Are you the one who has been stealing the money?"

"No Godfather," says Luigi.

The don puts the pistol to his head which has a dramatic effect on Luigi's story.

"Yes, yes, I took the money. It is in a large plastic bag in my refrigerator."

The don looks at his translator. "What did he say?"

"He says you are an old fart and he bets you don't have the balls to pull the trigger," said Mario.

*   *   *

TWO zoologists eager to preserve a rare gorilla species decided to advertise for a male volunteer 'for a special task.'

When Luigi fronted he was told the 'special task' involved mating with the gorilla, and the sum of $1000 was mentioned.

Luigi thought it over for a time and finally said: "I will agree on three conditions."

"What are they?" asked the eager scientists.

"First, I want a curtain across the cage so I can do it in private. Second, if any kid is born I want it raised a Catholic, and third, about the money. Can I pay by instalments?"

JAPANESE

THE Japanese tourist fronted the bank teller and presented his travellers cheque. When he counted the cash he said: "How come I get less money today than yesterday?"

"Fluctuations," said the clerk.

"And fluck you lot too," said the Jap.

* * *

What do Japanese men do when they have erections?
Vote.

* * *

JAPANESE cunnilingus is a constluctive cliticism.

* * *

A JAPANESE orgasm is a gland finale.

* * *

A PELVIC examination in Japan is a nookie lookie.

* * *

LACKA-NOOKIE is one of Japan's most dreaded diseases.

* * *

SACKA-NOOKIE is Japanese for bloomers.

* * *

THE Japanese call girl went broke.
Nobody had a yen for her.

* * *

THE Japanese firm making vibrators is Genital Electric.

* * *

AND there is a new Japanese camera.
When you trip the shutter it goes "crick."

* * *

WE know a bloke who is half Japanese and half Black.
Every December 7 he attacks Pearl Bailey.

* * *

THERE was a great Lord in Japan
Whose name on a Monday began
It carried through Tuesday
Till twilight on Sunday
And sounded like stones in a can.

* * *

THE Japanese are beginning to own so much of
Queensland that travellers will soon have to leave their
shoes at the New South Wales border.

* * *

A SAILOR named Harold had an affair with a geisha
girl in Japan. A few months later he received a letter
from her:
"Dear Harry. You gone three months. Me gone three
months. Should I carry Harry, or hari-kari?"

* * *

THE sumo wrestler won the world championship as
the biggest and the toughest, and as a sort of bonus his
manager fixed him up for the night with a geisha girl.
When she called at the manager's office next morning for her pay she was in a grumpy disposition.
"Whoever told that gorilla he could screw?" she
asked.
"Who's going to tell him he can't," said the manager.

* * *

THERE was a young lass from Japan
   Who danced nude on stage with a fan
   Then came a day
   When the fan blew away
   And blow me if it wasn't a man!

*   *   *

HE was thrilled when his wife became pregnant but much to his surprise the baby turned out to have blue eyes, light skin and blonde hair.

His wife shrugged off his concern.

"Occidents will happen," she said.

JEWS

JAKE sat at the table with such a worried look that his son asked what was troubling him.

"Ethics, my Son, It's a serious problem," said Jake.

"Take today for instance," he continued. "One of our regular customers paid with a hundred dollar note. After he left I found that there was a second hundred dollars stuck to it."

"Well, what's the problem, dad?"

"Ethics my son. Should I tell my partner or shouldn't I?"

* * *

DID you know Jesus Christ was Jewish?

Yes, he went into his father's business. He never got married. And his mother doted on him.

* * *

THERE were several cars involved in a highway accident that had just happened as Greenberg stopped his car and ran to a man lying on the side of the road.

"Have the police come yet?" he asked.

"No," moaned the injured man.

"Has the ambulance arrived?"

"No."

"And has the insurance assessor been yet?"

"No," moaned the man.

"Listen," said Greenberg, "you don't mind if I lie down next to you?"

* * *

THE reporter was interviewing the socialite who had organised the Charity Ball and couldn't take his eyes off a massive diamond on her left hand.

"Oh, that," she said, "It's the famous Guggenheimer diamond."

The reporter was dazzled by it.

"Unfortunately it has a curse attached to it," said the socialite.

"A curse?" gasped the reporter, "What curse?"

"Mr Guggenheimer," she said.

* * *

WHAT'S six inches long, has a bald head and drives Jewish women wild?

A hundred dollar note.

* * *

MOYSHE settled down in his favourite kosher restaurant. "Oi waiter, do you have matzo balls?"

"No," he said, "I always walk like this!"

* * *

ISAAC was the first to admit he was a little kinky. "I'm a monster," he told the madam, "I like to beat women and I've got my own whip. Have you got anybody for a wild pervert like me?"

"Olga's just the ticket," said the madam, "but whipping comes pretty high. It will cost you $500."

Olga insisted on the money up front. Once the cash was handed over Isaac went to work with his whip.

After ten minutes an exhausted Olga gasped: "I can't take much more. When are you going to stop?"

"When?" roared Isaac between frenzied strokes, "When you give me my money back."

* * *

WHAT'S the difference between an Italian woman and a Jewish woman?

One has real orgasms and fake diamonds.

* * *

WHAT'S a 'Catch 22' situation for a Jew?

Free pork!

* * *

THE Talmudic scholar wondered how it could possibly be a Christian world when the sun was named Sol.

* * *

THE kid said: "What's Christmas, Dad?"

So Dad took him to a department store where he met Santa Claus and saw the toy department. "That's Christmas, Son!

Little Isaac said to his father, Moishe, "What's Christmas, Dad?"

Moishe took the lad to a vast and empty warehouse. "That's Christmas, Son!"

* * *

MRS Plotkin complained to the head mistress that her little son, Izzie, was being teased in the school yard and was being called 'Jew Boy'.

"I want you to do something about it," said Mrs Plotkin.

The teacher said she would do so immediately and gathered the class together and said the taunting had to stop.

"It's very serious," she told the children, "How would you like to be called a 'Jew Boy'?"

* * *

TWO Jewish gentlemen were seated together on the flight from Sydney to Melbourne. They had been in the air for thirty minutes when the younger man asked the other if he had the time.

There was no answer. "Can you tell me the time please?"

Again there was no answer and the younger man detected some kind of deliberate resistance.

The aircraft was on its descent path when the older man quickly looked at his watch and said it was ten past three.

There was silence for a while before the young man said. "Why didn't you tell me the time earlier?"

"Well, you know what it is like on flights. People get talking to each other. We could become friendly, especially when we are both Jewish. I would be obliged to invite you home. I have a lovely daughter and you are a young man, quite handsome. Romance could blossom and before long you could be asking for her hand in marriage. And to put it bluntly, I don't want no son-in-law who hasn't got a watch."

* * *

MOYSHE had started in the second hand trade but was now one of the richest businessmen in the city. As his Rolls Royce stopped in front of the Ritz one night, an old school mate who had fallen on hard times was waiting for him.

"Hey Moyshe, remember me?"

"Eddie Rozenbloom, of course I do. Haven't seen you in years. How's business?"

"Moyshe," says Eddie. "I've hit a bad patch. In fact I was wondering if you could let me have a five dollars for a bed."

"Sure Eddie. Bring it around in the morning!"

* * *

THE Jewish beggar approached a man and said: "Could you give me a hundred dollars for a sandwich?"

"A hundred? Why that's ridiculous."

"Just a yes or no will do, fella. Don't tell me how to run my business."

* * *

JAKE the joke teller was in good form at the pub. "The bus stops and these two Jews get off ..." he began.

Suddenly a bloke gets off his stool and protests: "Hang on, I'm Jewish and I'm sick and tired of hearing about two Jews doing this and two Jews doing that. Pick on some other mob for a change."

"Okay," said Jake, "point taken."

So he starts again. "The bus stops and these two Eskimos get off and one said 'So there we were at my son's bar mitzvah ....'"

"IZZIE," whined his wife, Rachel, "you know that dress you bought me last week? Well Mrs Guggenheimer next door has bought one just like it."

Izzie looked up from his book, "And you want me to buy you a new one?"

"Well, it's a lot cheaper than moving," said Rachel.

* * *

THE irony of keeping up with the Guggenheimers, of course, is that you spend money you don't have to buy things you don't need to impress people you don't like.

* * *

WHEN Mrs Finklestein got caught in the rain after buying a brand new hat, she hoisted her dress up over her hat and dashed for cover.

145

It brought a comment from a taxi driver: "Hey Missus," he said "Your arse is sticking out in the rain."

"Don't I know it," said our heroine, "but that arse is 45 years old and this hat is brand new."

* * *

IZZIE came home early one day and caught Rachel screwing with the baker.

"I'm ashamed of you," he shrieked. "Why are you screwing the baker when its the butcher we owe money?"

* * *

MOYSHE had a little scheme which always seemed to work. When the taxi delivered him to his address he would fumble in his waistcoat for the money and then search around the floor of the cab claiming to have dropped a fifty dollar note.

"Stay here while I get some matches from that tobacconist's stall so I can strike a light to find it," he would say.

As soon as Moyshe got out of the cab it would invariably drive away.

* * *

THE new tax inspector was intrigued to find that for many years Mr Abraham Finklestein had consistently claimed deductions for substantial amounts to charity.

The inspector became downright suspicious when he found that these annual donations were being made to St Mary's Catholic Church, and that Mr Finklestein could produce hundreds of cancelled cheques going back for years, all made out to the church, and each endorsed by the priest.

The inspector decided to question Fr. O'Malley over Mr Finklestein's generosity.

"Generosity?" said the priest. "Yes I know Finklestein well, but he is hardly generous."

"But we have his cancelled cheques going back over years," said the tax man.

"Oh those," said the priest. "Indeed he helps us there. We take up a big collection each mass, and as the banks are closed on Sundays, Mr Finklestein will always give us a cheque for it to save us worrying about the cash over the weekend."

* * *

THE rabbi was surprised to receive a call from the tax inspector. "The synagogue is exempt from taxes," explained the rabbi.

"Oh, it's not you we are enquiring about," said the taxman, "it's one of your community, Isaac Goldstein."

The taxman explained that on his tax return Goldstein indicated that he donated $50,000 to the synagogue.

"Is this true?" asked the taxman.

"The money hasn't arrived yet but I am sure it will be here as soon as I remind dear Isaac."

* * *

A YOUNG woman looking as if she was in a photo finish with the stork staggered into the maternity ward and grabbed a nursing sister. She said she needed immediate attention.

"Ah," said the sister, "due are you?"

"No, Church of England."

* * *

HYMIE was the world's first public relations officer and worked with Moses on the flight of the Israelites. When they reached the shores of the Red Sea, hotly pursued by Pharaoh's army, Moses sent for his PR man.

"Where are the boats? You forgot the boats," Moses roared at Hymie.

"When were boats in the contract?" asks Hymie.

Moses was in a rage. "I must have boats. Do you want me to part the sea and walk across it?"

"Great thinking Moses," said Hymie. "If you do that I will get you two whole pages in the Old Testament!"

*   *   *

A JEW had settled in a train compartment when an African American entered and sat opposite. The black man opened a bag and took out a Yiddish newspaper and began to read it.

The Jew was intrigued. He watched for ten minutes before he leant over and said: "Being black isn't enough?"

*   *   *

LATE one dark night a secret operative disguised as an Arab slipped into the entrance of a Tel Aviv apartment and crept up to the stairs to the fifth floor.

He counted the doors until he arrived at No.7 where he knocked quietly; two loud knocks, a pause then three soft.

The door opened and an old man said: "I'm Goldstein the pawnbroker, what do you want?"

The shadowy visitor said: "Wet pigeons never fly at night."

"What?" said Goldstein who had been disturbed from his favourite television program.

"Wet pigeons never fly ..."

"Oh no," said the old man, "I'm Goldstein the

pawnbroker. You want Goldstein the spy, No.7 down on the fourth floor," said the old man.

*   *   *

AN Orthodox Jew who was worried about his son's gambling sent him a message to remind him of his religious commitments. "And don't forget Yom Kippur starts on Sunday."

"Put $50 on it for me, Pops," replied the son.

*   *   *

A JEWISH mother gave her son two ties for his birthday, a striped one and a spotted one.

Next day she saw him wearing the striped one.

"So what's the matter with the spotted one? You don't like it?"

*   *   *

THE Jews are the most confident race in the world.

They cut the end off their dick before they know how long it will grow.

*   *   *

WHAT do you call an uncircumcised Jewish baby?

A girl.

*   *   *

OF all the pornographic movies Jewish films are the worst.

They consist of five minutes of sex and ninety-five minutes of guilt.

*   *   *

THERE was a Jewish Kamikaze pilot.

He crashed his plane into his brother's scrap metal yard.

*   *   *

THE first Jewish astronaut was Nose Cohen.

*   *   *

PREP school son was studying his arithmetic and asked for help from his dad. "What's two and two, Dad?"

"Depends, Son. Are we buying or selling?"

* * *

"PAPA," said the lad. "What's Yiddish for a hundred per cent?"

"Izzie, my son, a hundred per cent is Yiddish."

* * *

THE Jews have discovered a new disease.

It is Waldheimer's Disease. People who suffer from it forget they were ever Nazis.

* * *

THE Jewish lawyer wore a worried frown. "It's my son," he confided to the rabbi. "He has come out of the closet and declared himself a homosexual."

"But the situation could be worse," he continued, "at least he is in love with a doctor."

* * *

WALKING down the street Mr Glubbernheim paused to reach into his pocket and drop a dollar into the tin held by the organ-grinder's monkey.

"I'm surprised Hymie," said his wife, "I didn't think you liked gypsies."

"I know," he said, "but their little ones are kinda cute."

* * *

A JEWISH nymphomaniac is a woman who allows her husband to make love to her after she has been to the hairdresser.

* * *

WHY does a Jewish wife close her eyes while having sex?

God forbid she should see her husband having a good time.

* * *

OLD Abraham Cohen was knocked down by a truck and was carried to the median strip and laid gently on the grass. A woman got a pillow from her car and placed it under his head.

"Are you comfortable?" she asks.

"Ah well," he says, "I make a living."

* * *

AT the synagogue social Sam realised he had lost his wallet with $500 in it. He approached the microphone on stage and made an announcement.

"Gentlemen. I have discovered I have lost my wallet in the hall somewhere. I will give a fifty-dollar reward to anyone who finds it."

A voice in the crowd said: "I'll give seventy-five."

* * *

MOYSHE and Izzie were out in the bay when their boat struck a rock and sank. Moyshe was the stronger swimmer and took hold of Izzie with one hand as he paddled towards the shore with the other.

However Moyshe soon got exhausted and asked Izzie if he could float alone for a while.

"Where in trouble like this," spluttered Izzie "and you want to talk business?"

* * *

IZZIE Goldstein had just returned from his monthly sales schedule and had an incredible story to tell his wife, Rachel.

When he got to Sydney there was an airport strike and he was delayed overnight. All the hotels were booked so he had to ask Schmidt, one of his customers, if he could put him up for the night.

Schmidt gladly offered to share his double bed and even offered Izzie a fine meal with wine.

In the middle of the night Goldstein felt a hand on his privates. Possibly his companion was dreaming. But there was no mistake when he felt an erect penis pushed against his bum.

"What did you do?" said Rachel with alarm.

"What could I do," said Goldstein, "Schmidt is my best Sydney account."

ABRAHAM wandered into Sam's pawnshop and placed a leather coat on the counter. "How much will you give me for this jacket?"

Sam checked it over. "$20, and that's my best offer."

"But that jacket is worth $100."

Sam was adamant. "$20 or nothing."

"Are you sure that's all it's worth?" pressed Abe.

"Positive."

"Okay," said Abe. "Here's your $20. The jacket was hanging in your doorway and I was wondering how much it was worth."

*　*　*

THE police sergeant entered the home of Mrs Bernstein to find her at the kitchen table eating her soup.

"Sorry to disturb you," he said, "but I have some terrible news."

"What is it?" she asked, slurping her soup.

"I'm afraid your husband has been killed in an accident," said the cop.

Mrs Bernstein continued to slurp her soup.

"I said," pressed the cop once more, "your husband has been killed."

"I know what you said (slurp slurp), believe me, as soon as I finish (slurp) this soup I am going to let out one almighty scream."

*   *   *

THERE was a sound reason why the Israelis did not get involved in the Gulf War.

The last time they listened to a talking Bush they wandered the desert for forty years.

*   *   *

TWO Jews were lined up before the Nazi firing squad when the officer asked if they had any last requests.

One said he would like a cigarette and when the Nazi came close enough, the condemned man spat in his face.

"Please Izzie," said his friend, "don't make trouble."

*   *   *

IN a small school in Dublin the teacher told the class she would give fifty pence to whoever could name the holiest man in history.

Only one hand went up, that of little Izzie O'Cohen. "That would be St Patrick, Miss," he said.

Teacher handed over the money and said to Izzie, "How come the only boy to know the answer was Jewish?"

To which Izzie replied: "In my heart of hearts I know it was Moses, but business is business."

*   *   *

WHEN asked to name the four seasons Izzie replied:
"I only know two. Busy and slack."

*   *   *

SAM Goldstein was at the funeral of a good friend when one of the mourners remembered he owed the deceased ten dollars.

"I am a man of my word," he said placing a ten dollar note in the coffin.

It reminded another of the deceased's debtors. "I am also a man of my word," and he shuffled forward to place another ten dollars in the coffin.

"You two have pricked my conscience," said Sam, "for I also owe our dear departed friend ten dollars."

Sam came forward, wrote a cheque for thirty dollars, threw it in the coffin and took twenty dollars change.

*   *   *

WHEN Abe won five million in the lottery he decided to give two million to his parents, two million to his family, $500,000 to himself and the rest to the Nazi Party.

His family was shocked. "Why?" they asked.

Abe rolled up his sleeve to show them. "They gave me the numbers," he said.

*   *   *

GOLDSTEIN ran a little sandwich shop and was eventually audited by the Tax Commission.

"I don't understand it," said the agent. "You have a small shop, you only sell sandwiches and the odd cup of coffee, yet you claim ten trips to Israel each year as business expenses."

"That's right," said Goldstein, "we also deliver."

*   *   *

THE reporter from the 'Wall Street Journal' asked Finklebaum, the stockbroker, "What's the latest dope on Wall Street?"

"My son," replied Finklebaum.

* * *

HOW do you tell an Italian gangster from a Jewish gangster?

The Jew is the one wearing the Italian suit.

* * *

THE aircraft was flying into Honolulu when the man in the window seat spoke to his fellow passenger for the first time.

"How do you pronounce it, Hawaii or Havaii?"

"Havaii." said the passenger.

"Thanks."

"You're velcome."

* * *

THE hall was packed for a public meeting in the Jewish district and while they were waiting for proceedings to start Finkleberg looked agitated and squirmed in his seat. He finally stood up and announced loudly: "Is there a Christian in the audience?"

A little lady, three rows back stood up.

"Would you mind changing seats with me, lady?" said Finkleberg, "I'm sitting in a draft."

* * *

YOUNG Hymie went off to America and after three months phoned his mother from Hollywood. "I'm married, Momma," he said.

"Oh, no, you haven't married a Goy have you?"

"No Momma."

"Then what's her name?"

"Goldberg, Momma."

"Oh, thank goodness for that. What's her first name?"

"Whoopie, Momma."

MRS Goldberg was heartbroken when young Moyshe told her he was getting married to Rosie McEvoy.

"Oh, why are you not marrying a lovely Jewish girl? Why are you marrying a shikseh?"

"Jewish girls are terrible, Momma," said Moyshe, "they grow fat and get varicose veins."

"So do all the shiksehs," cried his mother.

"Yes, but who cares about shiksehs?" said Moyshe.

* * *

MRS Plotkin was waiting for an appointment with Dr Goldstein and the only other person in the waiting room was a young businessman reading the Financial Review.

"Excuse me, young man," she said. "Are you Jewish?"

"No I'm not," he replied.

A little later she repeated the question. "Are you sure you are not Jewish?"

"Definitely not," he said without looking up from his newspaper.

But she kept her eyes on him, and a little later. "Are you really certain you are not Jewish?"

The young man threw his paper aside. "Okay," he said in utter exasperation, "I am Jewish."

Another five minutes went by. "That's funny," she said. "You don't look Jewish."

* * *

MOYSHE finished his business in Hong Kong early on the Friday and after many enquiries finally found the local synagogue.

Complete with his prayer shawl he attended the service and began to pray, surrounded by Chinese.

156

He was spotted by the rabbi who introduced himself and asked why he was there.

"Well, whenever I am in a foreign city I like to pray in the synagogue," he said.

"You are a Jew?" asked the rabbi with some surprise.

"Of course," replied Moyshe.

"You don't look like a Jew," said the rabbi.

* * *

IZZIE and Rachel went to Switzerland for a holiday and while in the mountains Izzie decided to try his hand at skiing. Down the slope he went and disappeared with a scream over a crevasse. When he didn't return that night a Red Cross rescue team was despatched to the area.

They searched all night and most of the next day until they discovered some tracks.

"Mr Guggenheim, Mr Guggenheim," they kept shouting. "It's the Red Cross."

And finally a feeble voice was heard in reply. "I've given already."

* * *

THE high-class society hooker had always refused to sleep with Izzie. She told him frankly that she hated Jews.

However, she finally agreed when Izzie offered her $500 for one night.

"Okay," she said, "provided we don't have the light on so that I don't have to look at you."

He agreed. And that night she was truly amazed at his virility. He had made love to her at least twenty times, stopping only to go briefly to the bathroom and back between each lively session.

She finally broke the silence. "Good gracious Izzie," she gasped, "I didn't know you were so lusty."

"Ah aint Izzie, ma'am," said a black man's voice. "Izzie's downstairs selling tickets."

* * *

IT was interval at the opera when Mrs Sternberg rose from her seat and called: "Is there a doctor in the house? Is there a doctor in the house?"

A man in a tuxedo pushed his way towards her. "I'm a doctor," he said.

"Oh Doctor," she said, "Have I got just the loveliest daughter for you!"

* * *

WHEN the rabbi was hit by a speeding car and lay injured on the road, his old friend the Catholic priest was first on the scene and thought it was an excellent opportunity for conversion.

"Do you believe in the Father, Son and the Holy Ghost?" whispered the priest.

The rabbi opened his eyes. "I'm dying and he asks me riddles!"

* * *

MOYSHE was on his death bed and raised his head gently. "Moira, are you there?"

"Yes, Moyshe, I am here."

A moment later Moyshe said, "Izzie, are you there?"

His son, Izzie assured him he was by his side.

"Joshua," said the ailing Moyshe, "are you there?"

"I'm here Poppa," said Joshua taking his hand.

Moyshe raised himself on his elbow, "Then who the hell is minding the shop?"

* * *

TWO men were standing side by side in the loo when the smaller of the two looked up and said: "You are a Jew, right?"

"Yes," said the taller.

"And you come from the Greensberg district!"

"Yes."

"And at your circumcision you were cut by the cock-eyed Rabbi Finklebaum?"

"Yes, how do you know all these things?"

"Because Rabbi Finklebaum always cut with a left bias and you are pissing on my boots."

* * *

WE know a rabbi who keeps a scrapbook of all his clippings.

* * *

GOLDSTEIN and Plotkin had spent a lifetime in competition climbing the social ladder, but Izzie Goldstein's bar mitzvah was to be the calendar event of the year. It began at the London Ritz where guests were delivered in white Rolls Royces. The cabaret featured Liza Minelli and Barbra Streisand accompanied by the London Philharmonic Orchestra. The food was flown in from Vienna.

Then the one hundred guests were flown first class to Kenya where they set out on safari riding a team of elephants.

Two hours out from the village there was an elephant jam and the safari came to a halt.

"What's the hold-up?" demanded Mr Goldstein of the lead elephant boy.

A runner came back with the message: "There appears to be another bar mitzvah up ahead, by the name of Plotkin," he said.

IT was with much wringing of the hands that Rachel discovered her husband, Hymie, had a mistress.

Rachel, however, was not the sort to kill the goose that lays golden eggs, rather, she decided to find out what the mistress had that she didn't.

After long interrogation Hymie finally relented. "Well to tell you the truth, Rachel, you are too cold. When we make love you don't do anything. You just lay there, whereas she moans and groans with feeling."

"Is that all," thought Rachel. "Is that all there is to it?"

That night she dressed in her most alluring lingerie, slipped Hymie a shot of his favourite cognac and got him into bed.

Half way through the business she decided to give her most passionate moans and groans.

"Oh Hymie, darling," she began. "I've had the most terrible day. Our shares have dropped two points. The washing machine broke down. You don't give me enough housekeeping money ..."

* * *

A TOURIST walking down the Jewish business district asked an Orthodox gent where Plotkin's jewellery store was located.

The Jew was loaded with parcels and began handing them over until the tourist was holding them all.

When his arms were completely free he shrugged his shoulders: "How should I know?" he said.

* * *

MOYSHE is on his deathbed and and finally realises that he is about to cash in his worldly chips.

He calls for his wife, Beckie and says, "I want to leave the business to Izzie."

"No, not Izzie, he's too much of a gambler. Leave it to Abie," said his wife.

"Okay, the Rolls I will leave to Michael."

"Na, not Michael. He has smashed up three cars this year," said Beckie.

"Okay," said Moyshe, "then the summer house I will leave to Rachel and her husband."

"Na, don't let that schmuck get his hands on that property, leave it to Rachel herself."

Moyshe raised himself on his elbow. "Listen Beckie. Tell me who's dying here?"

* * *

MR GOLDBERG ran a clothing factory and had the reputation of wringing a full day's work from his employees. Abe had worked there for thirty years and had never been late...until today.

He limped in on crutches an hour late with his head bandaged. Mr Goldberg pointed to the clock and asked him to explain.

Abe said he was on his way to work when he stepped on his son's skate and crashed down seven flights of stairs. He tumbled out into a laneway only to be hit by a truck.

Goldberg listened to the story and then said: "And this takes an hour?"

* * *

THE eldest son took his father aside and said he had a problem. "I have had a bit of a fling, Dad, and unless I come up with a thousand dollars she will sue me."

Dad reluctantly wrote a cheque to save the family name.

A week later his second son approached him. "Father, I have had a bit of a fling and unless I pay a thousand dollars she will sue me."

Dad coughed up another cheque to save the family name.

A week later his daughter approached him. "Father, I am ashamed to say that I have had a bit of a fling and ...

Her father interrupted, and rubbing his hands said, "At last. We make a collection this time."

*   *   *

A JEW boarded the overnight train and found himself sharing a sleeping compartment. As they were preparing for bed the Jew said. "Excuse me, I wonder if I could borrow a towel." The man lent him a towel.

"Excuse me," said the Jew again, "I appear to have left my pyjamas at home." The man lent him a tracksuit.

"Excuse me," said the Jew yet again, "will you lend me your toothbrush?'

This time the man refused.

When he was met by his son at Central Station he was asked if he enjoyed the journey.

"No, I had to share with an anti-Semite," he replied.

*   *   *

ON their 50th wedding anniversary Rebecca asked Sam to drive her to an adjoining neighbourhood and had him stop outside a block of housing units.

"They are ours, Sam. We own them," she said proudly.

Sam was stunned. When the news eventually sunk in he said: "But how did you do it?"

"Sam," she said proudly, "you remember I always charged you ten dollars for your conjugal rights? Well I saved all that money and invested it in this property."

"Oh, Rebecca," said Sam, "if only I had known I would have given you all my business."

* * *

WHILE Abe Rosenberg waited at the Pearly Gates, St Peter thumbed through his lengthy personal file with an ever-darkening frown. Finally, he said, "I am afraid you can't come in Mr Rosenberg." Abe was shocked.

"But look at this file," said St Peter, "it's nothing but good deeds, practically every day. The problem is Abe, we've got popes, archbishops and rabbis up here and if we let you in with this impeccable record, it would cause great embarrassment to the social order, not to mention putting a few pontifical noses out of joint. Here you are, a mere tailor, coming up here with a clean slate."

Old Rosenberg didn't protest. He was that type of bloke.

"Tell you what," said St Peter leaning forward on the counter in a confiding manner. "I'll zap you back to earth for the afternoon. You've got six hours to blot your copy book with a little sin. Do you think you could commit just one minor infringement? Then we could let you in without disturbing the heirarchy up here."

Rosenberg said he would do his best, and in a flash he found himself sitting in his lounge chair by the fireplace in his flat.

The mantlepiece clock chimed 12 noon and he began thinking. "What sin could I commit?"

He didn't smoke. He didn't like strong drink and no way would he risk a dollar on a horse.

He spent the first three hours racking his brain before he remembered the middle-aged spinster in the flat above, Miss Leonski. Yes, it was definitely a sin to make love to a woman to whom you were not married.

And hadn't Miss Leonski gone out of her way at the last Body Corporate social function by deliberately sitting beside him and offering him tea and biscuits?

"That's what I'll do," he thought, and putting on his hat and coat he made his way up to her flat and knocked on the door.

"Oh, Mr Rosenberg," she said, "this is a surprise. Last thing I am hearing of you is that you are very sick, maybe dying. Will you come in for a cup of tea?

Rosenberg sat there sipping tea, checking his watch and mentally noting that his life was fast ticking away while he was wasting time with small talk.

By five o'clock he was beginning to panic as he realised there was no tactful way to dive into sin.

So suddenly he jumped up, grabbed Miss Leonski, pushed her into the bedroom, ripped off her clothes and threw her onto the bed.

Then he sinned.

And while he was at it, he thought that if this was to be the only sin in his life he might as well give it his best shot.

About five to six he began to feel life slipping away and he got out of bed to reach for his clothes. He turned to smile down at Miss Leonski and said: "Miss Leonski, I want to thank you. This afternoon you have shown me the way to Heaven."

Miss Leonski looked up with a tired little smile. "Mr Rosenberg," she said, "you shouldn't mention it. Only me and the good Lord will know what a good deed you have done for me today!"

MEXICANS

WHY didn't Mexico have a team at the 1984 Olympics in Los Angeles?

Because anyone who could jump, run or swim was already there.

* * *

WHAT do you call a Mexican with a sheet of corrugated iron?

A home owner.

* * *

What do you call a Mexican with several sheets of corrugated iron?

A real estate agent.

* * *

WHAT happens to a Mexican who jumps out of a plane at 45,000 feet without a parachute?

Who cares?

* * *

WEARING a big sombrero Pedro walks into the bar and asks for a glass of tequila. A man sitting at the bar, also wearing a big sombrero says: "That's a coincidence. I also am drinking a glass of tequila. And I am wearing a big hat, just the same colour as yours."

"Where did you get such a fine sombrero?" asked Pedro.

"Back in a little town near the Rio Grande," said the hombre.

"That's a concidence," said Pedro. "That's where I come from."

"Well I must buy you a drink," said the hombre. "We had a big family there and my father was a sheep herder."

"Mine too," said Pedro. "This is amazing. Let me buy you another."

"Actually, my father was shot for sheep rustling ..."

"What?" said Pedro. "I can't believe this. So was mine. Shot by the Gringos."

It was the hombre's turn to look incredulous. "That's exactly what happened to my papa."

By then the bartender turned to the innkeeper and said. "Looks like a long night. It always is when the Gonzales twins come to town."

* * *

AFTER their marriage and bridal night in the town, Pedro and his new bride set off for Pedro's farm up in the hills in a wooden cart drawn by a donkey.

But the donkey wouldn't move. Pedro cajoled, then swore, but it wouldn't budge. He then got off the cart, picked up a short log and gave the donkey a severe whack over the head.

"That's one," he said, as the beast started to move forward.

An hour later the donkey stopped again. Pedro cajoled, then swore at it, but it wouldn't budge. He got down from the cart and gave it an almighty biff between the eyes with the short plank.

"That's two," he said as the donkey faltered forward.

When the donkey stopped for the third time and refused to move, despite a series of whacks over the head, Pedro said: "Well that's three," and he pulled out a shotgun and gave the donkey both barrels between the eyes. It dropped down dead.

It was too much for his new wife who uttered her first protest. "Fancy treating an animal like that," she said. "You beat it unmercifully. You are not only a cruel man but also a stupid one. That donkey was worth a hundred dollars. You are an extravagant fool."

"That's one," he said.

NEW ZEALANDERS

LITTLE Bo Peep she lost her sheep
  And didn't know where to find them.
  But a search revealed
  They were in the next field
  With a dirty big Kiwi behind them!

              *   *   *

TOBY had a little lamb
  His case comes up next Friday.

              *   *   *

HOW do you set up a New Zealander in small business?
  Buy him a big business and wait.

              *   *   *

WHAT'S long, hard and fucks New Zealanders?
  Grade Three.

              *   *   *

A KIWI farmer was counting his sheep.
  "301, 302, 303, 304, hello darling, 306, 307 ..."

              *   *   *

THE New Zealand couple eventually worked out the problem of the eternal triangle.
  They ate the sheep.

              *   *   *

THE farmer's wife gave him a plate of grass for his dinner.
  "What the hell's this?" he exploded.

"If it's good enough for your girlfriend it's good enough for you," she said.

* * *

WHY do New Zealand horses run so fast?

Because they've seen what they do to the sheep.

* * *

TWO farmers approached the Pearly Gates.

St Peter addressed one, "You must be a farmer from Australia?"

"Crikey, how did ya know, mate?"

"By the soil on your boots," said St Peter, and addressing the other said, "and you must be a farmer from New Zealand."

"Gee," said the Kiwi, "how did you know?"

"By the wool on your fly," said St Peter.

* * *

WHY did the New Zealander invent velcro?

Because the sheep started to recognise the sound of a zip.

* * *

IT was smoko and three shearers sat against the fence when a flock of sheep walked by.

"I wish that one was Miss Universe," said one.

"I wish that one was Mr Universe," said another.

"I wish it was dark," said the third.

* * *

WHEN a tourist coach passed through a small country town in New Zealand one of the passengers noticed a sheep tied to a lamppost on the corner in the main street.

"Oh that," said the guide, "that's the Recreation Centre."

* * *

A BLOKE went into the fish shop and asked for some 'fush 'n chups.'

"Are you a Kiwi?" said the proprietor.

The Enzedder was sick and tired of this so he spent the next three months at an elocution class.

He finally returned to the shop and asked in perfect English for some 'fish and chips.'

"Er, you're a Kiwi, eh?"

"How the hell did you know that?"

"Because this has been a hardware shop for the last two weeks."

* * *

THE potato farmer had recently arrived from Rotorua and had taken up a farm in Gembrook. "You look worried," said his mates in the pub. "What's bothering you?"

"Sex!" he replied.

They gathered around for more information.

"Well," explained the Kiwi, "as you know this is my first harvest here. I've got a wonderful crop of spuds, but not enough sex to put them in."

* * *

WHAT do New Zealand blokes use for contraception?

Their personalities.

* * *

THREE couples went into a restaurant in Auckland and asked for a table for sex.

"And three pillows," they added.

* * *

WHY are there so few swimming pools in New Zealand?

Because everyone who can swim is already in Australia.

KNOCK, knock.
Who's there?
Ann.
Ann who?
Ann other New Zealand wicket falls.

RUSSIANS

A RUSSIAN reported to the police that his parrot was missing.

The official took down its colour and description and asked: "Does the parrot talk?"

"Yes, but any political opinions he expresses are strictly his own."

* * *

TWO strangers stopped to admire a new car parked by the curb in Moscow.

"Beautiful machine," said one, "a great triumph for Soviet technology and engineering."

"But that's an American car," protested the other. "Don't you know an American car when you see it?"

"Of course I do, but I don't know you."

* * *

THREE travellers were discussing the Old Testament.

"Adam and Eve must have been English," said the pommie. "Only an English gentleman would offer to share the only apple with a lady."

"You're mistaken," said the Frenchman. "Only the French could be so much in love as those two."

"Both wrong," grunted the Russian. "Who but Russians could walk around with no clothes, nothing but an apple between them and think they were in paradise?"

* * *

AT an art exhibition in Moscow one exhibit was a huge success. It was a painting of a loaf of bread and a sausage.

Everybody wanted to know the artist's name and address.

*   *   *

IVAN lay dying on his bed when there was a knock on the door.

"Who's there?" he asked.

"The Angel of Death," came the reply.

"Thank Christ," gasped Ivan, "I thought it was the KGB"

*   *   *

IN the Gulag they did it tough. One day the commandant marshalled all the inmates together and announced he had good news.

"For the first time in five years we are changing the sheets," he said. "Those in Hut A will change them with those in Hut B."

*   *   *

PRAVDA started a Letters to the Editor column in which readers were invited to freely express any political criticism or opinion they cared about.

The only stipulation, letters had to be signed with name, address and next of kin.

*   *   *

CALLED in by the KGB for questioning the old Jew was told he was suspected of plotting against the State, but he could redeem himself if he knew Soviet history.

"Who was Karl Marx?"

"I dunno," said the Jew.

"And what about Lenin?"

"Never heard of him."

"Are you telling us the truth?"

"Of course," said the Jew, "Do you know Izzie Smirtzvitz?"

"No," said the officer.

"Do you know Shlomo Guggenheim?"

"No," said the KGB man.

"Well, there you are," said the Jew. "You've got your friends and I've got mine."

*　*　*

RUSSIAN astronomers suffered a setback in funding last year, but it didn't stop them from improvising to make sure all scientists witnessed solar movements during the last eclipse. They issued an official decree:

Face south and bend your body at the waist to form a 90 degree angle. Bend the knees at a 45 degree angle. Then get a shaving mirror and hold it between you knees. With a bit of luck, and if all the angles are correct, you should see Uranus.

*　*　*

SHE saw a man walking down a Moscow street with one shoe.

"Excuse me," she said, "Do you realise you have lost a shoe?"

"You are mistaken," he said. "I just found one."

*　*　*

WHAT do you get from consuming Ukranian dairy products?

The Trotskis.

*　*　*

THE Russian women entered the shop and said to the attendant: "I see you have no bread here?"

"Not true," he said. "We sell milk here, but we have

175

no milk. The shop which has no bread is next on the left."

* * *

ON her weekly shopping round in Moscow she found a long queue at the bakery, so she walked on. She found a long queue at the butcher shop, so she walked on. At the vegetable market the queue was even longer.

Frustrated at the situation she decided to buy some vodka at the liquor store, but the queue extended around the block.

"I've had enough of this," she declared finally, and loaded her husband's army revolver. "I'm going to the Kremlin to put an end to the Secretary General and his miserable way of running this country," she said.

When she got there she found a hundred people in line ahead of her.

* * *

THE two Russians were talking about the future of their country.

"What do you think our future will be three or four years from now?"

"How should I know," said his comrade. "One never knows what our past will be like in three or four years."

* * *

WHAT'S the difference between a Russian woman and the Abominable Snowman?

One is over seven feet tall, smelly and covered in hair. The other is a legend.

* * *

WHAT do you call an attractive woman in Russia?
A tourist.

* * *

CUSTOMS officer was inspecting a sweet young thing's suitcase and discovered six pairs of French knickers. "What are these for?" he asked.

"Sunday, Monday, Tuesday, Wednesday, Thursday and Friday," she replied.

"And what about Saturday?" he asked.

She replied with a smile and a wink and minced by.

Next was a big Russian woman who flung her suitcase onto the counter.

"And what are these for?" said the customs officer discovering twelve pairs of thick flannel bloomers.

She replied: "January, February, March, April.........."

* * *

SINCE the collapse of the Soviet Union the Russians have adopted many customs of the west, particuarly the social niceties.

So when Ivan found himself sharing a compartment with a woman on the train to Siberia he welcomed the chance to display his conversational skills and repartee.

On the afternoon of the first day's travelling he said: "Where do you come from?"

"Minsk," she replied.

On the second day he said: "What do you do there?"

"I am a cook," she said.

On the third day he said: "Enough of this romantic chit chat. Get your knickers off."

* * *

BORIS Yeltsin was being interviewed by western journalists on his assessment of the Cold War. He said the most crucial turning point was the assassination of President Kennedy in 1963.

"Why?" asked the reporter. "What if it went the other way and Kruschev was shot instead of Kennedy?"

Boris reflected for a moment: "Well, I don't think Mr Onassis would have married Mrs Kruschev," he said.

* * *

IT was a shabby pub in Moscow's red light district. One of the hookers walked in and said, "Gimme a glass of Smirvitz."

The barman did so and she scoffed the lot in one gulp then dropped to the floor in a dead faint.

The barman appealed to the only two drinkers to help him carry her into a back room where one of them said: "Hey, let's give her a quickie while she's out."

They did so and an hour later she sat up, scratched her head, said "Where am I?" got her bearings and left.

Next evening she came in at the same time and asked for a glass of Smirvitz, drank it in one gulp and dropped to the floor again. The same three carried her to the back room and did it again.

This went on for a third and fourth night.

On Friday night she came in and the bartender reached for the Smirvitz bottle.

"No Vladimir," she said. "I'll have Bacardi tonight, that Smirvitz makes my fanny sore."

SCOTS

A SCOT arrived at the Pearly Gates.
"Name?" asked St Peter.
"Jock McTavish," replied the Scot.
"Piss off," said St Peter. "We're not making porridge for one."

* * *

JOCK McPerv was so mean he used to reverse charge his obscene telephone calls.

* * *

THE reason Scots have blisters on their dicks is because they are such tight-fisted wankers.

* * *

WHAT do Scotsmen do with their old condoms?
They keep rooting with them.

* * *

WHEN Jock had a vasectomy he asked the doctor if he was entitled to severance pay.

* * *

HOW does a Scot take a bubble bath?
He has baked beans for supper the night before.

* * *

DID you hear about the Scot who found a crutch.
He broke his wife's leg.

* * *

A SCOTTISH gentleman is one who gets out of the bath to piss in the sink.

* * *

WHEN the Scot went to the clinic for a check-up the doctor told him he had too much sugar in his water.

So next morning he pissed on his porridge.

* * *

JOCK's fiancee peered at her engagement ring.

"Oh Jock, is it a real diamond?"

"Och, if it isnae, I've been done out of a fiver," he replied.

* * *

JOCK brought home a packet of salted peanuts and gave his fiancee one. Later she said: "Can I have another peanut?"

"Why?" said Jock, "I assure you they all taste the same."

* * *

START of a Scottish recipe:

First borrow three eggs.

* * *

THERE was the Scot who took a cab to the bankruptcy court, then invited the driver in as one of his creditors.

* * *

McTAVISH stopped a young man in the street. "Aren't you the chap that hauled my son from the lake yesterday?"

"Yes," said the life saver, "but think nothing of it. It was nothing."

"Nothing indeed?" roared McTavish. "Where's the lad's bloody cap then?"

* * *

GOLF was invented in Scotland and there are still clubs there which have signs on the course which read: MEMBERS WILL REFRAIN FROM PICKING UP

LOST BALLS UNTIL THEY HAVE STOPPED
ROLLING.

* * *

IT was a tight game in the Scottish Highlands.

"How many shots was that?" said McTavish when
they finished the fifth.

"Six," said McSporran.

"Well, I had five, so that makes it my hole."

When they finished the sixth McTavish said. "Well,
how many shots was that then?"

"Hang on," said McSporran. "It's my turn to ask."

* * *

YOUNG Jock McTavish got down on his knees to
propose to her when a 20p coin dropped from his
pocket and rolled under the sofa.

In the twenty minutes it took him to find it she had
lost interest.

* ' * *

McTAVISH was as shrewd as they come and when he
sat down with the lawyer he said: "I'm not into throwing money about, but I will certainly pay if you can
give me an undertaking that you can win my case."

The lawyer said that was fair enough and told
McTavish to outline the story.

McTavish launched into a terrible tale of breach of
contract, lying, cheating and fraudulent business prac-
tices.

"That's an open and shut case," said the lawyer, "I
will cheerfully accept such a brief."

"Oh that's bad news," said McTavish.

"Why?" asked the lawyer.

"That was my opponent's side of the story."

* * *

THEY asked why Jock was looking pretty glum.

"I just found a pay envelope in the street," he said.

"Then you should be laughing," said his Scottish mates.

"Nay, look at this," said Jock. "Look at the bloody tax that's been deducted."

* * *

TWO Scottish migrants met in Sydney. They hadn't seen each other since they migrated from Scotland together twenty five years ago. They hugged and slapped each other on the shoulder.

"Let's have a drink, like we did in the old times in Glasgow," said one.

"Aye, and don't forget, it's your shout," said the other.

* * *

A SCOT, a Jew and an Englishman were dining together in a restaurant. When the waiter cleared away the coffee the Scot was heard to ask for the bill.

Next day the newspaper headlines declared:

JEWISH VENTRILOQUIST
SHOT IN RESTAURANT
* * *

JOCK was the type of bloke who always let his friends pick up the dinner bill.

He had an impediment in his reach.

* * *

WHAT is the difference between a Scotsman and a canoe?

A canoe sometimes tips.

* * *

A SCOT met a doctor on the street and hoping for some free advice asked: "What should I do for a sprained ankle?"

The doctor, also a Scot, replied: "Limp."

* * *

SERGEANT McTavish of the Highland Regiment swaggered into a pharmacy. He placed a battered condom on the counter and asked the chemist how much would it cost to repair it.

The chemist held the damaged item up to the light. "I could launder it and disinfect it, vulcanise a patch on the holes and tears on the side and insert new elastic around the top, but if you take my advice it would be almost as cheap to buy a new one."

McTavish could recognise sales talk when he heard it and said he would think it over.

He returned next morning. "You've persuaded us," he declared, "the regiment has decided to invest in a new one."

* * *

A TRUE Scot never sends his pyjamas to the laundry unless he has a pair of socks stuffed in the pocket.

* * *

McTAVISH heard about a doctor who charged $20 for the first consultation, but only $5 for subsequent visits.

So when he entered the clinic he said: "Well, here I am again, Doc."

"Good. Keep up the treatment I prescribed the first time," said the doctor who was also a Scot.

* * *

A SCOT brought a round of drinks at the pub the other night. He has since asked police to appeal for witnesses to the accident.

A SCOT went to London for two weeks' holiday. He took a shirt and a five pound note. When he returned he hadn't changed either of them.

* * *

McTAVISH donates a lot of money to charity but he likes to do it anonymously.

In fact, he doesn't even sign the cheques.

* * *

THE Scots even enjoy being constipated.

They hate to part with anything.

* * *

DO you know what McTavish did with his first 50p piece?

Married her.

* * *

DID you hear about the Scotsmen who started a squash club?

Ten of them pooled their finances and bought their own bottle.

* * *

JOCK was due for his annual medical check-up and as usual arrived with a liberal specimen in a very large bottle. After the test the doctor announced that Jock was fine. There was nothing abnormal in the specimen.

Jock happily returned home to relay the good news. "Agnes," he said, "you and I, the kids and Grandpa are all in good health."

* * *

THERE was a young Scot named McIvers

Whose knackers were two different sizes

One was so small
'Twas no ball at all
But the other won several first prizes.

*   *   *

JOCK McTavish went to the Op Shop to buy a suitcase for his holiday. He found one at a reduced price. The manager asked if he wanted it wrapped. "Nae mon. Just put the brown paper and string inside."

*   *   *

HE spent the first week at Bondi. And that's all he spent.

*   *   *

IF Jock and Sandy were alone in a bar together they would die of thirst.

*   *   *

HE wouldn't shout if a shark bit him.

*   *   *

HER husband seldom bought her anything. He was a man of rare gifts.

*   *   *

McGREGOR the chemist wrapped the bottle and pushed the parcel across the counter.

The chap was walking down the street when McGregor came running after him in great distress.

"Oh, I'm so glad I caught you," he said. "I've made a terrible mistake and given you arsenic instead of phensic."

"Oh, is there a difference?" asked the chap.

"Indeed there is. That will be another 5p please."

*   *   *

HE took his kids to the beach and bought them an icecream, but they still squabbled and fought.

They wanted one each.

*   *   *

JOCK was so mean that when he found a bottle of indigestion mixture, he ate a jar of pickles.

* * *

JOCK was down in the dumps and his office mate wondered why, because he left the pub the previous evening with a lovely blonde on his arm.

"What happened?"

Jock said he took the blonde to dinner, bought her chocolates and champagne and they went back to his flat for the night.

"Well, why so gloomy?"

"I spent a fortune," said Jock, "and another bloke has just told me I could have got the same result with a couple of beers and a packet of potato chips."

* * *

AN Englishman, a Scotsman and an Irishman were on the Titanic when she struck the iceberg.

As she started to sink the purser shouted: "We are about to meet our maker. We'd better do something religious."

The Englishman said a prayer. The Irishman sang a hymn. The Scotsman took up a collection.

* * *

IN his later years Shamus began to be a little deaf but was too mean to buy a hearing aid.

So he scrounged some thin wire and put one end in his top pocket and hooked the other end behind his ear.

It made no difference to his deafness, but it prompted people to speak to him more loudly.

* * *

JOCK walked into the fish shop and ordered two pieces of fish, two pickled onions, plenty of vinegar and salt "and wrap the lot up in today's newspaper."

* * *

THE rich Sultan of Istanbul was dying from a disease that baffled the medical world for months before they discovered that only a blood transfusion would save him. It was a rare blood group and a search throughout the globe revealed that there was only one man that could match the Sultan's blood group. It was Jock McTavish from the Highlands.

Jock donated the blood. It saved the Sultan's life and shortly afterwards Jock received a gift of $5000.

Two years later the Sultan had a relapse and Jock was asked to supply more of his unique blood. Again the Sultan recovered and soon after Jock received a gift of $2000.

When the Sultan fell ill for the third time Jock once again came to the rescue with more Celtic blood. The Sultan recovered and sent Jock a thank you note.

* * *

JOCK was walking down the street in his kilt when a curious woman asked if there was anything worn under the tartan.

"Nothing's worn," he replied, "everything's in perfect working order."

* * *

THE Scotsman gave the waiter a tip.

It didn't even run a place.

* * *

THE chaps in the bar invited Jock to a small bore shooting club. When he got there they stood him on a box and started firing at him.

WHEN a Scottish millionaire in his eighties decided to marry an eighteen year old chorus girl the vicar protested.

"I don't believe in marrying for money," he said.

"Good," replied the millionaire, "then I won't insult you by offering you a fee for performing the ceremony."

* * *

HAVE you heard about the Scotsman who gave an Englishman, a Welshman and an Irishman ten pounds each?

Neither has anyone else.

* * *

THEN there's the Scot who drinks Scotch and Horlicks. When it is his turn to shout he is fast asleep.

* * *

A SCOT pushes his way to the bar. "I've had an attack of the Yaws," he says to the barman.

"What's Yaws?" he says.

"Double whisky," says the canny Scot.

* * *

A SCOT ordered a pot of beer and as the barman handed it over he said, "D'yer think yer canna fit a nip o whisky in it too?"

"Certainly," said the barman.

"Then fill it ta the top wi beer."

* * *

THREE Scots were in church one Sunday when the collection plate came their way. One fainted and the other two carried him out.

* * *

THE young Scotsman's delight was obvious as the train pulled in to Victoria Street Station.

"First time in London?" enquired the passenger opposite.

"Aye," said Scotty, "and not only that, I am on my honeymoon."

The passenger looked surprised. "Then where is your wife?"

"Oh, she's been here before," said Scotty.

* * *

OLD Mrs McTavish was dying and for almost a week her husband had never left her bedside. But it was Friday night and McTavish always had a wee dram with his mates.

He lent close to her ear. "Darling," he whispered. "I've got to go out for a wee bit. Now if you feel yourself slipping away, before you breathe your last breath would you mind blowing out the candle?"

* * *

SHAKING her collection tin the Salvation Army lass approached Old Jock at the bar and asked him for a dollar for the Lord.

"How old are ye, lass?" asked Jock.

"I'm twenty," she said.

"Well, I'm 82 and I'll be seeing the Lord afore you, so I'll give him the dollar meself."

* * *

LETTER to the Editor: "If you don't stop making jokes at the expense of Scotsmen I shall discontinue borrowing your newspaper."

* * *

A SCOTTISH music lover married a woman because he was charmed with her voice. So charmed indeed, that he didn't realise how ugly she was until the first morning of the honeymoon when he sat in bed looking at her without her makeup.

He stared at her for some time, then grabbed her by the shoulders and roared: "Sing ya bugger, sing. Fer Chrissake sing."

* * *

DOWN at the Edinburgh Arms the worst drunk at the bar is always Duncan Disorderly.

* * *

A SCOTTISH hotel is an establishment where they pinch the towels off the guests.

* * *

McTAVISH took all his money out of the bank for a holiday. After it rested in his pocket for a week he put it all back.

* * *

WHEN the police put a price on Jock's head he turned himself in.

* * *

SHE said she would never go to a restaurant with Jock again. "He reads the menu from right to left," she said.

* * *

THERE were no serious injuries in an accident on the highway when a truck collided with a taxi.

The truckdriver escaped unhurt, but the sixteen Scotsmen in the taxi were treated for shock, as they had paid for the trip in advance.

* * *

JOCK picked up a lovely young woman in the pub and hailed a cab to take her home. He was so infatuated with her he could hardly keep his eyes on the meter.

* * *

SCOT McTavish was lugging a heavy suitcase. He hailed a cab. "How much to the train station?"

"Five dollars," said the driver.

"How much for my suitcase?"

"Nothing."

McTavish opened the door, slung his case in and said: "Here, take it to the station then."

* * *

WHEN the taxi company lowered its rates from two dollars flagfall to a single dollar there was a protest meeting at the Celtic Club. The Scots were annoyed that in most cases they were saving around five dollars a night by walking home, now they would only save around $2.50.

* * *

McTAVISH was the meanest of Scottish conmen. When he had need to write a letter to his brother Hamish, he would address the letter to himself with his brother's name and address on the back, then post it without a stamp.

When it was duly delivered to his address McTavish would refuse to pay the duty and refuse to accept the letter. It was therefore returned to the sender whose name was on the back.

* * *

AN old farmer and his son had scratched out a living on their farm for thirty years. One day the son came home yelling for joy that he had won the £500,000 first prize in the lottery.

"Here Dad, here's your share," and he slapped a hundred pound note on the table.

The old man looked at it a while. "When I was young," he said, "I never had time to smoke, drink or gamble because working this farm took all my time. In fact, I never had time to marry your Ma."

The young man considered this. "Well that's a nice state of affairs," he complained. "Of course you know what that makes me?"

"Yeah," said the old man, "and a bloody mean one at that."

*   *   *

FARMER McTavish had groomed the prize bull for the annual show and was confident of winning a blue ribbon, but on the very eve of the big event he was aghast to find the bull had gone cock-eyed.

He made a panic call to the vet who was quickly on the scene and summed up the problem in a professional and composed manner. He simply picked up a length of plastic pipe from the barn floor, inserted one end in the bull's rectum and blew forcefully in the other.

The bull's eyes popped straight ahead.

But next day, as McTavish unloaded the bull into his stall at the show, he was distraught to find the cock-eyed affliction had returned.

He shoved the pipe up the bull's bum and blew for all he was worth, but to no avail. In desperation he made another panic call to the vet, who once again arrived in his usual calm manner.

"I did what you did," said McTavish, "But it doesn't work."

"Show me," said the vet.

Once again McTavish shoved the pipe in and blew his best.

"No, no," said the vet. He pulled the pipe out, turned it round and plunged the opposite end into the beast. He gave one puff and the bull's eyes popped straight.

"Oh, so I was using the wrong end of the pipe?" said McTavish.

"No," said the vet. "It makes no difference."

"Then why did you turn it around?"

"You don't think I would use the same end you've had in your mouth do you?" said the vet.

* * *

TIMES were hard so McTavish decided to put his wife on the street as a woman of the night. At the end of the week he grabbed her handbag and emptied the contents on the kitchen table. In cash it amounted to $75.50p.

"What miserable bastard gave you 50p?" he said.

"They all did," she replied.

* * *

SHE had told the court the defendant had robbed her.

"Yes," said the judge, "you claim this man stole a hundred dollars you had pinned inside your knickers?"

"Yes, judge, that's him."

"But why didn't you put up a fight, scream or kick?"

"Your Honour, at the time I didn't know he was after my money."

SPANIARDS

CHRISTOPHER Columbus was the first conman. He was an Italian in charge of a Spanish ship. He didn't know where he was going. When he got there he didn't know where he was. When he got back he didn't know where he had been. And the government paid for the trip.

* * *

IN Spain it is not uncommon for parents to name a boy Jesus. There was one such boy in the choir at St Miguel's and although the kid was tone-deaf and couldn't sing a note he was of such angelic appearance that the priest didn't want to waste such beauty and placed him in front of the choir.

"Don't sing," said the priest, "just mouth the words and pretend to be singing."

Jesus was in the forefront of the choir when the bishop made his annual visit to St Miguel's. The bishop told the priest he was impressed by the choir.

"But you know," he said, "that little dark boy in front. He wasn't singing at all. He was just opening and shutting his mouth."

"Oh, Jesus. He can't sing."

"No, but Christ Almighty, he could try couldn't he?"

* * *

THE Spanish platoon was ready to go over the top.

"It will be man-to-man fighting," yelled the commandant.

Pedro raised his hand: "Can you introduce me to my man so that we could come to an understanding?"

* * *

A TOURIST went into a Madrid restaurant and asked for the speciality of the house. He was served a magnificent plate bearing two king-sized rissoles.

The tourist tucked in, found them to be delicious and called the waiter to express his appreciation.

"What do you call that dish?" asked the tourist wiping his lips with the napkin.

"They are gonads," said the Spanish waiter. He went on to explain that the gonads were the testicles of the bull killed in the adjoining bull ring that very day.

"Always fresh, Senor," said the waiter.

It was quite a shock for the tourist, but he had to admit they were tasty, satisfying and cheap.

In fact, the very next evening he returned and asked for the same dish.

When they were served he called the waiter back to complain about the size of the two miserable rissoles which sat forlorn and lonely in the centre of the plate.

"Yes, Senor," agreed the waiter, "they are much smaller than yesterday, but you see Senor, today, the bull wins."

* * *

THE tourist in the swank hotel in Barcelona could not help but notice that Manuel the waiter had his thumb in every dish he served. When the soup arrived the digit was once again deep in the bowl. Next came the chilli concarne with Manuel's thumb well inserted in the gravy.

It was too much for the tourist. "Hey, is it a Spanish custom for waiters to leave their thumbs in the food?"

"No Senor," replied Manuel. "It ees just that I have zee arthritis in the thumb and I need to keep it warm."

The news shocked the tourist.

"You bastard," he said, "putting your thumb in my food. You can jam your thumb up your arse."

"That ees what I do in the kitchen," said Manuel.

TURKS

WHEN the sultan entered his harem unexpectedly, his
wives let out a terrified sheik.

*　*　*

THE sultan had ten wives.
   Nine of them had it pretty soft.

*　*　*

IN the harem the lonely girl calls
   But the guard takes no notice at alls
   When asked if he cheats
   On the sultan, he bleats,
   "Oh I would, but I ain't got the balls."

VIETNAMESE

HUNG Le, Australia's Vietnamese comic asks: "How do you know when a Vietnamese has robbed your house?"

He says because the dog is missing and your homework's done.

*   *   *

VIETNAMESE migrant got excited when he saw a hot dog stall. "You beauty," he said, until he took a closer look.

"That's disgusting," he said. "In my country we don't eat that part of the dog."

*   *   *

SIGN on a Vietnamese restaurant door: "Dogs not allowed—Out."

*   *   *

HUNG Le said he came to Australia aboard a very leaky prawn boat. "It was so leaky even the prawns were wearing life jackets," he said.

*   *   *

WHEN Vietnamese Louie rolled a big win at the casino he looked around town for the finest house on the choicest piece of real estate. He found that the Rothschilds, the great financiers, owned the most palatial home. So he began building an identical mansion beside it.

When it was finished Baron Rothschild compli-

mented Vietnamese Louie on his attention to detail.
The building was identical in every respect.

"But it's worth more than yours," said Louie.

"How come? I don't see that," said the baron.

"In every way the two places are alike until you try
to sell them," explained Louie. "When the prospective
buyer asks me about the neighbours I tell them we live
next to the famous Rothschilds. But when they ask you
about the neighbours you will have to admit it's Vietnamese boat people."

WELSH

WHY do the Welsh always sing?
  Because they have no locks on the dunny doors.

* * *

WHAT do you call a Welsh vasectomist?
  Dai Abollickal.

* * *

WHAT do you call a Welshman with the runs?
  Dai O'rrhoea!

* * *

DID you hear about the Welshman who looked up his family tree and found that half of them were still living in it?

* * *

WELSHMEN think so much of their women they have put a picture of one on their national flag.

* * *

HOW do Welsh women make yogurt?
  They stare at a bottle of milk.

* * *

HOW do you stump a Welshman?
  Ask him to spell his name.

* * *

WHY are there no Welsh ventriloquists?
  Because nobody would know which was the dummy.

* * *

A WELSHMAN was fined $100 for having sex with a goat.

His friend was fined $50 for acting the goat.

* * *

BEING of the Celtic race the Welsh are reputed to have a sixth sense. Which is quite remarkable because they have none of the other five.

* * *

TAFFY had a little lamb.

His case comes up next week.

* * *

WHAT do people sit on in Wales?

Their brains!

* * *

WHAT do you get if you cross a Welshman with a boomerang?

A nasty smell you can't get rid of.

* * *

TAFFY applied for the job as a postman. Knowing that the Welsh are thick, the postmaster decided to give him an intelligence test.

"How far do you think it is from here to the moon?" he asked.

"If that's the size of the round you can stick the job up your bum," said Taffy.

* * *

TAFFY entered the pharmacy.

"I'd like some deodorant, if ye please?"

"Aerosol?"

"No ya great mullock, it's fer under me arms."

* * *

A GROUP of rowdy drunks singing in chorus was making its way down the street before stopping outside a cottage.

"Is this where Taffy lives?" they would shout between bawdy songs.

Finally a woman flung a window open and told them to be quiet.

"Is this where Taffy lives?" came another call.

"Yes," she replied.

"Well then, can you come down and let him in so the rest of us can go home?"

* * *

TAFFY had only been married six months when he confided to his mate: "I've just had a terrible shock. I have just discovered my wife is a liar."

"How do you know?" asked his mate.

"She said she was out with Betty last night. I know that's not true because I was out with Betty last night!"

* * *

THEY had been married a week and one morning while they were lying in bed, she was idly fondling his dick and said "Taffy darling, didn't you say you were the only man with one of these?"

"That's right, luv."

"No, you've been telling fibs," she said. "Your brother has one too."

"Oh, that was my spare one. I gave it to him."

"Silly man," she said. "You gave the best one away."

MULTI-NATIONAL

AT an international medical conference the Russian doctor told how they transplanted a new heart into a man and he was working within one month.

"That's nothing," said the American. "We put a heart, lungs and a new liver into a man and within one month he was up looking for work."

"That's bugger-all," said the Australian. "We put a fart in Canberra and in no time at all he put half the population out of work."

* * *

AT a United Nations function in New York the Norwegian consul approached a small group of diplomats and made a bid to start small talk. "Pardon me," he said. "What is your opinion of the meat shortage?"

The American looked perplexed: "What's a shortage."

The Pole scratched his head: "What's meat?"

The Russian shrugged: "What's an opinion?"

The Israeli asked: "What's pardon me?"

* * *

WHEN Paddy emigrated from Ireland to Australia, it lifted the IQ of both countries.

* * *

"I'M Murphy, Irish, and proud of it."

"I'm McTavish, Scotch, and fond of it!"

* * *

THE Irishman was bonking a Scottish lass in the park and she wasn't impressed with his performance.

"I thought Irishmen were supposed to be big and thick," she grumbled.

"And I thought the Scots were tight," he replied.

* * *

FOUR women, one English, one American, one German and one French, were all asked the same question: "What would you do if you were shipwrecked on an island with a regiment of soldiers?"

The Englishwoman said she would hide. The American said she would seek the protection of the commanding officer. The German woman said she would be out marching and it wouldn't bother her.

The French woman thought for a moment; "I understand ze question, but what seems to be ze problem?"

* * *

PUT two men and a woman on a desert island and it can depend on the nationalities what will happen.

If they are Jewish the two men will sit down and argue for months on the right to the woman.

If they are Greek they will play cards for her.

If they are English they are as likely to ignore her and be more interested in each other.

If they are French they will agree to share the woman.

If they are Italian one man will kill the other.

If they are Australian they will take turns and brag about it to each other next day.

* * *

THE train was rattling towards a long tunnel and in one compartment sat an Englishman, an Irishman, a pretty young woman and a little old lady.

The train entered the tunnel and all went black. There was a loud kiss followed at once by an even louder smack.

When the train emerged from the tunnel the four occupants were still in their seats and busy with their own thoughts about what happened.

The pretty young woman was thinking: "Why would that Irishman want to kiss an old lady?"

The old lady was thinking: "What a hussy sitting there as if nothing had happened when I know that Englishman kissed her."

The Englishman was thinking: "I didn't do a damned thing, so why should I get my face slapped?"

And the Irishman was thinking: "How about that! I kiss my own hand, slap an Englishman in the mouth and get away with it!"

*   *   *

AN Englishman, an Australian and a Scotsman were invited to a party. The Englishman took six bottles of Guinness, the Aussie took six bottles of beer, and the Scotsman took six of his friends.

*   *   *

THREE soldiers met in the pub. The Australian stood a round, the Englishman stood a round and the Scotsman stood six feet tall.

*   *   *

IF a paddock full of Irishmen is a paddy field, then a paddock full of Ockers must be a vacant lot.

RELIGION

(General)

IT has always been Politically Incorrect to ridicule the church. The penalty not so long ago was to be burnt at the stake especially if you were a woman.

But thanks to the pranks of the notorious English church with its transvestite vicars and eccentric ecclesiastics, the church has become a legitimate butt of ridicule.

Let's face it, there are no laughs in the Bible. There is little humour in Hell or Purgatory and no doubt it is totally improper to giggle in Heaven.

A GORILLA left the zoo's reading room quite confused.

He had read the Bible and Charles Darwin's Origin of the Species and didn't know if he was his brother's keeper or his keeper's brother.

* * *

A BURGLAR was rummaging through a house house in the dark. He froze when he heard a voice say: "Jesus is watching you."

Sweating with fear, he heard the voice repeat: "Jesus is watching you."

He finally found the courage to switch on the light, and discovered a parrot, which said again:

"Jesus is watching you."

With a sigh of relief the burglar said to himself: "Whew! Just a bloody parrot."

"I might be just a bloody parrot," said the bird, " but you'll find Jesus is a dirty big Doberman."

* * *

MY mother-in-law converted me to religion.

I never believed in Hell until I met her.

* * *

THE clergy have been making fools of themselves for some time. "Would you believe it," said the verger to the vicar, "someone's stolen my umbrella. I don't know what things are coming to because I believe it was someone in this parish."

"Dreadful state of affairs," agreed the vicar. "I'll tell you what. I will give a strong sermon next Sunday on the subject of sin and I will go through each of the ten commandments. You stand beside me and scrutinise the congregation and when I come to 'Thou Shalt Not Covet Thy Neighbour's Goods' see who is looking fidgety or guilty."

So he does. Next Sunday morning the whole village is in church and the vicar starts thundering through the commandments. But when he finished the verger wasn't there.

Asked to explain why he left so suddenly the verger said: "When you got to the one, 'Thou Shalt Not Commit Adultery' I remembered where I'd left my umbrella!"

* * *

HIS dad asked what he had learned in Sunday School that morning.

"I learned about a cross-eyed bear whose name was Gladly," replied the youngster.

Dad was puzzled and had to press the point further to finally discover it was a hymn: 'Gladly, Thy Cross I'd Bear'.

*　*　*

LARGE sign on the cathedral door read: 'This is the House of God, and these are the Gates of Heaven'.

And below in smaller print: 'This door is locked between the hours of 6 pm and 10 am'.

*　*　*

A LARGE sign outside the church read: "If you are tired of sin, come in."

Underneath, written in lipstick was an adendum: "If not, ring Dulcie on 041-2468."

*　*　*

A VICAR reported to his bishop that he was too ill to take morning service that Sunday, and then ducked off to the golf course to play a quiet 18 holes.

It didn't go unnoticed by one of the angels on high who dobbed him in to God. "He shouldn't be allowed to get away with that," said the angel.

God nodded agreement and said "Leave it to me."

The vicar hit off on a 500 metre par-five hole, a mighty shot which sent the ball soaring straight down the fairway. Three bounces and it reached the green to slowly roll across to the pin, and plonked in for a hole-in-one.

"I thought you were going to punish him," said the angel.

"I have," said God. "Who is he going to tell?"

*　*　*

A REPORTER on a religious newspaper was polling the religious beliefs of the world leaders and sought an interview with Bill Clinton.

He was shown into the oval office and was impressed to see among the bank of phones with hotlines to Britain, Russia and the Pentagon, a purple phone on the end.

"That's my direct line to God," said Clinton.

"Gosh," said the reporter. "How much does it cost to call God?"

"Oh, just on a thousand dollars a minute, but the communication is essential."

Binyamin Netanyahu was the reporter's next assignment and in the Prime Minister's office in Tel Aviv he noticed another purple phone among the rest.

"No doubt that's a direct line to God?" said the reporter.

"Indeed it is," replied Peres.

"How much does it cost?"

"Oh, about thirty cents I think," said Peres.

"But it costs the US President just over a thousand."

"Ah yes," said Netanyahu, "but from here it is a local call."

* * *

THE radio announcer was delighted to hear the way in which his little son said his prayers, concluding with: "And here again, dear God, are the headlines."

THE travelling parson had decided to retire from his circuit in the bush and wanted to sell his horse. Old Jack was down from the high country and recognising a strong horse when he saw one, soon struck a bargain with the parson.

But when Jack swung up in the saddle, the horse refused to move.

"Oh, I forgot to tell you he is a very religious horse,"

said the parson. "I have trained him reverently and he will only go when you say the words 'Jesus Christ', and he will only stop when you say 'Amen'."

Old Jack thanked the parson, said "Jesus Christ" and the horse took off at a fast clip.

They were travelling back to the high country when thunder clouds darkened the sky, and a bolt of lightening cracked to the ground.

The horse bolted in fright and a low branch struck Old Jack in the face momentarily blinding him. As the horse galloped madly through the bush he tried to think of the word to make it stop, finally yelling "Amen".

The horse skidded to a halt and when Old Jack opened his eyes he saw that his mount had stopped right on the edge of a frightening mountain precipice.

"Jesus Christ," he said.

*   *   *

PAT and Mick were digging up the road outside the local knock shop when they noticed the vicar's furtive approach before he ducked into the entrance.

"Did yer see that?" said Pat. "The dirty Protestant minister sneaking in for his share o' sin. What a hypocrite."

After further denouncement of the vicar they began digging again until Mick spotted a rabbi making a tentative but swift entry into the brothel.

"Didja see that?" said Mick. "The Jews are no better."

About an hour went by before they spotted Father McGuire hurrying into the whorehouse.

"Mick," said Pat, "take off your hat. One of those poor girls must be dying in there."

AFTER countless centuries of temperature changes the wall between Heaven and Hell began to crack. St Peter called Lucifer and said it was his turn to provide the money to fix the dividing wall.

"Rubbish, we're not paying," said the evil one.

"Okay, then we will sue," said St Peter.

"Really," grinned the Devil, "and where do you intend to find a lawyer?"

*　　*　　*

IT all started in the Garden of Eden, and one day Adam was intrigued by the antics of a buck rabbit. "What's he doing?" he asked God, and was told that the rabbits were simply making love.

He saw two birds doing something similar, and upon enquiry from on high was told they were also making love.

"Why haven't I got anybody to do that with?" he asked God, who replied that he would fix it first thing next morning.

Sure enough, when Adam awoke, there was Eve lying beside him. He took her by the hand and they ran into the bushes.

Ten minutes later Adam emerged from the bushes. "Hey God, what's a headache?"

*　　*　　*

AND apparently religion is very old:
　　AN old archeologist named Tossel
　　Discovered a marvellous fossil
　　He knew from its bend
　　And the knob on the end
　　'Twas the peter of Paul the Apostle.

*　　*　　*

"I DON'T like the look of the new missionary," said one cannibal to the other.

"That's alright," said the other, "just eat the potatoes."

*　*　*

ISRAELI prime minister Binyamin Netanyahu invited the Pope to a game of golf. Since the Pope had no idea of the game he convened the College of Cardinals and asked their advice.

"Call Greg Norman, make him a cardinal, tell Netanyahu you're sick and send Cardinal Norman in your place."

Honoured by the Pope's request Greg Norman agreed to represent him.

When he returned from the game the Pope asked how he had done. "I came in second," said Norman.

"You mean Netanyahu beat you?"

"No, Your Holiness, Rabbi Nicklaus did."

*　*　*

THE sermon for the evening was 'Christian Perfection', and the minister was quick to point out that this was an ideal state of grace unattainable by the likes of the sinners in the nondescript congregation before him. Nevertheless, in the course of his sermon he challenged anyone present to stand and proclaim they were perfect. To his astonishment a bloke in the fifth pew got to his feet.

"Do you dare claim you are perfect?" thundered the cleric.

"No, not me," replied the man, "I am standing proxy for my wife's first husband!"

*　*　*

LEANING on the bar, two drinkers were arguing about religion. "What do you know about the Lord's Prayer," said one. "I'll bet you ten cents you don't know the first line."

"You're on," said the other, and put his ten cents on the bar.

"And now I lay me down to sleep," proudly recited the first.

"You bastard," said his mate pushing the money towards him, "I didn't think you knew it!"

*   *   *

MURPHY lived next to McTavish, one a Catholic, the other a Protestant, but they were good neighbours.

One day McTavish, hassled by his tribe of kids, said to Murphy: "You Catholics don't use birth control, yet you've got no children and I've got five."

"We use the Safe Period," explained Murphy.

"Never heard of it," said McTavish, "What's the Safe Period?"

"Every second Tuesday when you go to Lodge," said Murphy.

*   *   *

THE vicar, the priest and the rabbi were always arguing about which was the true religion. But they were friends enough to make a pact that whoever died first, the other two would each put $300 in the coffin to ensure admittance to the Pearly Gates.

It came to pass that the vicar died first. The other two attended the funeral service and as good as his word, the priest approached the coffin and put in his $300.

The rabbi followed, wrote a cheque for $600, put it in beside the vicar and took his $300 change.

THE two men dressed in black were the only occupants in a compartment on a long train journey. After a time one said, "Excuse me, but would I be right in thinking you are a Catholic priest?"

"Yes. And would you be a rabbi?"

"I am," said the first.

They had a lot of time to kill and eventually the rabbi said: "Have you ever broken a commandment?"

The priest admitted that he had 'taken a woman.'

After a while the priest said: "Have you ever eaten pork?"

The rabbi looked around as if to check nobody else was in the compartment, then nodded his head. "Yes," he whispered.

The long silence was broken by the priest. "Sex is much better than pork isn't it!"

* * *

A JEWISH tailor was troubled by the way his son had turned out and went to see his rabbi about it. "I brought him up in the faith, gave him a very expensive bar mitzvah, cost me a fortune to educate him. Then he tells me last week he has decided to be a Christian. Rabbi, can you help me, what will I do?"

"Funny thing you should bring that problem to me," said the rabbi. "Like you I brought my boy up in the faith, put him through university, cost me a fortune, then one day he comes and tells me he has decided to become a Christian."

"What did you do?" asked the tailor.

"I went to the synagogue and prayed to Almighty God for an answer."

"And what happened," pressed the tailor.

God's voice came into the synagogue as clear as a

214

bell: "Funny thing you should bring that problem to me," he said.

* * *

OF course it was a certainty that Jesus was Jewish. He lived at home until he was 30, he went into his father's business, his mother thought he was divine, and he thought she was a virgin.

* * *

WHY wasn't Christ born in Australia?

Well, where would you find a virgin, and where would you find three wise men?

* * *

ACTUALLY there were four wise men. While following the star on the way to the manger, one of them said he knew a short cut.

* * *

THE city council had just taken delivery of the new mayoral car and called on the three denominations to consecrate it at a special ceremony.

The priest chanted a blessing and sprinkled it with holy water. The parson chanted a blessing and waved the cross over it. The rabbi chanted a blessing, went round the back and cut an inch off the exhaust pipe.

* * *

GOD spent a lot of time hacking out the commandments on one tablet of stone, then he offered them to the first tribe he saw.

They happened to be Germans, and after studying the bit about 'Thou Shalt Not Kill' decided it was not their cup of tea. Killing was a natural thing to do wasn't it?

God offered them to the French. They took one look

and said "What's all this ban on adultery. That's not for us," so they refused.

God then offered them to the Jews.

"How much?" said Moses.

"They are free," said God.

"Okay, we'll take two."

*   *   *

THE priest, the vicar and the rabbi were discussing how they divided the collection between God's work and themselves.

"We lean more towards the fundamentalist side," said the rabbi. "I take the money outside and literally fling it up to heaven and what God wants he keeps, what falls back on the ground, I keep."

*   *   *

AFTER the healing of the centuries-old rift between the Catholic Church and the Jewish Orthodox faith, the leaders attended the International Inter-Church Council and for the first time they sat down together.

"We've been meaning to give you this for a long time," said the Rabbi handing the Pope an envelope.

It was the bill for the Last Supper.

*   *   *

AT the same Inter-Church Council an argument developed on whether God was black or white. It went on for weeks until the assembly finally agreed on a joint prayer to put the question directly to God himself.

There was an immediate and thundering reply that reverberated around the cathedral: "I am what I am!"

There was a stunned silence.

"That settles it then," said the Archbishop of Canterbury. "He's white."

"What do you mean?" protested Archbishop Tutu.

216

"Well, if he was black," said the Archbishop of Canterbury, "he would have said: 'Ah is wot ah is!'"

*　*　*

THE minister pranged his brand new car when a woman stopped to check her make-up in the rear-vision mirror. It was only the car's first time on the road and the minister got really angry.

He got out and roared at the woman: "Why don't you go forth and multiply!"

*　*　*

ST PETER, with a clipboard under his arm, was interviewing a new arrival at the Pearly Gates.

"What's your name?"

"Marmaduke."

"When you were on earth did you ever smoke or gamble?"

"No."

"Did you ever lie, cheat, steal or swear?"

"No."

"Did you ever drink or chase women?"

"No, indeed I did not."

"Well what took you so long?"

*　*　*

A CATHOLIC priest and a Protestant minister had a lively argument about their respective faiths. At last they agreed to differ.

In parting the priest said: "You worship God in your way and I'll worship Him His way."

*　*　*

THE vicar was invited to give an address to the local branch of Alcoholics Anonymous.

"I have lived in this town all my life," he said. "And

217

there are thirty-five hotels in this town and I can honestly say I have not been in one."

"Which one was that?" came a voice from the rear of the hall.

* * *

FATHER Kelly rang the local council to complain about a dead goat on the road in front of the church.

The protestant clerk who took the call thought he would be smart.

"I thought you lot looked after the dead."

"We do," said the priest calmly, "but we are obliged to advise the relatives first."

ANGLICANS

(Protestants, Presbyterians and all that lot)

THERE once was a vicar from Kew
  Who preached with his vestments askew
  A lady called Morgan
  Caught sight of his organ
  And promptly passed out in the pew.

* * *

THE meek had a meeting today and decided they don't want to inherit the earth.

* * *

THE vicar was selling raffle tickets for the Society of Retired & Incontinent Bellringers and knocked on the door of frail old Mrs Billingham.

"Would you care to support the Society for Retired & Incontinent Bellringers? " he asked.

"What's that?" said Mrs Billingham. "I'm hard of hearing."

"Would you care to buy a ticket?" repeated the vicar in a louder voice.

"What's that?" she answered, cupping her hand round her ear.

In disgust the vicar turned and walked away.

"Don't forget to shut the gate," said Mrs Billingham.

"Bugger the gate," muttered the vicar.

"And fuck the Society for Retired & Incontinent Bellringers," said Mrs Billingham.

* * *

AS Rev Smithers droned on the little boy's eyes began to wander around the church until he spotted the war memorial plaque.

"Daddy," he whispered, "what's that for?"

"It's for the men who died in the service."

Growing pale the boy said: "Was Rev Smithers giving the sermon then, too?"

* * *

"I DON'T mind people looking at their watches when I'm making a speech," said the vicar, "but it is damned disconcerting to see them take them off and shake them to see if they have stopped."

* * *

THE vicar asked the pert young widow to give a little talk to the Temperance Society because he said the men liked her short addresses.

* * *

THE new vicar in town even entered the country pub in a bid to introduce himself and approached an old-timer at the bar with outstretched hand.

"My name is Paul," he said.

The old-timer studied him for a moment and then said: "Did those Thessalonians and Galatians ever write back to you?"

* * *

THEY were discussing the declining attendances at church. "But it does have its advantages," said the spinster.

She explained: "Sometimes the congregation is so

small that when the vicar says 'Dearly Beloved' it is as if he is proposing to you."

* * *

THE clergyman had delivered a fiery sermon against the evils of dancing and made it clear that he was fundamentally opposed to this past-time. After the congregation had filed out he was approached by a young dancing enthusiast. "Just what's wrong with dancing?" he asked.

"Well, for one thing," said the minister, "it's the close touching of the bodies."

"Not so," protested the parishioner, "it's all in the mind of those who look at it with the wrong attitude."

"Then let's suppose," argued the minister, "that you came home from work and found me holding your wife in that manner. What would you think?"

"I'd think that you'd better be dancing," was the reply.

* * *

THE vicar was delighted to see Old Ned working up a sweat in his front garden. He leaned over the fence and gushed: "Your garden is looking lovely. Isn't it wonderful what man and God can do when they work in harmony?"

"Maybe," said Ned wiping his brow. "But you should have seen this yard when God had it on his own."

* * *

THE young vicar got married and on his honeymoon night was surprised to find his bride already in bed when he entered the bedroom.

"Oh dearest," he said, "I had hoped to find you on your knees at the bedside."

"Oh, alright," she said, "but I had hoped to see your face tonight."

* * *

TWO vicars were lamenting the present generation's slack state of morals.

"I didn't sleep with my wife before we were married," said one indignantly. "Did you?"

"Not sure, old boy, what was her maiden name?"

* * *

THE vicar's term at the parish was up and he was about to be transferred. The regular parishioners had gathered at a tea party in his honour.

"We'll really miss you," said one little old lady. "No matter who they send as a replacement he will never be as good as you."

The vicar was flattered, but he assured her his successor would be an adequate and caring pastor.

"No, no," the old-timer insisted, "it's always the same. We've had six ministers here in my time and I can assure you each one has been worse than the one before!"

* * *

THE Queen had a baby and they fired a 21-gun salute.

The nun had a baby and they fired the dirty old Canon.

* * *

THE squire took his son to the library for a heart-to-heart. "Look here Cecil," he said, "You are thirty-five now and your mother thinks it is high time you were married. What about marrying Lady Genevieve?

"I don't love Lady Genevieve," he said.

"Well what about Lady Cynthia?"

"I don't love Lady Cynthia. Actually I love Lord Fonsonby."

"Well you can't marry him. He's a Catholic."

* * *

FROM the pulpit the vicar announced that one of his flock, Miss Helen Hunt, had found a purse containing money, a variety of personal items and what he believed to be a small packet of white balloons.

"So whoever has lost this purse, go to Helen Hunt for it!"

* * *

THE woman was about to be stoned to death for her sinful ways when Jesus pushed his way through the crowd.

"Stop," he cried. "Let whoever is without sin cast the first stone."

With that, a rock flies over the crowd and whacks the woman between the eyes.

Jesus spots the culprit: "Not you again, Mother," he says.

* * *

LYING on the psychiatrist's couch, the dean told the doctor he feared he might be gay.

"What makes you think that?"

"Well, my grandfather was gay, and so was my father," said the dean.

"That doesn't mean you're gay," said the shrink. "We don't believe it is hereditary."

"Yes, but my brothers are also gay," pressed the dean.

"That's uncanny," said the doc. "Isn't there anyone in your family sexually attracted to women?"

"Yes," said the dean, "there's my sister."

THE drunk boarded the train and plonked himself down beside a vicar and began to read the paper.

He looks up after a bit and says: "Tell me Rev, what causes arthritis?"

It was just the opening the vicar wanted. "I will tell you what causes arthritis my man," he said with passion. "It's immoral living, too much drinking and smoking and no doubt sins of the flesh. How long have you had it?"

"Oh it's not me, Rev," said the drunk. "It says here the Archbishop of Canterbury's got it."

*   *   *

THE vicar walked around to the back of the church and saw three boys sitting on the ground with a handful of coins at their feet.

"What might you boys be doing?" he enquired.

"We're having a competition," explained one. "Whoever tells the biggest lie gets the money."

The vicar was visibly shocked. "When I was a boy," he said, "I never told untruths."

They said "Okay, you win," and gave him the money.

*   *   *

IT was hard times and he knocked on the vicarage door for a hand-out.

"I want to ask you one question," said the vicar when he had heard the man's hardluck story. "Do you take alcoholic drink?"

"Before I answer that," said the swaggie thoughtfully, "is that in the nature of an enquiry or an invitation?"

*   *   *

THE country vicar had not seen young Johnny at Sunday School, so when he found the lad beside a country road minding his dad's cattle, he thought it an appropriate time to deliver an impromptu sermon.

"They are fine bullocks, Johnny, do you know who made them?"

"Dad did," replied Johnny.

"Oh no," the vicar smiled. "God made those bullocks."

Johnny shook his head. "God made them bulls. Dad made them bullocks."

* * *

AS the proud father handed the baby to the vicar at the christening font, the cleric said: "And what will we call this little chap?"

"It's a girl," whispered the father. "You've got hold of my thumb!"

* * *

THE notice board outside the church declared the stern warning: 'What would you do if Christ returned this week?'

The graffiti scrawled underneath said: 'Move McNally to full foward and Christ to centre half.'

* * *

THE vicar called at the home of Miss Smithers, secretary of the church auxiliary, who had been in bed for a week with the flu.

"I prayed for you last night," he said.

"No need to," she replied. "I'm in the phone book."

* * *

THE vicar said to the young lad: "Tell me, who went to Mount Olive?"

"Popeye," was the quick reply.

FAITH is a wonderful thing, and when a group of Christian postal workers noticed an envelope simply addressed, 'To God' they couldn't keep their sticky fingers from opening it.

They found it to be a sad letter from an old man suffering from a terminal disease, asking God to send him a hundred dollars so that he could see his elderly wife was looked after when he died.

The letter said: 'I have always believed in you, yet never asked you for anything except this favour.'

The postal workers were touched. They had a quick whip around and gathered all the money they could, stuffed the notes in an envelope and had it delivered back to the old man on the next round.

Two days later they noticed a second letter addressed to God. Moved by the speed in which the old man wished to thank his Creator they opened it.

It read: 'Thanks for the money which came so promptly. However, it was only $80 when it arrived. I reckon those thieving bastards at the post office snitched the rest.'

*   *   *

STANDING at the door as the parishioners filed out of church the vicar shook a man's hand. "Nice to see you coming along to church again," he said. "Is it because of my sermons?"

"No," said the prodigal, "not yours, my wife's."

*   *   *

IN Sunday School the teacher asked little Johnnie which parable in the Bible he liked best.

"Simple," said Johnnie. "It's that one about the bloke who loafs and fishes."

*   *   *

AFTER his first appearance in the pulpit Rev Moggs asked the bishop what he thought of his performance.

"Did I put enough fire into my sermon?"

The bishop pondered for a moment. "Might have been better if you had put more sermon into the fire," he said.

* * *

A PARISHIONER was asked what the new preacher, Rev Moggs, was like.

"Oh a good enough bloke except for his dreary sermons. After you've been listening for two hours you look at your watch and it's only been 15 minutes."

* * *

A BLOKE died and when he regained consciousness he found himself in a big crowd floating on a cloud. There were hundreds of other crowded clouds in what seemed a traffic jam at the Pearly Gates. Heaven was closed.

"What's up?" he asked.

A bishop next to him explained that the gates had been shut for a hundred years. "It appears they are adjudicating on a question of doctrine," he said.

They floated about on the clouds for days, weeks and months before a great shout echoed through the skies. People began to jump up and down and slap each other on the back. The gates opened and the clouds began slowly drifting in.

They turned to the bishop for an explanation. "What's up?" they asked.

"Looks like they have made that decision," he said with elation, "Yes, hurrah, we're in. Fucking doesn't count."

227

ATHEISTS

THE atheists organised a dial-a-prayer service.

When you phone up, nobody answers.

* * *

ATHEISM is a non-prophet organisation.

* * *

AN atheist is a man with no invisible means of support.

* * *

ALTHOUGH the atheist and the bishop had often debated 'the big question' they remained good friends. One day the bishop fell seriously ill and was told by his doctor not to have too many visitors. But when his long-time atheist friend called he was ushered into the bishop's bedroom.

"I do appreciate you seeing me when your friends have not been admitted," said the unbeliever.

"It's like this," replied the bishop, "I feel confident about seeing my friends in the next life, but I was concerned that this might be my last chance of seeing you."

* * *

A SINCERE atheist is one who eats pork on Good Friday and wipes his bum with his right hand.

It's the only way he can insult three religions with one stroke.

* * *

I AM an atheist, and the church I do not attend is Catholic.

*   *   *

AN atheist was strolling along the cliffs by the sea when he slipped and went over the edge. He instinctively grabbed at a small bush growing from a crevice. It halted his fall, but as he looked down past his swaying legs at the jagged rocks below, he wondered how long the frail bush could hold him.

He hung there terrified. Then he looked up at the edge of the cliff above him and called loudly: "Help, is there anybody there?"

From somewhere above the clouds a deep thundering voice replied: "Yes, my son. I hear you. Trust in me, have faith. Let go the shrub."

He thought it over for a minute. Then he looked up and shouted: "Is there anyone else there?"

*   *   *

IF God is good
   Why do his peoples
   Put lightning rods
   On top of steeples?

*   *   *

ROSES are red
   Violets are bluish
   If it wasn't for Jesus
   We'd all be Jewish

BORN-AGAINS

THE trouble with born-again Christians is that they are a worse pain in the neck the second time around.

* * *

AN evangelistic preacher came to a small country town and asked a young boy to direct him to the church where he was to deliver a hell-fire sermon that evening.

After the boy had given him directions the preacher said, "You should come along tonight. Bring your friends and I will tell you how to get to Heaven."

"You must be joking," said the kid. "You didn't even know how to get to the church."

INDEED it was a hell-fire sermon on repentance and damnation. "If a man is caught stealing he should be buried with his hand uncovered to set an example," he said.

"If a man is convicted of telling lies then he should be buried with his tongue left sticking out of the ground. And if a man is guilty of adultery ..."

"Hang on," interrupted Murphy from the back row. "If you're gonna say what I think you're gonna say the cemetery in this town will look like an asparagus patch."

* * *

WHAT do you get when you cross a Jehovah's Witness with a Bikie?

Somebody who knocks on your door and tells YOU to 'Piss Off!'

*　　*　　*

A MINOR religious sect in India worships the Goddess of the Harvest, Kali.

Every morning they visit Kali's temple and make an offering; a watermelon.

They present the offering and then sing their sacred song: "Here's another melon Kali baby!"

*　　*　　*

AN elderly couple were watching a TV evangelist ranting and raving about faith healing. He told his viewers he was about to transmit some spiritual healing through the telly set and he urged his listeners to place one hand on their heart and the other on the organ which needed healing.

The old lady put one hand on her heart and the other on her arthritic hip.

The old man had one hand on his heart, the other on his genitals.

"For goodness sake, Jake," said the old woman. "He aims to heal the sick, not raise the dead."

*　　*　　*

TWO women had become friends after meeting each other at various fertility clinics in their quest to become pregnant.

"And now look at you," said one, "You must be six months gone."

"Yes," said the mother-to-be, "I finally went to Dr Python the faith healer."

"Oh, we tried that," said the first woman. "My husband and I went there for months."

"No," whispered the pregnant one, "you've got to go alone."

* * *

ALL hotel rooms have a copy of the Gideon bible as a comfort to travellers and it was natural for the tub-thumping evangelist to reach for it and flick through a few pages before going downstairs for a nightcap.

He soon engaged the barmaid in conversation and was still chatting her up at closing time. He had the gift of the gab and eventually suggested she come up to his room for a blessing. After a few more drinks and a bit of hands-on healing they were ready for a tumble under the blankets.

"Should we be doing this?" she giggled as she undressed. "After all, you are a man of the cloth."

"I assure you it is alright. It is written in the Bible," he said, dropping his trousers.

During her post-coitus cigarette, which is a very reflective time for women, she said to the Bible-basher: "Show me the passage in which it says we should have done what we did?"

The evangelist picked up the Bible and turned to the fly-leaf to show her the quote: 'The barmaid downstairs is a certainty.'

* * *

BUDDHISTS and all manner of eastern religions

* * *

THE Buddhist monk knocked on the sacristy door.

"I'm afraid my Carma has run over your Dogma," he told the priest.

* * *

HAVE you heard of Salman Rushdie's latest book?"
It's called 'Buddha Knew Bugger-All'.

* * *

THE Moslem strip-tease dancers had tantalised the men to a frenzy.

"Show us yer faces, show us yer faces," they yelled.

* * *

THE mystic was so convinced she would be coming back after her death she had her tombstone inscribed: 'To be continued'.

* * *

TIBETAN monks have it hard where celibacy is concerned. One can hardly sneak out to the knock shop, like the western clergy in towns and cities, when you are closeted in a monestry high in the Himalayas.

One novice assigned to such an isolated existence thought he had the problem solved when he noticed several of his colleagues nicking out the back gate with a little parcel under their arm. Obviously a gift for an anticipated favour.

He followed with care down to the stables and was momentarily alarmed to find the monks lining up to have their wicked way with a yak.

So he got on the end of the queue and eventually had his turn.

"Well?" said the yak when he was finished, "where is my present?"

A little embarrassed the monk said he didn't bring one.

"Typical," she protested, "another case of fuck you yak I'm alright."

CATHOLICS

AN international conference on Family Planning was organised by the world's church leaders.

Unfortunately, the Catholic representative had to pull out at the last moment.

* * *

THE Vatican has taken over the railways and called it the Transportus Coitus Interruptus.

Everybody gets off one stop before their destination.

* * *

CATHOLIC girl's prayer:
    Oh, Blessed Virgin we believe
    That thou, without sin, did conceive
    Teach us then, how thus believing
    We can sin without conceiving.

* * *

PEOPLE who use the rhythm method of contraception are usually called Parents.

* * *

MANY believe that the Pope's phone number is Vat 69.

It's not. It's Et Cum Spirri 2-2-0.

* * *

SIN is so bad at our parish lately that the church has added an extra confessional box with a sign over the door: 'Eight items or less'.

* * *

THE priest was partial to the whisky bottle and when the young couple stood before the altar to be married the bride noticed he was slurring the wrong words.

"Father," she said, "you are reading the burial service."

"Doesn't matter," he whispered back. "You'll be under the sod tonight either way."

*   *   *

BRIGID had been a devout Catholic so it was a surprise to everybody when she married out of the church. But although married to a Presbyterian she always attended mass.

One Sunday morning she rose as usual, slipped out of her nightie and began to dress. As she pulled on her stockings she was conscious of her husband watching with a lustful eye and noticed the bedsheet rise just below his navel.

Then she rolled off her stockings, took off her pants and climbed back in to bed.

"I thought you were going to church," he said.

"The Catholic Church will stand forever," she said, "but how long can you trust a Protestant prick?"

*   *   *

FATHER Flannigan was concerned about the amount of heavy drinking among the men of the parish. He decided to preach a sermon to prove that the animals of the world did not fall for the same folly as men.

He told the story of the Mexican peasant who depended on his donkey for survival.

"Out of gratitude one day the peasant offered the donkey a bucket of beer, but the donkey refused it. The peasant offered the donkey a bucket of water and he drank it," said the priest.

"Why is it that the donkey drank the water but would not drink the beer?" asked the priest.

At the back of the church Murphy supplied the answer: "Because it was a bloody donkey, that's why!"

* * *

MORE than anything else Father Kelly loved to go to the fights on Friday night. Every week he would be ring-side cheering his favourite fighters. The curate was intrigued with such obsession and wanted to know why the priest had such a fascination for boxing.

"Come along and I'll teach you everything about the sport," said Fr Kelly.

Next Friday night they took their places at ringside and Fr Kelly pointed out the red corner, the blue corner, the rules of the match, where to put the bets on and a history of the fighters.

"He's our boy in the red corner," said the priest.

"What's he doing now?" asked the curate.

"He's getting last minute instructions from his trainer."

The curate was becoming involved. He then saw the fighter make the sign of the cross.

"What's he doing now?"

"He's just blessed himself."

"Will that help?"

"Not if he can't fight," said the priest.

* * *

FATHER Gilligan and his bishop were both keen golfers and while enjoying their regular weekly game, the priest tackled the bishop on an important religious question.

"Your Excellency," he said, "is there a golf course in Heaven?"

The bishop said he didn't know, but he was saying a novena through the week and he would make some enquiries during this special prayer session.

The following week they were having another round when the priest raised the question again.

"Oh yes indeed," said the bishop, "they have a fine golf course in Heaven, and you're booked in for next Saturday."

* * *

THE Catholic priest settled himself in the corner of his favourite restaurant and ordered a six-course gourmet meal with starters, soup, entree, turkey, sweets, the lot. "And a bottle of your finest chardonnay," he said to the pretty waitress, slapping her on the bum.

Two protestant spinsters, who heard all this while sipping their frugal tea and biscuits, glared down their noses at him.

He glared back: "Do you think God made all the good things in this life only for the sinners," he said.

* * *

THE curate told the parish priest that a new family had moved into town. "And the mother has eleven children," he said.

"Good to see an old-fashioned Catholic family raising so many sons and daughters for the church," said the priest.

"Oh, no. They're not Catholics, they're Presbyterians."

"What? How disgusting. They must be sex mad. Absolutely no self-control," said the priest.

* * *

237

YOUNG Father Kelly had been the curate for three years and was now leaving for a parish of his own.

A send-off was arranged at which all the ladies of the parish attended.

Presenting him with a farewell gift a young woman gushed: "We don't know what we will do without you, Father. Until you came we didn't know what sin was."

* * *

PATRICK had difficulty understanding the doctrine concerning miracles. Even though the priest explained the subject with great clarity and patience, Patrick was still none the wiser.

"Father, could you be giving me an example?"

"All right then, turn around."

Pat turned away from the priest who then gave him a mighty kick up the backside.

"Did you feel that, Pat?"

"Indeed I did."

"Well," said the priest, "that would be a bloody miracle if you hadn't."

* * *

FR FLANNIGAN was at the races and was astonished to see and hear one of his parishioners roaring the most frightful abuse and lurid language during a race.

It was Murphy. "Use the bloody whip ya stupid short-arsed knuckle-headed bastard," he roared at the jockey.

After the race Fr Flannigan took Murphy aside. "There's no need for language like that," he said.

He told Murphy to take it quietly. "Now when I have a bet I just pray to the Lord that the horse gets away from the barrier cleanly, then I pray he gets a good position, I pray that he makes the home turn cleanly and I pray that he leads into the straight."

Murphy promised the priest he would try it in the next event.

Sure enough, Murphy's horse jumped clean from the barrier, got into a good position, made the home turn and was leading as they turned into the straight.

"Thanks Lord," said Murphy, "Now I'll take it from here... Use the bloody whip ya short-arsed bastard ..."

*   *   *

MURPHY was on his death bed and knew he was cashing in his chips so he had Teresa call the priest.

"Father, I want to renounce the Catholic faith and become a Mason."

"Have ye taken leave or your senses my son?" said the priest.

"No Father. It's just that, if somebody's got to die, isn't it better that it be one of them bastards than one of us?"

*   *   *

MASON or Catholic, Murphy was still on his death bed and the priest suggested that he should at least renounce the Devil.

"I don't know Father," he said. "I'm thinking it might not be a good time for making enemies."

*   *   *

THERE was a big statue of the Virgin Mary at the side of the altar, big enough for the priest to sit out of sight when he wanted a quiet moment.

He was resting there one afternoon when a little girl from the parish school came into the church and approached the statue.

"Dear Our Lady," she said, "Can I bring my friend

Lulu to the parish picnic on Sunday? She's not a Catholic."

The priest heard this and thought he would play a prank. In his deepest voice boomed: "No!"

The girl was nonplussed. "I'm not talking to you. I'm talking to your mother."

*　　*　　*

SISTER Agatha had spent the whole afternoon instructing the children about confession and repentance.

"Now," she said, summing up, "what do we have to do first before we can ever hope to obtain forgiveness?"

Mick's hand shot up. "Sin," he said.

*　　*　　*

AN elegant dowager approached the priest.

"My good man, I would like you to arrange a Christian burial for my cat."

The priest dismissed her with the curt reply: "We don't say prayers for the likes of cats."

"Oh, pity," she said. "I was prepared to pay a thousand dollars for a special ceremony."

"Why didn't ye say it was a Catholic cat?" said the priest.

*　　*　　*

WHEN the cardinals' convention was hit by a bomb it sent fifty of them to Heaven in one stroke where they all began to shuffle through the Pearly Gates as if they owned the place.

"Hang on. Just a moment," roared St Peter. "You lot have to go through the religious test like anybody else. How many of you have committed sins of the flesh?"

240

There was an awkward silence before, one after the other, forty-nine hands went up.

"Right," said St Peter. "You forty-nine go off to Purgatory, and take that deaf bastard with you."

* * *

THE Pope and Casanova arrived at the Pearly Gates on the same cloud. While the Pope hung around the gates meeting and greeting a few friends Casanova went straight in.

When the Pope finally entered he bumped into Casanova at the reception centre and said "I want nothing more than to kneel at the feet of the Virgin Mary. Do you know where I can find her?"

Casanova said, "Yes, but you are just too late, Father."

* * *

FATHER Murphy was sent to a small Eskimo village in the northern wastes of Alaska. After a year the bishop paid him a visit.

"How do you stand the weather my son?" asked the bishop.

"Oh I don't care how cold it gets," said Father Murphy, "I have my Rosary and my vodka to keep me warm."

"That's good," said the bishop. "Come to mention it, I wouldn't mind a vodka right now."

"No problem," said the priest. "Hey Rosary, bring two vodkas, pronto."

* * *

THE Pope called his cardinals together and in a shocked voice said: "I have some terrible news."

He said he had just received a phone call from God and it's a She!

241

"After all we have said about women," said one of the stunned cardinals.

"Yes," said the Pope, "but worst of all, she rang from Salt Lake City."

* * *

THE doctor told the young man the reason for his depression was stress. "Take life easier," was the doc's advice. "Do you drink?"

"No," said the young man, "never have."

"There is no harm in a quiet drink," said the doctor, "even a smoke to relax, and sex at least once a week. In fact, in your case it is essential."

Two months later the patient returned and was evidently in much better health. He told the doctor he enjoyed a glass of beer each night and had taken up the pipe.

"And sex?" asked the doctor.

"Hard to find it every week," admitted the patient, "especially for a parish priest in a small country town like this."

* * *

SUFFERING from depression the priest was advised by his psychiatrist to take a rest from stress with a short break in Paris. "Nobody will know you there," said the shrink.

Indeed, he got to like the sinful city and even went to a strip show. And when a gorgeous blonde danced by he lurched out in a bid to grasp her bum.

"Oh, no you don't, Father," said the blonde.

"How did you know I was a priest?"

"Because I'm Sister Priscilla, and we've got the same shrink," she replied.

* * *

THE priest took Paddy aside. "I've been told that you went to a football match last Sunday morning instead of coming to Mass."

"No Father, not true, and what's more, I've got the fish to prove it."

*   *   *

THE Pope dies and arrives at the Pearly Gates on the same cloud as a lawyer. They are both ushered in and St Peter assigns the lawyer to a mansion with a golf course while the Pope is confined to a single room with a radio.

Even the lawyer was surprised. "How come?" he asked.

St Peter replied: "We have near on a hundred popes, but you are the first lawyer."

*   *   *

THE Protestant minister met his friend the priest and said he dreamed about a Catholic Heaven last night.

"It looked like a nice place, with plenty of pubs, bright music and people dancing about," he said.

"That's funny," said the priest. "Only last night I dreamt about a Protestant Heaven. It looked nice with lots of flower beds, pretty trees and gardens."

"And what were the people doing?" asked the vicar.

"What people?" replied the priest.

*   *   *

THERE was a small knot of football supporters on the terrace and a voice from somewhere in the middle of this group shouted: "Is there a priest here! Is there a priest about?"

A small chap with a white collar pushed his way through the crowd. "I'm not a priest," he said. "I am an Anglican vicar, can I help in any way?"

"Na, you'd be useless," replied the footy fan. "We need a bottle opener."

* * *

CATHOLIC priests are often at the races, but Pete the Punter was surprised to see the priest sprinkle holy water over one nag which duly went out and won by half a street.

Pete followed him closely and witnessed another holy water sprinkle and another win, at ten-to-one.

Next time he had the money ready and as soon as the priest annointed yet a third horse, albeit a skinny nag, Pete was off to the bookies.

After the horse had dropped dead on the home turn Pete tackled the priest for an explanation.

"If you were a Catholic," said the priest, "you would have known the difference between a blessing and the last rites."

* * *

A DRUNK sat opposite a priest on the train and studied him for ten minutes. Finally he said, "Tell me, yer Worship. Why do you wear your collar back to front?"

"Because I am a father," said the priest.

"But I'm a father too," said the drunk.

"No, I am a father to hundreds in my parish."

"Then maybe it's your trousers you should be wearing back to front," said the drunk.

* * *

THE monastery was in financial trouble and decided to go into the fish and chip business. One night a customer rapped on the door which was opened by a monk.

"Are you the fish friar?"

244

"No," replied the robed figure, "I'm the chip monk!"

* * *

PADDY, his wife and their seven kids were waiting at the bus-stop when they were joined by a blind man. When the bus arrived it was almost full and the conductor said only eight could board.

"Okay Teresa," said Paddy to his wife, "You take the kids on board and me and the blindman will walk."

Without giving the blind man an option in the matter, Paddy helped his family scramble aboard and the bus took off.

He and the blind man then set off walking down the road and all went well until the constant tap-tap-tap of the blind man's cane began to irritate Paddy.

"Tap-tap-tap, that bloody tapping is driving me crazy. Can't you put a bit of rubber on the end of it," he complained irritably.

The blind man was quick to respond. "If you had've stuck a bit of rubber on your own stick we would be on that bloody bus."

* * *

TWO priests were chatting philosophically.

"Do you think the Pope will ever allow priests to marry?" said one.

"Not in our lifetime," said the other, "maybe in our children's."

* * *

IT was one of those silent orders where the only utterances allowed were the morning and evening rituals to greet the head monk. "Good Morning Head Monk" they would chant at breakfast and "Good Evening Head Monk" just before retiring.

After fifteen years this ritual was getting on Brother Paddy's wick and causing rebellion to swell within him. Finally he planned a revolt.

Next day, when the brethren chanted "Good Morning Head Monk," he would deliberately chant "Evening!"

The prospect nearly sent his rocks off. He was all of a tremble at the breakfast table and when the head monk entered he stood with the rest of them and in the chorus of "Good Morning Head Monk" Paddy threw in his rebellious "Evening!"

The head monk was very perceptive. There was an awesome silence until his monotone baritone loudly proclaimed: "Someone Chanted Evening!"

* * *

AGAIN it was one of those monastic orders where the monks were silent, except on the day of their patron saint, St Titus.

The first year Brother Basil asked for another blanket. The second year he asked if he could have porridge instead of wheaties. The third year he asked if he could have sugar in his tea. The fourth year he asked if he could leave the order.

"You might as well," said the head monk, "You've done nothing but bloody whinge since you've been here."

* * *

THE district inspector of Catholic Primary Schools called at St Patrick's and decided to put Grade V to the test with some basic questions on the faith.

When he came to young Johnny he asked: "Who knocked down the Walls of Jericho?"

"It wasn't me," was the instant reply.

The inspector was taken aback. Johnny's parents obviously needed a word about their responsibility in religious instruction so he noted the address and knocked on the door that evening.

When Johnny's Mum opened the door the inspector introduced himself and said: "When I asked your boy who knocked down the Walls of Jericho, his answer was that it wasn't him." he said.

In a defiant pose she answered: "If my Johnny said he didn't do it then he didn't do it."

This was too much for the inspector and he asked to see the man of the house. Paddy was in bed, but when the inspector revealed the purpose of his visit, he reached for his trousers. "Okay, okay, how much did this bloody wall cost anyway?"

* * *

ONE priest confided in another. "I don't know what to do to repress these feeling of sexual desire."

"Take a cold shower," said his colleague.

"But I've taken so many cold showers that when it rains I now get an erection."

* * *

FATHER O'Grady was preaching on the difference between knowledge and faith. "In the front row we have Teresa and Shamus with their six children," he said.

"Teresa knows they are her children, That's knowledge. Shamus believes they are his children. That's faith."

* * *

THE parish priest made his way to the front door of the farmhouse through a swarm of fighting kids. He knocked on the door repeatedly but there was no answer. He moved along the porch to the bedroom window, looked in and was shocked to see them hard at it on the bed.

The priest made a discreet retreat through the fighting kids and went to the next property where the farmer met him at the gate.

The priest said: "Your neighbour sure likes making babies."

"He sure does," agreed the farmer. "His wife is in hospital having her tenth, and my wife is over there helping him out."

*　*　*

"GIRLS," said mother superior addressing the class which was about to graduate and leave the convent.

"You are about to go into the sinful world. I must warn you against certain men who will whisper rude suggestions to you, buy you drinks, take you to their rooms, undress you and offer you money to do rude things."

"Excuse me, Mother," piped up a rather buxom girl, "did you say these wicked men would give us money?"

"Yes, child, why do you ask?"

"Father Flannagan only gives us lollies."

*　*　*

A RICH Catholic tourist who had come to the Vatican in the cherished hope of seeing the Pope was ecstatic when the Pontif came into the crowd near him and placed his hands on the shoulders of a derelict.

Next day he was amazed to see the Pope approach the same bedraggled man and seem to single him out, ignoring the hundreds of wealthy tourists clamouring for a blessing.

So the tourist stopped the tramp and offered him a hundred dollars to swap clothes, to which the down-and-outer eagerly agreed.

Next day, dressed in the tramp's smelly rags the tourist was delighted to see the Pope turn and approach him.

With both hands on his shoulders the Pope bent forward and whispered: "I've told you twice to piss off. Now beat it!"

* * *

A PRIEST and a nun partnered up for a game of golf. As the priest swung the first drive he missed and sent a large divot flying through the air.

"Shit, I missed," he said.

The nun was shocked.

Several holes later he missed a vital putt.

"Shit, I missed," muttered the priest.

This time the nun could not contain herself. "Father, you must watch your language."

The priest apologised. "May God strike me dead if I swear again," he said.

But on the 18th he chipped the ball into a bunker.

"Ah shit, missed again," he said.

Suddenly a bolt of lightening flashed down from a black cloud and struck the nun dead.

And a thunderous voice from above boomed: "Ah, shit, missed again."

* * *

WHEN the diocese finally sent an assistant to Father O'Sullivan, the old priest had some misgivings when the young curate arrived with luggage that included a bag of golf clubs and two tennis racquets.

And he had no sooner settled in when he asked Fr

O'Sullivan for an advance until pay day. "Can you spare $25.50?" he asked.

"What for?" asked the old priest.

"For a nookie," replied the younger man frankly.

Not wanting to appear ignorant, the priest handed over the money, but it troubled him for the rest of the day until he chanced to meet Mother Superior.

"What's a nookie?" he asked her.

"$25.50" she replied.

* * *

THREE young priests had been driving interstate when they stopped at a country pub for their usual three pots of bitter. Yes, we all know Catholic priests drink, but what made them nervous was the pretty barmaid with a shapely set of knockers set off by a deep cleavage.

The young priest approached the bar. "Could I have three pots of titters?" he stammered.

"Cheeky lad," she said as the priest retreated in embarrassment.

"I'll get the drinks," said the second priest, but as he approached the bar he couldn't keep his eyes off them.

"We'll have three tits of potters," he blurted.

The third priest had to take the issue in hand. He approached the bar with confidence. "Three pots of bitter please Miss," he said precisely, "and you should dress more modestly, young woman, or St Finger is going to point his Peter at you."

* * *

THE Pope's physician finally diagnosed the ailment as suffering from a prolonged life of celibacy. A blockage of the canals. He said it was unnatural to be without a woman and it was seriously affecting the pontiff's health.

The Pope resisted. The physician implored the cardinals to intercede assuring them it was a matter of life or death.

Finally, with great reluctance, the Pope agreed and specified a long list of conditions. He said it had to be a secret affair. She had to be a Catholic.

"Oh, and one more thing," he said, "make sure she has big knockers!"

*   *   *

THE French peasants watched the tour bus go past with the strange sign on the side.

It read: SU CITCELSYD RUOT FO SEDRUOL.

When it passed them on the return trip a day later it read: US DYSLECTIC TOUR OF LOURDES.

*   *   *

THE family shunted their crippled granny's wheelchair to the front of the throng at Lourdes but the hustle and bustle got out of control and suddenly the wheelchair and granny went whizzing down the slope, splash, into the magical waters.

When they pulled granny out she was drowned. But there was a set of brand new tyres on the wheelchair.

*   *   *

MURPHY was awarded a million dollars after an industrial accident that left him confined to a wheelchair for life.

However, the insurance detective suspected fraud and told Murphy he would pursue him for the rest of his life.

"In that case," said Murphy, "you'd better follow us

to Lourdes next month where you will see the greatest bloody miracle of all time."

* * *

WHEN Murphy was coming back through customs he assured the officer that the six large bottles in his luggage contained holy water, from Lourdes.

The officer took the top off one and tasted it.

"This is whisky," he said.

"B'Jeesus," said Murphy. "It's another bloody miracle."

* * *

A YOUNG Scottish lass called Alice
Peed in the presbytery's chalice
The padre agreed
'Twas done out of need
And not out of Protestant malice.

* * *

THE back door slammed. "Christ! That'll be my husband," she said.

He just had time to gather his clothes and dive, still naked, into the wardrobe. He remained hunkered down there for a time until a voice said: "Jeez, it's dark in here!"

"Who's that?" whispered the shivering lover, surprised to hear somebody else in the wardrobe.

"It's me, Tommy," said the voice, "And I know who you are. And if you don't give me fifty dollars I'll yell for my dad."

"No, no. Don't do that," and frantically fumbling through his trousers he offered a handful of notes to the kid in the dark.

Next morning while down the street with his mum,

Tommy said he was going to buy a brand new skate-board.

"What with?" asked his mother.

"I've got fifty dollars."

"Where did you get it?"

"Can't say."

"You must have done something wrong," she said, slapping him around the ear. "Confession is the only thing for you my lad," and she took him into the church and pushed him into the confessional box.

"Jeez, it's dark in here!" he said.

"Now don't start that again," said the priest.

*   *   *

TRAVEL seems to induce confession, so when three priests found themselves in the same compartment of a train on a long journey to a Eucharistic council, they began to bare their souls and admit to certain sins.

"It's women with me," said the first. "I find them very hard to resist and I have fallen several times."

"It's the grog with me," said the second. "Struggle as I may there have been times when the proceeds of the poor box have gone on Demon Drink."

The third priest was quiet. "I suppose you succumb to gambling," prompted his colleagues.

"No," he said. "My problem is gossip. I am a blabbermouth and I can hardly wait to get off this train."

CONFESSION

CELIBATE priests must be masochists. They torture themselves by giving up their sex lives, only to have people come in and tell them the highlights of theirs.

LITTLE Patrick to little Isaac: "Our parish priest knows more than your rabbi."

Isaac: "That's because you tell him everything."

* * *

A WOMAN confessed to her priest: "Father, I spent an hour this morning just looking in the mirror and thinking how beautiful I was. Will I have to do penance?"

"No," he said, "You only do penance for sins, not mistakes."

* * *

THE little old lady entered the confessional and knelt to confess her transgressions.

"I have had sex with a man," she said.

"When did this happen, my daughter?"

"Forty-five years ago," she said.

"Then why haven't you confessed this before?"

"Oh, I have. Several times."

"But daughter, you only have to confess a sin once. Why are you telling me about it again?"

"Because I like talking about it," she said.

* * *

PADDY crept around the back of the country parish presbytery and nicked one of the priest's chooks. He then promptly went to confession.

"I stole a chook, Father," he began. "I know it was very wrong and I am sorry. Can I give it to you for repentance?"

"Certainly not," said the priest. "I don't want it. Return it to the man you stole it from."

"I've tried, but he says he doesn't want it," said Paddy truthfully.

"In that case you might as well keep it and say ten Hail Marys."

* * *

JENNY the gymnast had her first sexual encounter with Pete the pole vaulter. Next morning she felt ashamed and couldn't get to confession quick enough.

The priest was sympathetic and gave her absolution. Jenny was so elated she did spontaneous cartwheels down the aisle just as Mrs O'Flaherty came in.

"Oh Gawd," said the old lady, "is that today's penance? The very day I've forgotten to wear my knickers?"

* * *

PRIEST: "Are you troubled by improper thoughts?"

Fred: "No. I rather enjoy them."

* * *

"FATHER," said Murphy, "I feel I don't need forgiveness for the various adulteries I have scored this month."

"And why not?" asked the astonished priest.

"Cos all the married women I slept with were Jews," he said.

"Ar, you're right me son," said the priest, "That's the only way to screw the Jews."

* * *

O'FLAHERTY confessed that he had committed sins of the flesh with a new woman in town. And worse, she was a Protestant. "She is an actress in the new show at the Town Hall, Father," he said. "Her name is Pussy Pink and she is a seductive, voluptuous red head, and if you saw her Father, you would understand."

The priest granted absolution but was intrigued about the description of the town's new vamp.

The following Sunday he saw a well-built redhead sway down the aisle all the way to the front pew.

Nudging the organist he said: "Hey, Gilligan, is that Pussy Pink?"

Gilligan turned and squinted at the woman as she crossed her legs. "No, Father," he said, "It's just the sunlight coming through the stained glass windows."

* * *

O'FLAHERTY was in confession and the priest asked: "Now tell me son. Did you ever sleep with a woman?"

"No, not me, Father."

"Now son, I'll ask you again," said the priest, "did you ever sleep with a woman?"

"No, er, well, no, Father."

"Now son, there's just me and God listening. I will ask you for the last time, did you ever sleep with a woman?"

"Well, come to think if it, Father," said O'Flaherty, "I believe I did doze off once or twice."

* * *

BRIGID was still a new bride and sought some advice from Father McGinty in the confessional box.

"Father," she whispered, with a little embarrassment, "Is it alright to have intercourse before receiving communion?"

"Certainly, my lass," he replied, "just as long as you don't block the aisle."

*   *   *

WHEN the sliding door opened in the confessional box he started: "Father, I had sex with a pair of lovely eighteen-year-old nymphomaniac twins five times last week."

"What kind of Catholic are you?" demanded the priest.

"I am not a Catholic," he replied.

"Then why are you telling me this?"

"I am telling everyone!"

*   *   *

"FATHER, yesterday I made love to my wife."

The priest explained that there was nothing wrong with that.

"But Father, I did it with...lust."

Again the priest reassured the man that it was no sin.

"But Father, it was the middle of the day."

The priest was growing uncomfortable with the description but assured his parishioner that it was a natural act for man and wife.

"But Father, it was sheer passion. As she leant over the deep freeze I just jumped on her and we did it on the floor. Am I banned from the church?"

"Of course not," said the exasperated priest.

"Oh good. We're both banned from the supermarket."

* * *

WHEN the priest finally noticed the little boy sitting close to the confessional box he grabbed him by the ear. "You young rascal," he said, "have you been listening to confessions all evening?"

"No Father," said the kid, "I've only been here since Mrs Murphy told you about throwing her leg over the baker."

* * *

SATURDAY night is confession night but Father O'Riley stopped Pat as he entered the church. "Pat, the church is full. Can you come back tomorrow night? You haven't committed murder since last time have you?"

"Indeed I haven't," said Pat and he turned to leave.

On the way out he met Shamus. "Go home Shamus and come back tomorrow. They are only hearing murders tonight!"

* * *

AS Rabbi Rozenbloom was passing St Patrick's, Fr O'Callaghan rushed out in an agitated state. "Izzie, you're just the man," said the priest. "Can you help me out of a tight spot?"

The priest explained that he was double booked. He had to officiate at the funeral of the local bishop but couldn't find another priest to take over the confession session.

"Surely you can stand in for me. It's only an hour."

The rabbi said he didn't know anything about confession. Jews were not into confessing anything.

"There's nothing to it," insisted the priest. "Come

with me now and listen to the first few, then you can take over."

When they got to the dark confessional the rabbi sat behind the priest and listened to the procedure.

A woman came in: "Father I have sinned."

"What have you done my child?"

"I have committed adultery."

"How many times?"

"Four times Father, and I sincerely repent."

"Put $2 in the poor box and say ten Hail Marys and you will receive absolution," said the priest.

Then a second woman came in. "Father I have sinned."

"What have you done my child?"

"I have committed adultery."

"How many times?"

"Twice, Father."

"Put $1 in the poor box and say five Hail Marys, and you will be forgiven," said the priest.

As soon as the woman had left the priest whispered to the rabbi, "You have got the hang of it now, quick, take my place, I have to rush."

The rabbi settled down in the priest's position and soon enough another woman knelt at the other side of the grill.

"Father, I have sinned," she said.

"What have you done my child?"

"I have committed adultery."

"How many times?"

"Just the once, Father."

"Well, you had better go and do it again. It's two for a dollar this week."

* * *

"FORGIVE me Father, but I have had an obsession about stealing wood from the timber mill where I work. I have suffered with this problem for years. What shall I do?"

"That's alright my son," said the priest. "But because this sin has been perpetuated for so long I must ask you to make a novena."

"If you've got the plans Father, I've got the timber."

* * *

TERESA went to confession and told the priest she had sinned three times that week. She said she had slept with Shaun on Tuesday, Paddy on Wednesday and Shamus on Friday night. "Oh Father what should I do?"

"On your way home, my child," he said, "call in at Con the Fruiterers, buy a lemon and suck it."

"Oh Father, will that cleanse me of my sins?"

"No. But it should take that damn smile off your face."

* * *

ON Saturday nights the three lads always went out on the town together, but Shamus always made a point of going past the church first so he could duck into confession while the other two waited outside.

"It's been a week since my last confession Father," said Shamus, "and I'm sorry to say that I have sinned of the flesh once again."

"Was it that O'Flannagan hussy from the dairy?"

"No Father."

"Was it the cheeky Costanzo girls in the fruit shop?"

"No Father."

"Don't tell me it was the widow Murphy flauntin' her wares again?"

"No Father."

"Well do your usual penance and be off with you then," said the priest.

Shamus rushed out of the church to his waiting mates. "Got at least three good tips for tonight," he said.

* * *

AS drunk as a skunk Paddy wandered into the church and stumbled into the confessional box.

Moments after he sat down there was a tap-tap on the partition.

"Forget it, pal," said Paddy, "There's no paper in here either."

* * *

THERE was a young lady called Tessa
   A quite unrepentant transgressor
   When sent to the priest
   The rude little piece
   Would try to undress her confessor

NUNS

WHEN two novices saw Mother Superior approaching they gave a her a cheery hello, but all they got in return was a rather grumpy response.

"Looks as though she got out of the wrong side of the bed this morning." said one novice.

"Yes, and she's still got Father Kelly's slippers on," said the other.

* * *

HELP a nun kick the habit.

* * *

A NUN who walks in her sleep is called a
Roamin' Catholic.

* * *

MONKS do it out of habit
While nuns were once novices at it.

* * *

TWO nuns were riding their bikes along a cobblestone lane.

"I've never come this way before," said one.

"No. It must be the cobbles," said the other.

* * *

BECOME a nun and feel superior.

* * *

THERE was once a monk from Siberia
Whose manners were rather inferior
He did to a nun

What he shouldn't have done
And now she's a Mother Superior

*　*　*

MOTHER Superior was engrossed in a crossword puzzle for some time and muttered that something was wrong.

"What's a four-letter word relating to women that ends in U-N-T?"

"Oh dear," said Sister Priscilla, "I think that would have to be AUNT."

"Of course," said Mother Superior. "Do you have an eraser I could borrow."

*　*　*

DID you hear about the priest who asked the nun for a kiss?

"Okay," she said, "as long as you don't get into the habit."

*　*　*

SISTER Prudence and Sister Priscilla were travelling sedately along the highway when Dracula pounced onto the bonnet of their car and began making obscene gestures through the windscreen.

It scared the daylights out of Sister Prudence who screamed to her companion: "Show him ya cross. Show him ya cross."

Sister Priscilla stuck her head out of the window and said: "Get off the car ya bastard or I'll show you just how really cross I can be when I get my bloody hands on yer."

*　*　*

THREE nuns died at the same time, arrived at the Pearly Gates simultaneously and intended to go straight in, but St Peter barred their way.

"Just because you are nuns," he said, "doesn't mean you barge straight in without the religious test."

"You," he said to the first one. "What was the name of the first man?"

"Er, Adam?" she answered, and the bells clanged and the trumpets blew and in she went.

"You," said St Peter addressing the second, "What was the name of the first woman?"

"Er, Eve?" she ventured, and the bells clanged and the trumpets blew and in she went.

"You," he said to the quaking third nun, "What were the first words Eve said to Adam?"

"Oh, gee. That's a hard one." And the bells clanged and the trumpets blew and in she went.

* * *

WHEN a bus load of nuns went over a cliff they were soon lined up at the Pearly Gates where St Peter produced a large vat of holy water for the nuns' test.

"If any of you have touched a man's genitals you will have to wash your hands before passing the gates," he said.

Three of the nuns came forward, washed their hands and passed through.

Then a fourth approached the holy water, washed her hands then sheepishly opened her habit and washed her breasts before passing through the gates.

A fifth nun approached the holy water, lifted her skirt and splashed some between her legs.

The nun next in line was heard to mutter: "Hey go easy, I've got to gargle that stuff in a minute."

* * *

TWO novices were climbing back into the dormitory window, trying to sneak in as quietly as possible when one said, "This makes me feel like a burglar."

"Me too," said the other, "but where would we find two burglars at this time of night?"

* * *

THE young novice soon realised that the absence of sex in the convent was a problem. She confessed to Mother Superior that it was unhealthy and she was restless.

"Comfort yourself with a candle," she was advised.

"I've tried that," she said, "but you get tired of the same thing wick in and wick out."

* * *

THE young novice was assigned her first job at the convent: to sweep the steps of the church and keep the entrance clean. But she was having a terrible time with the pigeons. They were flapping, cooing, and shitting all over the steps she had just cleaned.

She would wave her arms and say: "Piss off. Piss off."

It annoyed the priest who asked Mother Superior to have a discreet word with the novice.

"Your language is unseemly and entirely unnecessary,"

Mother Superior told her, "All you have to do is say 'Shoo-shoo', and swipe them with the broom and you will find they will soon fuck off."

* * *

TWO young nuns were assigned to do the shopping and drove to the supermarket in the convent's Mini Minor. When they couldn't find a parking space one elected to do the shopping while the other drove around the block.

The first nun finally returned to the car park with a loaded trolly and asked a council worker: "Have you seen a nun in a red Mini?"

"Not since I stopped drinking," he replied.

* * *

WHEN the novice returned from the presbytery Mother Superior said: "Why were you so long, Sister?"

"Father Murphy was showing me how to blow the Horn of Plenty."

"The old villian. He told me it was the Trumpet of Gabriel."

* * *

MOTHER Superior was addressing the graduation ceremony and giving motherly advice. "In the outside world you will meet many temptations," she warned the girls. "You must remember the teachings and ideals you learned here at the convent."

She preached on at length and finally said: "There will be many a wicked man trying to take sexual liberties with you. Resist, and remember that one hour of pleasure could ruin your whole life. Any questions?"

"Yes, Sister. How do you make it last an hour?"

* * *

WALKING into a liquor store Sister Genevieve asked for a bottle of whisky. "Oh it's alright. It's for Mother Superior's constipation."

Later that afternoon the licensee was shocked to see the nun in the park looking the worse for wear.

"I thought you said that whisky was for your superior's constipation," he said.

"Don't worry," slurred Sister Genevieve, "when she sees me she'll shit."

* * *

A PRIEST was driving along a country road when he noticed a sign by the road: 'Sisters of Mercy Whorehouse, 10kms'.

He could hardly believe his eyes, but a few minutes later he was confronted with a second sign with a similar message, then a third: 'Sisters of Mercy Whorehouse, next turn right'.

Bent on getting evidence of this sorry state of affairs and report it to the bishop he knocked on the door which was opened by a nun.

"I saw your sign on the road and ..."

"You've come to do business?" said the nun, "Entry fee is $50," she said.

He reluctantly paid the money and she directed him, through a series of passageways to another door.

"Knock there," he was directed.

This door was opened by another nun who confided that it would cost another $50 to go through the next door, "where it all happens."

He paid up and walked through to find himself out in the car park with a large sign confronting him: 'You have just been screwed by the Sisters of Mercy'!

* * *

TWO nuns had gone to the circus, but after the show they were dismayed to find heavy rain had created a deep puddle between the big top and their bus stop. They didn't want to get their habits or their shoes wet.

Two clowns came to their rescue and offered to piggy-back them across the water.

Halfway across one clown stopped and said to his mate: "Do you realise that this is virgin on the ridiculous?"

* * *

THE nun began to lecture him on the evils of drink as he tried to enter the pub. "Listen Sister," he said, "how can you knock it if you've never tried it?"

The argument continued along these lines. "If you tasted one drink you would know what you are talking about," he said.

Finally she agreed he had a point. "Just a small ladies drink then," she said, "whatever that is."

He suggested gin.

"Well I don't want to be seen drinking from a hotel glass. Here," she said, unhooking a tin mug from her belt, "I'll taste it in this."

So he went up to the bar and asked for a beer and a gin in the mug.

The barman muttered, "Ar don't tell me that nun is still out there."

* * *

MOTHER Superior had listened to the parish priest ramble on for hours about the increasing number of splinter groups in religion.

Finally she blurted out: "Is that all you can think about, Sects! Sects! Sects!"

* * *

SISTER Priscilla was sent down to get the convent's Peuguot from the service station.

"What kind of a car was it, Sister?" asked the mechanic.

"Can't remember, but it starts with a P."

"It's not here then," said the mechanic, "All ours start with petrol."

* * *

IT was Sister Priscilla's task to drive into town and pick up the mail every morning but she was showing an increasing reluctance to do the job.

"What's wrong?" asked Mother Superior. "I thought you enjoyed the daily excursion away from the convent."

"I do," said Sister Priscilla, "but lately a young policeman has taken to stopping me each morning."

Mother Superior said Priscilla had nothing to fear provided she didn't do anything wrong. She sent her on her way.

She had hardly driven for two minutes along the country lane when the motor cycle policeman signalled her to stop.

"Oh no, not the breathalyser again," muttered Sister Priscilla as the cop approached unzipping his fly.

* * *

A NUN raced in to Mother Superior's office screaming and waving her hands. "Oh, Mother," she cried, "we seem to have a case of hepatitis!"

"Well, my dear, bring it in," said Mother Superior. "I'm sick to death of Bernie Smith's Bodega."

* * *

A COUPLE who went to the movies found themselves sitting directly behind two nuns; the ones with the large headgear.

Trying to see the screen past these obstacles, the girl muttered to her boyfriend: "It would be nice to go to Scotland, there are not so many nuns there."

The boyfriend replied audibly: "What about Russia, there are even fewer there."

One of the nuns turned around, gave the couple a sweet smile and said: "Why don't you both go to Hell, you won't find any there!"

*   *   *

SISTER Anastasia wandered away from her party at the zoo to take a second look at the gorilla. Actually, she leant too close to read his name and the brute reached out, grabbed her by the habit, pulled her through the bars and had his wicked way with her.

She was in such a state of shock that it was seven days before the other nuns could visit her in hospital.

"How do you feel?" they asked in chorus.

"How do you think I feel?" she replied. "It's been a week and he hasn't written, he hasn't phoned ..."

*   *   *

THE disc jockey was driving along the country road when he saw a young nun trying to hitch a ride. He stopped. She explained that she had been a bit naive in trying to walk the distance to church. It was further than she anticipated.

As they drove along she asked why he was up so early in the morning. "I'm a radio announcer on the morning shift at the local regional station," he said.

"Oh," said the nun. "I would do anything to be able to send a cheerio."

The DJ took another look and noticed that she was indeed a comely wench. "Anything?" he repeated.

When she indeed confirmed that it was her major wish in life he drove off the road into a shady glade and whipped out the old John Thomas, as unscrupulopus DJs are wont to do.

She bent down, grabbed it with two hands and said "Hello Mum, Hello Dad, this is Teresa here ..."

* * *

A NUN and a priest were travelling on a missionary assignment in the wilds of Africa. Their means of transport was a humble but honest donkey which carried them both for quite extraordinary distances each day until finally, it dropped dead.

They set up camp and prayed to be rescued, but after a week they began to realise that their plight was serious.

"I think we are about to die," said the priest. "But before we do, Sister," he said, "I have always wondered what a woman really looks like. Would you take your clothes off for me?"

It was warm weather, and what the hell, Sister thought she might as well. Anyway, she had a request of her own.

"You know Father," she said, "I have only seen women naked and I have often wondered about men."

"No worries," said the priest who took it as a signal to quickly shed his gear.

She took one look at the rising appendage and said: "Crikey Moses, what in blazes is that thing?"

"That Sister, is the staff of life," he said proudly. "If I put it in you it will create new life."

"You don't say," she said in wonder, "Well don't stick it in me. Stick it in the bloody donkey and let's get out of here."

DISCRIMINATION

UNDER the heading of Discrimination we gather all the Politically Incorrect jokes based on Ageism, Sexism, and those ethnic minorities who didn't get a chapter to themselves. They can be roasted here.

HOW do the ethnics-you-don't-like teach their kids to put their underpants on?

They use a colour code. Yellow to the front, brown to the back.

* * *

DID you hear about the migrant who came out to this country, married a prostitute and brought her down to his level?

* * *

NOTING that there were distinct advantages in being white, a young Negro got some chalk and applied it to his face and hands.

When he presented himself to his mother she screamed abuse at him and told him go and show his father.

His father also swore at him and gave him a few thumps behind the ear.

He left the house holding his head. "Crikey," he said to himself, "I've only been a Whitey for ten minutes and already I hate those black bastards."

* * *

JACK and Jill worked for a company which was experiencing a financial crisis and the boss had to sack one of them. But which one? He thought the woman would understand his problem better so he called her in.

"Jill, things are tough," he said, "you know I have either to lay you or Jack off."

"Well, you'll have to jack off because I've got a headache," she said.

*   *   *

LETTER received by the Bureau of Ethnic Affairs:

'Gentlemen. I have always wanted to have an affair with an ethnic. How do I go about it?'

AGEISM

AGEISM is another area where some seek protection through political correctness. The author is an old bastard himself and frankly, I've never had so much fun in my life as I have as a senior citizen. We certainly don't need protection.

DO not resist growing old. Many are denied the privilege.

* * *

A PENSIONER was told that the doctor wanted a stool specimen, a urine specimen and a sperm specimen.

"What's he talking about?" said the deaf pensioner to his wife.

"He wants you to leave your underpants here," she replied.

* * *

THE old gent went for his annual medical. "Your hearing is getting worse," said the doc, "and you must cut out drinking, smoking and sex."

"What!" cried the old geezer, "Just so I can hear better?"

* * *

THEY were talking health and Old Jake was adamant that there was a big difference between cholesterol and fat.

"You can hardly wake up in the morning with half a cholesterol," he said.

*   *   *

GRAMPS finally agreed to his son's wishes to give the rest home a trial. On his first morning a nurse brought his breakfast and noticed he had a 'morning glory'.

"I'll take care of that," she said, grabbing the erection firmly and proceeded to give the old fellow a gratifying hand job.

Later, during his morning shower, Gramps happened to drop the soap and while picking it up 'Wham!' He got shafted by one of his fellow residents.

When his son called in that evening he recounted the day's surprising events.

"Well," said the son, "Win some and lose some. It wasn't too bad was it?"

"As maybe," said Gramps, "the trouble is I don't get a boner all that often these days but I'm always dropping the soap."

*   *   *

IT was one of those cruises full of geriatric passengers and the sprightly octogenarian, finishing his jog around the deck, approached a spinster on her deck chair.

"Guess how old I am?" he ventured with a twinkle in his eye.

The old lady reached out and put her hand up his shorts. She took a firm hold of his family jewels, felt their weight and moved them gently from side to side.

Withdrawing her hand she said with confidence: "You'll be eighty-two next January 3rd."

"That's amazing," said the old codger, "How do you know?"

"Because you told me this morning you forgetful old bugger."

*   *   *

BY the time you reach seventy-five years of age you've learnt everything.

All you have to do is to try and remember it.

*   *   *

WHAT'S pink and wrinkly and hangs out your underpants?

Your grandmother.

*   *   *

WHAT'S got seventy-five balls and screws old ladies?

Bingo.

*   *   *

THEY struck up a romance at the Twilight Retirement Home and he put the hard word on her.

They were quickly in his room where they started to undress. "By the way," she said as she flung off her blouse, "I have acute angina."

"Well I hope it's better than those tits," he replied.

*   *   *

OLD Beryl and Dave struck a relationship in the nursing home. They would meet in the television room after the evening meal, spread a rug across their adjacent chairs and Beryl would quietly give Dave a hand job.

Then one night Beryl was alarmed to see another woman sitting next to Dave, the rug spread across their knees and tell-tale bobbing movement beneath it.

"How could you, Dave?" said Beryl.

"I'm sorry," said Dave, "but she's got Parkinson's."

THE tearful widow asked the solicitor about her husband's will.

"I'm sorry to say he left everything to the Happy Valley Home for Indigent Gentlewomen."

"But what about me?" she sobbed.

"That's it. You are all he had left."

*   *   *

JAKE was determined to keep healthy in his old age, and when he turned sixty he decided to walk five kilometres every day.

He has now reached Port Augusta.

*   *   *

A YOUNG social worker used to call on Old Jake to cut up his steak and help with his meals. She noticed a bowl of almonds beside his tray.

"They were given to me as a present, but I don't want them," he explained. "You can have them."

She said thanks and began to nibble away on them.

"Funny present to give a man with no teeth," she remarked when she had eaten most of them.

"Oh no," he said. "They originally had chocolate on them."

*   *   *

A GERIATRIC is a German cricketer who captures three successive wickets.

*   *   *

AN elderly couple killed in a car accident arrived in Heaven. St Peter took them on a tour of the facilities and showed them into their ocean view apartment.

"Here are the buttons to press if you need food, wine, movies, trips, new cars, massages, etc. It's all there."

When St Peter had left the husband turned to the wife and snarled: "Shit Mabel, we could have been here years ago if you hadn't made us give up smoking."

*   *   *

THEY had agreed to a secret meeting on the porch of the Twilight Home immediately after supper.

With some excitement they moved their rocking chairs close together.

Then he said, "Fuck you."

She replied, "And fuck you too."

They thought about this for awhile until he said: "I don't think much of that oral sex, do you?"

*   *   *

EVEN the parish priest was a welcome visitor for short-sighted Mrs Flannigan.

"But that wasn't the priest," said her daughter after the man had left, "that was the doctor."

"Oh was it?" she exclaimed with relief, "I thought Father O'Reilly was getting rather familiar."

*   *   *

MRS Flannigan described herself as a sprightly old girl. "Actually I see seven gentlemen a day," she said. "I get out of bed with Will Power, then I go to my John, next it's breakfast with Uncle Toby, followed by Billy T.

Then the rest of the day is spent with either Arthur Ritis or Al Zymer until I finally go to bed with Johnny Walker.

*   *   *

THE old gent was backing his Rolls into the last available parking space when a zippy red sports car whipped in behind him to take the spot.

The young man jumped out and said: "Sorry Pops, but you've got to be young and smart to do that."

The old man ignored the remark and kept reversing until the Rolls had crunched the sportscar into a crumpled heap. "Sorry son, you've got to be old and rich to do that!"

*   *   *

AN old bloke was sitting at the bar sobbing with the odd tear dropping in his beer. "I got married to a lovely young widow last week," he explained to the barman. "She is a great cook, keeps my clothes in great nick and is insatiable in bed," he said.

"Then why the hell are you crying?" said the barman.

"Because I can't remember where I live," sobbed the old codger.

*   *   *

AN elderly couple toddle in to the pharmacy and the gent asks for a packet of condoms. "We are having a weekend away," he says.

The clerk eyes them suspiciously. "You are both over eighty, aren't you?" He went on to explain that with menopause well past the woman could not become pregnant.

"It's not that," said the old gent, "Emily here just loves the smell of burning rubber."

*   *   *

THE doctor had examined Old Jake's heart and summed up his advice with "No smoking, no drinking and no sex."

After much protesting by Jake, the doctor relented: "Okay, one cigarette only after meals, and no more than two glasses of light beer a day."

"What about sex?" pressed Jake.

"Very occasionally," said the doctor, "and only with your wife because it is important you avoid any excitement."

* * *

DID you hear about the eighty-year-old man who was acquitted of sexual assault because the evidence wouldn't stand up in court?

* * *

AN old chap in his seventies was concerned about his lack of sex drive and consulted his doctor.

"Well, what would you expect at your age?" said the medic.

The old geezer was still worried, "But my next door neighbour is over eighty and he says he gets it every night."

The doc thought for a moment. "Well, why don't you say it too?"

* * *

A COUPLE of old timers were discussing their sexual situation. "You know Jack," said one, "I understand that drinking stout will put lead in your pencil. Why don't we try a bottle?"

"I don't know about you," replied Jack, "but I don't have that many women to write to."

* * *

THREE old codgers had been playing cards for a few days when one noticed that they had run out of beer. They pooled their money, drew straws and Old Jake was sent for the beer.

An hour passed. Three hours passed and there was no sign of Jake's return. One said, "I think the old bugger has run off with the money."

Jake's voice was heard from near the door. "One more smart comment like that and I won't go at all."

* * *

THE old farmer had married a comely young wench of eighteen years and after a month of wedded bliss he visited his doctor for some advice.

"It's so tiring, Doc," he said. "I am still working the farm, and when I am out in the field and get randy I have to run back to the house, jump into bed, and afterwards, I have to walk back to the job again. It's knocking me out."

"No wonder," said the doctor. "You are eighty-two and she is only eighteen. She should be running out to you," he said.

He solved the problem by suggesting that the farmer take a shotgun out into the field, and every time he felt randy he could fire a shot to signal that his young wife should come running.

A month later the doctor bumped into the old man down the main street and out of curiosity asked him how the shotgun scheme was working.

"Oh it worked well for the first two weeks, but then the duck season opened and I haven't seen her since!"

* * *

THE vicar called on the rich eighty-year-old grazier who had recently married a twenty-year-old bride to see how he was coping.

"Can't keep my hands off her," he said.

The vicar mumbled his approval and went on his way.

He called back in a week. "How's the bride?" he enquired.

"Can't keep my hands off her," repeated the old farmer. "Worse, now she has run off with one of them."

* * *

OLD Horace complained that he couldn't do it like he used to with his young wife so the doctor advised them to sleep in separate rooms. "You will get better rest and when you go to her room you will give a better performance," said the doc.

He tried it for a month before coming back to the clinic. "Didn't it work?" asked the doc.

"Worked well," said Horace. He told the doc that he got randy twice in April but when he went to her room she said: "What, again? You were here just 15 minutes ago."

"Doc," said Horace, "I think I'm losing my memory."

* * *

THE old codger came to see the doctor for a check up. "I'm getting married next week," he said.

The doctor was surprised for he knew the old gent was eighty-four.

"Why would you want to get married?" he asked.

"I don't want to, I have to," said the old codger.

* * *

OLD Jake came back from the doctor's anxious to show his missus his new $3000 silicon chip hearing aid.

"It looks fine," she said.

"Half past seven," he replied.

* * *

WHEN Old Jake returned to the doctor he was given a bottle of medicine. "This is potent stuff," said the doc. "Don't take it every day."

The doctor wanted to make sure Old Jake understood. "So take it on alternative days, do you know what I mean? Take it tomorrow, then skip a day, then take it the next day and skip another day, and so on."

A month later the doctor saw Jake's wife in the street and enquired after the old codger.

"Oh, he's dead," she said.

The doctor was aghast.

"No, the medicine wasn't that strong," she said. "It was all that skipping!"

* * *

"WHAT'S the matter little boy?" asked the old codger when he saw the lad sitting on the kerb crying.

"I'm crying because I can't do what the big boys do," he said.

The old man sat on the kerb and started crying too.

* * *

OLD Jake tottered into the clinic. "Doc," he said, "you've got to do something to lower my sex drive."

"C'mon Jake," said the doctor. "Your sex drive is all in your head."

"That's what I mean. You've got to do something to lower it!"

* * *

THE old codger came to the doctor with the exciting news that he was going to marry a twenty-year-old bride.

"Well, I think at your age you should take things easy. In fact I think you should take in a lodger," said the doctor.

A year later he bumped into the old codger and asked how was married life.

"The wife's pregnant, I am happy to say," said the old man, and with a wink and a nudge he added, "thanks for that advice about taking in a boarder. She's pregnant too."

* * *

WHEN he fronted at the Sperm Bank counter the matron looked him up and down and asked what he was there for.

"I want to make a donation," he said.

"But you look about eighty-five," she said.

"I am," said the old codger, "but I have been a goer all my life. I can do it okay."

After further pleading the matron decided to give him the benefit of the doubt and handed him a jar. "Use that cubicle there," she said.

After ten minutes of grunting, groaning and heavy breathing she knocked on the door. "Are you okay?" she asked.

He came out with perspiration all over his face. He looked distressed and was out of breath.

"I have tried with my right hand, I have tried with my left," he said. "But I can't get the bloody lid off this jar!"

* * *

OLD Jake was reminiscing. "I can remember the time I gave up both booze and sex at the same time. Crikey, in all of my life that was the worst half hour I've ever spent!"

* * *

THE exhausted bush-walker stumbled into a drover's hut high in the Alps and was immediately welcomed by its lone inhabitant, a tough old mountain man.

The visitor was offered food and invited to sit by the log fire.

After the meal the old man pulled down an unlabelled bottle from a shelf and offered the visitor a drink. The bush-walker accepted, but when he pulled the cork and sniffed the evil home-brew he graciously declined and attempted to return the bottle.

"Drink it!" insisted the old-timer. When the lad declined again the old man reached for his rifle, cocked it and pointed it at the lad's head.

There was no other alternative but to take a swig of the vile firewater that had a kick like a mule. When the bush-walker gasped his way to recovery he handed the bottle back, and the old man handed him the rifle.

"Now you hold the gun on me while I have a drink," he said.

* * *

THE old codger wrote to his doctor:

'Dear Doc. For the past sixty years, or more, I have awakened in the morning with a roaring erection so strong I have never been able to bend it.

But this morning, on applying great pressure, I was able to force it down. Doc, is my dick getting weaker, or my forearm getting stronger?'

* * *

THE old codger staggered into the clinic. "I'm worried, Doc," he said. "I met this nymphomaniac last week and made passionate love to her. Since then my roger has become red and itchy. It has swollen to three times its size and there is a discharge beginning to appear."

The doctor examined his donger.

"You'd better sit down," he said. "You are about to come."

* * *

WHEN the family learned that Gramps was set to marry a twenty-year-old they were horrified. The eldest son took him aside and said: "Frankly, Dad, we're concerned that sex with a young girl like that could be fatal."

"So what," said the old codger, "If she dies, she dies."

* * *

GRAMPS went to the pharmacy. "You've got to help me with a potion," he said. "I've scored a date with a lovely young lady and I need something to get it up."

The pharmacy knew Gramps was eighty-two and past it. Nevertheless he sold him a jar of cream and sent the old man away happy and contented.

The pharmacist wondered if he had done the right thing and later that evening rang Gramps. "Did the potion help?" he asked.

"It was great," said Gramps. "I've managed it three times already."

The pharmacist was surprised, "And what about the girl?" he asked.

"Oh, she's not here yet!"

* * *

JAKE looked a little tired as he took his usual place in the sun lounge. "I'm exhausted," he said to Fred, "I pulled a muscle in the bathroom this morning."

"That shouldn't make you tired," said Fred.

"It does if you pull it 375 times," said Jake.

* * *

"NOT so much sex going on as there was in the old days, eh Bert?"

"Oh yes there is," said Bert, "It's just another crowd doing it."

* * *

OLD Bob has been missing from the senior citizens' club for some time and when he eventually fronted his mate said, "Gee you look pale, where have you been?"

Bob had to admit he had been three months in jail after being charged with rape.

"But you are eighty-four," said his mates.

"Yeah, that was the trouble," said Bob. "I pleaded guilty and the judge gave me three months for perjury!"

* * *

OLD Jake was alone in his hotel room watching television when there was a knock on the door. He opened it and a buxom young girl walked in.

"Oh, I am so sorry," she said, "I must be in the wrong room."

"No love," said Jake. "It's the right room, but you are just thirty-five years too late."

* * *

OLD Chippendale was a millionaire. He had married a ravishing twenty-year-old and it was the same old problem. He was past it.

On good advice he finally went to an audio-hypno-therapist who assured him that a simple audible signal would get it up immediately and the same audible signal repeated, would bring it down again.

"For example," said the doc. "Look into my eyes and I will program your mind so that the simple sound 'beep' will give you a roaring horn, and 'beep, beep' will safely bring it down again.

"But I warn you," continued the doc, "at your advanced age three sessions is all your system could stand. Any more and it could kill you."

"Three will see me out," chirped the old man elatedly. "You mean if I go 'beep' it will ..."

And immediately Chippendale had cracked an enormous erection.

"You can't go home like that," said the doc. "You've got to go 'beep, beep." And as soon as the words were uttered the erection subsided.

The old man sat there exhausted, yet delighted that it worked.

But while driving home a Morris Minor overtook him and went 'beep', then 'beep, beep' and he had an erection and a subsidence that caused him to pull over for twenty minutes to recover.

"One final spurt to go," he said to himself as he mounted the stairs to his bedroom, showered and donned his dressing gown.

"Darling," he said to his young bride, "get your clothes off and get on the bed. I'm horny."

She was quick to do so. "About bloody time," she said.

He flashed open the front of his dressing gown, jumped on the bed, yelled 'beep', and presented her with a gigantic throbbing erection.

"Wow," she said. "What a beauty. But what's all this 'beep beep' shit?"

* * *

IN his dotage Old Jake had become simple. On his daily walks he would talk to the trees and flowers. Going through the park one day he said "Hello trees, hello flowers," and when he saw a little ebony idol he said: "Hello little ebony idol."

To his surprise the idol replied. "Oh, please help me. I am not really a little ebony idol, I am really a beautiful young woman under the spell of a witch. It only needs sexual intercourse with me to break the spell.

"Well, I am a bit beyond that sort of thing," said Jake, "but let me talk to my brother, he's an idle fucking bastard."

* * *

IT was a regimental dinner testimonial:

"Today we honour a man who doesn't know the meaning of fear; a man who doesn't know the meaning of defeat, quit or surrender.

So we have all chipped in and bought him a dictionary."

* * *

TWO blokes in the Old Soldiers' Home were talking. "Do you remember those pills they used to give us in the army to keep our minds off girls?" said one.

"Vaguely," said the other.

"Well," said the first, "I think they are beginning to work."

* * *

WHEN old Fred went to join the Returned Soldiers' League they asked him if he had a war record: "Bloody oath. I've got Vera Lynn singing the White Cliffs of Dover."

* * *

289

THE reporter was pressing the old gent on his 100th birthday as to why he had lived so long.

"Two reasons," said the old-timer, "The first is my life-long practice of having two whiskies a day."

"And second?" asked the reporter.

"Cancelling my voyage on the Titanic," said the old gent.

*   *   *

THE cadet had been assigned to do the annual story on Colonel Frobisher. "He has the reputation of being England's bravest soldier," said the editor. "The story has been done before, but if you can get a new angle, then you are well on the way m'lad."

The cadet went off to the Old Soldier's Home with the advice of his chief still ringing in his ears. "If only there was a time Frobisher had been scared ..."

He found the colonel sitting in his wheelchair and soon came to the point. "Surely, Sir, surely there was a time when you were frightened?"

The colonel looked thoughtful for a while. "Well there was the time I was with the fusiliers in India and this rogue tiger had eaten two or three of the native chaps," he began.

"I remember tracking the beast through the jungle. I followed his tracks and got a glimpse of him hiding behind some tall grass. I cocked my gun and crept right up to the grassy patch and I was about to peep through when the monster leapt straight at me and roared 'Aaaarrgh!' I shit myself."

The cadet whipped out his notebook. "When was that?" he asked eagerly.

"Just then when I went 'Aaaarrgh!'" said the colonel.

THE Elderly Citizens' Club now has a community bus and each Sunday they go off on a mystery tour. To make it interesting the oldies dob in fifty cents in a sweep to guess the mystery destination.

Bert the driver has won it three times in a row.

SPINSTERS

Dear Sir, God bless you for the beautiful radio your Company donated as a prize at our recent Senior Citizen luncheon. I was the lucky one to win it.

I am 86 years old and live at the Country Home for the aged. All my people are gone and it was nice to have someone think of me.

God bless you for your kindness to an old forgotten lady.

My roomate is 95 and always had her own Radio but would never let me listen to it. The other day her radio fell and broke into lots of pieces. It was just awefull. She asked if she could listen to my new radio and I told her to get fucked.

Sincerely
Elsie McEvoy

TWO old ladies at the Twilight Home were talking.

"Did you hear old Jim Mullins had a massive stroke?"

"Always did," said her friend, "that's what made him so popular at our social functions."

* * *

SHE had always been a lively lady and when she was finally retired to the nursing home she refused to lead a boring life. She was determined to liven up the place. So she put a large sign on her door: 'SEX, $20 in bed, $5 on the floor'.

Nothing happened for the first few nights, but on Friday there was a timid knock and she opened the door to find Jock standing there. He handed her a $20 note.

"Hang on," she said. "I'll get the bed ready."

"To hell with the bed," said Jock. "I'm here for four on the floor!"

* * *

AS the bus was leaving the seaside for the return trip to the Twilight Home it lurched and caused old Henry to lose his balance. He fell onto Miss Prim and in the ensuing tangle his elbow poked the old woman in the breast.

"I'm sorry about that," said Henry, then added with a wink, "but if your heart is as soft as your breast, then I will see you in Heaven."

"And if your prick is as stiff as your elbow, I'll see you back at the Twilight Home," she smartly replied.

* * *

ON his morning round the doctor stopped beside the little old lady he had been treating for asthma. He checked her over, asked a few questions and listened to her croaky replies.

"What about the wheeze?" he said.

"Oh, fine," she replied. "I went three times last night!"

* * *

ELDERLY Miss Smithers had been called for jury duty and took her place beside a rather burly Italian. It was a sordid case of sexual harassment and although Miss Smithers found parts of the case interesting, the dreary legal argument would sometimes cause her to nod off.

The case reached the point when the attractive young victim was asked to repeat the rude suggestion the defendant had made. She was too embarassed to tell the court.

The judge asked her to write it down on paper so that it could be passed to members of the jury.

So it came as a little surprise when Miss Smithers was gently prodded on the elbow by the Italian on her left and handed a note which read: "I'm randy. I'd like to rip your knickers off."

She looked at the Italian, smiled, and put the note in her handbag.

* * *

AUNT Maud dreamt she was married.

But when she woke up she found there was nothing in it.

* * *

THE salesman had noticed the spinster at the next table give him a dirty look but he persisted with his meal. Nevertheless he was surprised when the waiter delivered a note from her. It read: "Young man, maybe you don't know it but your fly is unzipped. You should be ashamed of yourself. Exposing your person in a public place is disgusting. It's indecent. PS: I love you."

* * *

IN the supermarket the spinster approached a customer standing by a shopping trolley. "Excuse me," she said, "are you going to use that trolley?"

"No," he said, "I'm only here for one thing."

"Typical male," she sniffed.

* * *

SHE called at the police station to complain about the young man next door. "It's not safe to go out on the street," she said. "He's always sitting on his front porch whistling dirty songs!"

* * *

AN elderly spinster sniffed with disdain when asked why she didn't marry.

"I have a dog that growls, a parrot that swears, a fireplace that smokes and a cat that stays out all night. Why should I want a husband?"

* * *

THE spinster was coming home from evensong when a man jumped from behind a tree and said: "Don't move, this is a stick-up."

"I haven't got any money," she said, showing him her empty handbag.

"I'll see for myself," he said, and with that he began searching her. He felt around her waist, felt inside her bra, ran his hands up and down her legs and even searched her knickers.

Not finding a brass cent he turned to walk away.

"Don't stop searching," she said. "I can write you a cheque."

* * *

MISS Prim had phoned the local police station several times to complain about the man next door who walked around his apartment completely nude.

Finally the sergeant called around. "But you can't even see his window from here," he said.

"Try standing on that kitchen chair and looking through the skylight," she said.

* * *

THE spinster approached the salesman in the furniture store. "I can't decide between the armchair or the sofa," she said.

"Believe me, madam," said the salesman, "you won't make a mistake on the armchair."

"Right, then I'll take the sofa," she said.

* * *

STELLA the spinster had heard that men with big feet have big pricks, so when a tramp knocked on her door asking for a hand-out, she was quick to notice his very large shoes stretched across the entire width of the step.

She invited him in, gave him a hearty meal, a bottle of beer and took him to bed.

When he woke alone next morning he found $50 and a brief note.

"It said: 'Buy yourself a pair of shoes that fit'.

* * *

THE spinster had just settled into the seaside resort when she noticed the sign on the wall: 'If the electric blanket doesn't work switch it off and call in a man'.

* * *

MISS Prim complained to the police that the men on the building site were using foul language.

The cop told her that builders' labourers tended to call a spade a spade.

"No they don't," she said. "They've been calling it a fuckin shovel."

*   *   *

OLD Spinster's Prayer:

And now I lay me down to sleep
I wish I had a man to keep
If there's a man beneath the bed
I hope he heard each word I said.

*   *   *

YOUNG Spinster's Prayer:

Oh Lord I ask nothing for myself, but would you please send my dear mother a son-in-law?

*   *   *

SPINSTER'S advice:

Dear girls, be wary of Cupid
And hark to the lines of this verse
To let a fool kiss you is stupid
To let a kiss fool you is worse.

*   *   *

SHE was a teacher in her mid-forties and a spinster until she finally allowed herself to be seduced by the school inspector.

She sat up in bed and started crying. "Oh the shame," she sobbed. "How can I stand up in front of those children tomorrow and pretend to be worthy when I've been sinful so often."

"What do you mean, often?" said the school inspector. "I thought this was the first time."

"It is," she said, "but you are going to do it again, aren't you?"

* * *

THE elderly spinster had called the vet because her cat seemed to be off her food. He made a quick examination and pronounced that the cat was pregnant.

"Impossible," said the spinster. "Moggie never goes out. I feed her in here. She has had no contact with stray cats of any kind."

Just then a battered old ginger tom wandered out from behind the couch.

"There's the culprit," said the vet.

"Preposterous," said the spinster. "That's Moggie's brother."

* * *

TWO elderly spinsters were sitting on the front porch of their country house convincing each other they had made the right choice in life when a rooster chased a flurried hen past them.

The hen took evasive action, running around the house three times, then dashed onto the road, straight into the path of an oncoming car.

"See that," said one spinster, "she'd prefer to die."

* * *

SPINSTER Brown rang the police to say she had captured a man climbing into her bedroom window and that they could call around for him next morning.

* * *

THE sign outside the pet shop said: 'Special dog for spinsters', and sure enough, it soon attracted a well-dressed woman in her mid-forties who pretended to browse around the shop before she got to the point.

298

"And what does this dog do?" she asked.

"He's a big boy. A Great Dane," said Charlie the conman. "He does little tricks for lonely women, if you get my meaning, nudge, nudge, wink, wink."

"I don't know what you mean, but I'll buy him," she said.

A week later Charlie received a phone call. It was to complain that the so-called special dog was a non-performer. It hadn't done a thing.

"Are you in bed?" asked Charlie.

"Yes," she replied.

"Hmmm, I can't understand it. I'll come right over."

When Charlie arrived the woman was indeed in bed and the dog was sitting on a chair peering out the window.

"Damn it Roger," said Charlie taking off his clothes, "I'm going to show you this trick just one more time."

*   *   *

AFTER watching Little Red Riding Hood leave her home the wolf hurried through the woods and broke into the home of the little girl's grandmother.

"Alright Granny," he snarled, "Get outta bed. I'm gonna lock you in the closet."

Reaching under the blankets Granny drew out a shotgun. "Oh no you don't, big fella," she said, lifting her nightie, "you are gonna do what the story says."

MOTHERS and MOTHERS-IN-LAW

POLITICAL Correctness has given mothers-in-law too much protection lately. My mother-in-law thinks I'm effiminate, and compared to her I probably am. They have always been fair game and have always been able to look after themselves.

MARRIAGE Anonymous is a club for bachelors. If any member is tempted to get married they send over a mother-in-law in a dressing gown and hair curlers.

* * *

MY mother-in-law broke up our marriage.

My wife came home early one evening and found me in bed with her.

* * *

THE local Peeping Tom knocked on the door the other night and asked if the mother-in-law would mind closing her bedroom curtains.

* * *

USHER at the wedding reception: "Are you a friend of the groom?"

Woman: "Indeed I am not. I am the bride's mother."

* * *

ONE mother-in-law to another: "I have never made a fool of my son-in-law. I always allow him the opportunity to develop his natural abilities."

* * *

I NEVER forget a face. But in my mother-in-law's case, I am willing to make an exception.

* * *

"EVERY night she covers her face in mud and puts her hair in rollers."

"Does it help?"

"A little. But I can still tell it's her."

* * *

WONDERFUL woman my mother-in-law, seventy-five years old and never uses glasses. Drinks straight from the bottle.

* * *

FOR twenty years my mother-in-law and I were happy.

Then we met.

* * *

MY mother-in-law is musical and does a bit of singing. Yesterday she was practising and three factories knocked off for lunch.

* * *

MY mother-in-law has a speech impediment. Now and then she pauses for breath.

* * *

SAM rented a little cottage by the sea and wired his wife that the holiday was arranged and to come and join him. But he got a shock to see both wife and mother arrive with luggage.

First chance he got he took his wife aside and

whispered: "Didn't you get the telegram not to bring your mother?"

"Yes," she replied, "that's what she wants to talk to you about."

* * *

HIS wife was ebbing fast, yet she raised herself on one elbow and beckoned him to come closer.

"On the day of the funeral," she gasped, "it would please me if you would ride in the same car as my mother."

"Okay," he said grudgingly, "but it will completely spoil my day."

* * *

HARRY was explaining to his mate at the bar that he had yet another fight with his mother-in-law.

"But at least she came crawling to me on her hands and knees this time," he said.

His mate was impressed: "Why, what did she say?"

"Come out from under the bed you pathetic, snivelling little coward and I'll clobber you again!"

* * *

WHEN Harry's house burned down he went off to the insurance company and demanded his compensation money. But he was soon to learn that the company didn't operate that way.

"It is our policy to replace your house and anything else you lost exactly in the same style and condition," said the manager.

"Hell," said Harry. "In that case I would like to cancel the policy I took out on my mother-in-law."

* * *

BLOKE on a caravan holiday in Far North Queensland with his wife and mother-in-law was wakened one morning. His wife said her mother hadn't returned from her morning walk and she was alarmed. They searched along the river bank for a while before the wife let out a scream when she saw her mother paddling in the shallows and a large crocodile stalking her from behind.

"Oh my Gawd," screamed the wife, "Do something, quick!"

The man considered the situation for a moment and said: "The croc got himself into this trouble, let him get himself out of it."

* * *

THE same mother-in-law was kidnapped when they returned from their holiday. After three days they got a note from the kidnappers saying that if they didn't send the ransom money immediately, they would send her back.

* * *

HE complained to the doctor that he was worried about his mother-in-law. "She keeps blowing smoke rings through her nose when she talks to me."

"Nothing unusual about that," said the doc. "Lots of people blow rings when they are smoking."

"Yeah, but my mother-in-law doesn't smoke," he said.

POLITICIANS

THE frightening thing about Political Correctness is that politicians will legislate to make it law, and no doubt they will be in the queue seeking protection.

No matter who you vote for, a politician always wins and the worst thing about political jokes is that they keep getting elected. Politicians are ubiquitous.Everybody knows one, which makes them legitimate targets for lampooning in speeches or yarns. So let's laugh at them while we can.

THE Prime Minister was asked if he had heard the latest political jokes.

"Heard them?" he said. "I work with the bludgers."

*   *   *

ONE politician said he wouldn't mind a bit if women were in power.

The other said he wouldn't mind a bit and he didn't give a stuff who was in power.

*   *   *

COME to think of it, there is no difference between politicians and bull sperm. Only one in a thousand actually work.

*   *   *

WHEN a politician says a meeting was meaningful; it means that it was meaningless.

*   *   *

THE Prime Minister adjourned the cabinet meeting for lunch and went into the dining room where he told the waitress he would have steak and sausages.

"What about your vegetables?" she asked.

"Let the bastards order for themselves," he said.

* * *

Jokes on politicians are perennial, only the names have to be changed to make them current, or switched to suit your own political bent.

For example, when the Prime Minister (name your own bias) saw some grafitti outside the lodge proclaiming 'The PM is a dick-head' it angered him. It made him all the more furious to realise that it was written in piddle in the snow.

When he saw it repeated a second morning it was the last straw. He called in security. "Make it first priority to discover this offender," he told his spooks.

The forensic team went into action and after two days of scientific study announced to the Prime Minister that they had good news and bad news.

"The piddle source is the Leader of the Opposition," they said, "but it is your wife's handwriting!"

* * *

MAKE your MP work—Don't re-elect him.

* * *

"DADDY," said the little girl, "do all fairy tales begin with 'Once upon a time'?"

"No," said her father, "they often start with, 'Vote for me and ...'"

* * *

WHY is it that the only people who know how to run the country are driving cabs or cutting hair?

* * *

IT has just been revealed that the Prime Minister was a test tube baby.

Evidently nobody gave a fuck for him then either.

* * *

POLITICIANS are people who have to mind their appease and accuse.

* * *

WHAT's the difference between a flattened politician and a flattened kangaroo on the road to the State Capital?

There are skid marks leading to the kangaroo.

* * *

NEVER believe anything about a politician, until he has made an official denial.

* * *

THE Prime Minister is considering changing the name of his party to the Condom Party.

It stands up to inflation, it protects a bunch of pricks, it halts production, and it gives a false sense of security while the nation is being screwed.

* * *

MAGGIE Thatcher died and went to Heaven. As she approached the celestial chair God said: "Who are you?"

"I'm Baroness Thatcher, that's my chair you're sitting in."

* * *

AT the political rally the heckler yelled:

"Clinton should be bloody well hung!"

Hilary jumped up: "He is, he is."

* * *

"MR MINISTER!" boomed the back-bencher, "What are you going to do about the Abortion Bill?"

"Shhh, not so loud," said the Minister, "I'm paying it tomorrow."

* * *

THE election campaign had become fairly bitter and when the two opponents met at a social gathering it was a chance to make a pact to stop insulting each other.

"Let's make a clean fight of it," said Smith. "I promise to stop telling lies about you."

"That's fair," said Brown, "and I will stop telling the truth about you."

* * *

HE had listened to the politician's speech for a solid hour before going outside for a breath of fresh air.

"Is he still talking?" asked his mate outside.

"Yeah."

"What's he talking about?"

"He didn't say."

* * *

HE walked into the general store of a country town in the Wimmera and bought all the rotten fruit, tomatoes and eggs available. The greengrocer beamed: "I bet you are going to hear the visiting MP at the Mechanics' Hall tonight."

"No," he replied. "I AM the visiting MP!"

* * *

HOW come there is only one Monopolies Commission?

* * *

ON the headstone of a grave in the cemetery is the most unusual epitaph: "Here lies the body of a great politician, an honest man and the Member for Wills."

It is unusual because it is not often they bury three men in one grave.

* * *

ONE thing about our local MP. He's an honest politician. When he's bought he stays bought.

* * *

WHAT do you need when you have a politician up to his neck in concrete?

More concrete.

* * *

WHAT's the difference between a pot hole and a politician?

You would swerve to miss a pothole.

* * *

THE politician went to Harley St, London, for a dick transplant. It rejected him.

* * *

BILL Clinton was jogging in the park and preoccupied by affairs of State, slipped and fell in the lake.

A youth heard his cries for help and at great risk to himself dived in and saved him.

When he recovered the great man said to the lad: "Boy, you saved my life. Anything you can name you can have."

"I don't want anything," said the lad. "Just don't tell my dad."

* * *

MAGGIE Thatcher gathered her cabinet around her and stood up to outline the strategy of the next campaign. "I am going to describe the tactics in the simplest possible terms, so if there are any idiots in the room will they stand up now."

After a pause one politician got to his feet.

"So you are an idiot are you?" said Maggie.

"Not exactly, PM, I just didn't like to see you standing alone!"

*   *   *

THE proposition to put a king-sized statue of the Prime Minister in Central Park has been well supported. It will give shelter when its raining, shade in the summer, and the pigeons a chance to speak for us all.

*   *   *

"AND as for the problem of the pigeons around the Town Hall," said the mayor, "It's no use trying to dodge the issue."

*   *   *

OUR local Member of Parliament says at the forthcoming election he will stand on his record.

That's the only way he can stop people examining it.

*   *   *

DON'T vote. It only encourages the bastards.

*   *   *

THE romance was off to a shaky start from the beginning because she was conservative while he was traditional labor but they decided to live together on the basis of agreeing to disagree.

It went well for a short time until a television program set off the inevitable political argument.

When they retired to bed he remained on the left and she on the extreme right.

Eventually she made an overture: "There is a split in the Tory movement and it is quite likely that if a Labor member stood he could slip in unopposed."

"Too late," he said. "There's been too much stimu-

309

lation in the private sector and he has blown his deposit."

*　　*　　*

WHILE on safari in cannibal country a traveller came across a cafe in a clearing in the jungle. The sign out front advertised: Fried Missionary $5, Boiled Hunter $4-50, Grilled Safari Guide $5, Stuffed Politician $15.

When the traveller asked why so much for the politician the chef replied, "Have you ever tried to clean one?"

GRAFFITI

NO doubt about it, brevity is the soul of wit and ever since man could write he has written on walls in short, sharp slogans that were 'politically incorrect' until adopted by the general populace.

The walls of our cities have long been the only form of published expression available to crusaders of causes that have eventually changed society.

As Paul Simon wrote:
'The words of the prophet
Are written on the subway walls,
And tenement halls.'

Many crusades, from anti-slavery, Pankhurst's Suffragettes, the anti-war movement, to the environment issue have all used the walls as a serious expression of their cause.

Graffiti, with its brief message, and sometimes an appended reply, can also be entertaining.

* * *

TURK, Jew or Atheist
   May enter here,
   But not a Papist!
     To which a reply was later chalked:
Who wrote this wrote it well
For the same is written
On the Gates of Hell.

* * *

WHY do people write, 'Fuck the Pope' on walls?

Because there is usually very little room, or time, to write: 'Fuck the Moderator of the General Assembly of the Church of Scotland'.

* * *

THE country is stuffed through apathy!
  (What's Apathy?)
  (I don't know and I don't care).

* * *

GOD Lives!
  (So does Doubting Thomas).

* * *

JESUS Saves!
  (Moses invests).
  (But only Buddha pays dividends).

* * *

JESUS Saves!
  (But the Mongol hordes).

* * *

JESUS Saves!
  (He couldn't on my salary).

* * *

JESUS Saves!
  (Darwin survives).

* * *

JESUS Saves!
  (Does this mean no Easter holidays?)

* * *

THE meek shall inherit the earth
  (They're not game to refuse it).

* * *

THE meek shall inherit the earth
  (If that's okay by the rest of you?)

* * *

LEGALISE Mental Telepathy.
  (I knew you were going to say that).
                    *   *   *
GRAFFITI should be obscene and not heard.
                    *   *   *
GRAFFITI was Mussolini's Secretary for Defence.
                    *   *   *
AYATOLLAH Khomeini is a Shiite.
                    *   *   *
DEATH is life's answer to the question 'Why?'
                    *   *   *
DEATH is the price of evolution.
                    *   *   *
REINCARNATION is a pleasant surprise.
                    *   *   *
SUDDEN prayers make God jump.
                    *   *   *
THE cleaner's work has been in vain
  The phantom sprayer has struck again!
                    *   *   *
Sign on hotel wall:
  Count your change. Some of our staff
  are in business for themselves.
                    *   *   *
AN erection is like the Theory of Relativity;
  the more you think about it the harder it gets.
                    *   *   *
ALL the big women die young.
  That's why we are left with little old ladies.
                    *   *   *
IF it has to be a matter of Reds under the bed,
  please send me Natasha.
                    *   *   *
ORAL sex is a matter of taste.

ANARCHISTS Unite!

*　　*　　*

EUNUCHS Unite! You have nothing to lose.

*　　*　　*

YOU can tell the sex of a chromosome
   by taking down its genes.

*　　*　　*

ROSES are red, Violets are blue
   and Jean isn't wearing any.

*　　*　　*

LITTLE Red Riding Hood is a Russian contraceptive.

*　　*　　*

OEDIPUS was the first man to plug the generation
gap.

*　　*　　*

SADO-masochism means not having to say you are
sorry.

*　　*　　*

IF you feel strongly about graffiti, sign a partition.

*　　*　　*

LIFE is a sexually transmitted disease.

*　　*　　*

I CHOKED Linda Lovelace.

*　　*　　*

UNTIL I discovered women
   I thought love was a pain in the arse.

*　　*　　*

LOWER the age of puberty.

*　　*　　*

WAKE up to insomnia.

*　　*　　*

I AM an abject failure:
   Legalise Abortion!

*　　*　　*

SUPPORT fee enterprise:
  Legalise Prostitution!
               *   *   *
STAMP out philately!
               *   *   *
REPEAL the Law of Gravity.
               *   *   *
REPEAL the banana.
               *   *   *
DEPRESSIVE neurosis is nothing to laugh about.
               *   *   *
REALITY is for people who can't cope with drugs.
               *   *   *
BE Placid with Acid.
               *   *   *
GRASS is nature's way of saying: 'High.'
               *   *   *
HELP a nun kick the habit!
               *   *   *
HIRE the morally handicapped.
               *   *   *
SILENCE those who oppose freedom of speech.
               *   *   *
WE are the people our parents warned us about.
               *   *   *
LIFE is a hereditary disease. And terminal.
               *   *   *
IF you think life is a joke,
  consider the punchline.
               *   *   *
THOSE who think they know it all
  upset those of us who do!
               *   *   *
I'D give my right arm to be ambidextrous.

WHAT has posterity ever done for me?
* * *

NOSTALGIA isn't what it used to be.
It's a thing of the past.
* * *

LARGE cats can be dangerous,
but a little pussy never hurt anyone.
* * *

TO go together is blessed,
to come together is divine.
* * *

I AM virgin on the edge of intercourse.
* * *

WHICH is all very graffitifying.

FARTS

FARTS may not be politically incorrect but they have been socially unaccepted for a long time which is nearly the same thing. Fortunately, you can't keep a good fart down. No less a literary giant than Geoffrey Chaucer gave recognition to the humble fart in his 13th century account of 'The Miller's Tale'.

Before him, Aristophanes, the Noel Coward of his day, took great delight in having his characters discuss the intimate details of their farts.

Today, if you can fart in company then you are surrounded by true friends.

MADAM was quite the old stager
   Who as the result of a wager
   Consented to fart the complete oboe part
   Of Mozart's Quartet in F major
*   *   *

BUT the violinst was just a bit smarter
   For he was a magnificent farter
   He could play anything, from God Save the King
   To Beethoven's Moonlight Sonata.
*   *   *

STEPPING into the elevator the businessman quickly detected an offensive odour. The only other occupant was a little old lady. "Excuse me," he addressed her, "did you happen to pass wind?"

317

"Of course I did," she replied. "You don't think I stink like this all the time do you?"

* * *

AT the Twilight Home old Jake was dozing in his chair. Every time he leaned too far to one side a nurse would gently push him up straight.

Bert, a new arrival, asked how he liked the rest home just as a nurse pushed Jake up straight again.

"Oh the home is alright," said Jake, leaning to the left again. "It's just that they make it bloody difficult to fart."

* * *

THE reason farts
   Smell like they do,
   Is so that the deaf
   Can enjoy them too.

* * *

SHE was delighted when the most eligible bachelor asked her to dance, but while they glided around the floor doing the cha-cha-cha the effort caused him to let go a few whoofers.

"Oh what an original way to keep time," she said.

* * *

AS a young man Cecil B. Ponsonby was in the front pew for evensong when he felt a rumble in the stomach as the only belated warning of the thunderous fart that followed.

He was mortified with embarrassment. In shame he shut his eyes and held his head in his hands and didn't look up until he was sure every last soul in the congregation had left.

He slunk out of the church, fled home, packed a few belongings and went abroad.

His embarrassment was such that he remained over-seas, travelling the world, until he was an old and weary man. In his heart he longed to return to his home village once more before he died and so decided to make the trip.

He had aged, grown a beard and rationalised to himself that nobody would recognise him and that the shameful incident of his life would have long been forgotten.

Once again in the village of his youth he went to the little church and was surprised to see it now had a steeple.

"When was that built?" he asked the verger.

"The steeple? Oh, that was built seven years, three months and five days after Ponsonby farted in the front pew."

*   *   *

AT the Galloping Gourmet's annual feast Fred Flabby set a new record of eating thirty-five plates of baked beans. However the record was not counted due to a following wind.

*   *   *

WHAT do you get when you've been eating onions and beans?

Tear Gas.

*   *   *

PADDY the Irish cook was famous for his bean soup.

"I use exactly 239 beans," he said. "One more and it would be too farty."

*   *   *

THE Queen was showing the Archbishop of Canterbury around her new stables when a stallion nearby let go with a resounding fart that registered seven-point-two on the Richter scale. It rattled the windows and couldn't be ignored.

"Oh, dear," said the Queen blushing, "I'm frightfully sorry about that."

"Think nothing of it, Ma'am," said the Archbishop. "Actually, I thought it was the horse."

*　　*　　*

IT was so cold in the mountains that Old Jake woke one morning to find two ice cubes in his sleeping bag.

When he threw them on the fire they went: Phartsst! Pharsst!

*　　*　　*

IT is her first date with her supervisor from the office and she is edgy. They are going to a charity concert but she is gripped with nerves and a tightening of the stomach. Just as she hears the doorbell ring she is taken by a great desire to fart.

In great discomfort she stifles it.

Outside in dark street the young man ushers her into the front seat of his car but does not get in himself. "I'll just nip over to the shop and get some cigarettes," he says.

Immediately she takes the opportunity to let go a rip-snorting fart, lifting one cheek of her bum off the seat to let the blast go free. A few seconds later her date returns, settles behind the wheel and says: "Oh, I'm sorry. I forgot to introduce you to my parents," and turning round he indicates the two people sitting in the gloom of the rear seat.

*　　*　　*

HE sat next to the duchess at tea

It was just as he feared it would be

Her rumblings abdominable were simply phenomenal

And everyone thought it was he.

* * *

AN embarrassed young woman was farting uncontrollably when her date was due to arrive. She was an accomplished pianist so to drown the noise she offered to play the Storm Scene from the William Tell Overture.

She had concluded the piece when she felt another fart attack on its way and quickly asked him if he would like another tune on the piano.

"Well if it is that storm scene again," he said, "can you leave out the bit where the lightning strikes the shithouse?"

* * *

HER marriage into high society was an excuse for Lady Upstart to inveigle princes and diplomats to her candle-lit suppers and to put on airs and graces above her station.

It all got up the butler's nose.

But it turned out that on one of these society occasions her stomach was suffering a little internal turbulence and during an unfortunate lull in the conversation she let forth an audible fart.

Without batting an eyelid she turned briskly on the butler and said "Jeeves, stop that."

Jeeves was up to the mark. "Certainly Madam, which way did it go?"

* * *

THE Scot was so mean the only way he would take a bubble bath on Saturday morning was to eat baked beans for his supper on Friday night.

TWO old maids were discussing the merits of panty-hose.

"Don't like them at all," said one. "Every time I fart it blows my slippers off."

* * *

IT was the season's diplomatic dinner and at the head of the table sat Lady Carrington society matron and matriarch of the diplomatic corp. On her right was the British Consul and on her left was the French Consul.

Suddenly, in an unfortunate lull in the conversation her ladyship let go a loud and reverberating fart.

The Englishman leapt to his feet and apologised profusely to the startled diners. "I crave your indulgence," he said, "a serious war wound makes me particularly susceptible to flatulence and in stimulating conversation such as this, with excitement and laughter, I sometimes lose control. My humblest apologies. I hope you will forgive me." He sat down.

The French consul was puzzled. He knew it was her ladyship who had unleashed the whoofer, yet the Englishman had taken the blame.

Twice more she let farts rumble by and each time the Englishman jumped to his feet and apologised.

It was only when Lady Carrington left for the powder room that the Frenchman had the chance to lean across and asked for an explanation.

"Well, old chap, we can't let her get embarrassed about it can we. It is my duty as a British gentleman to take the rap. It's a matter of honour," he said.

The conversation was cut short with Madam's return. A few moments later she discharged a rip-snorting fart that shook the chandeliers.

This time both consuls jumped to their feet at the

same instant. The Frenchman waggled his finger at the Englishman: "Oh, no Monsieur. The honour of France is at stake. This one is on me."

*　*　*

THE sex surrogate had been hired by the rich farmer to teach his son the intricacies of love and she was delighted to find he was a fine strapping lad.

She even skipped some of the basics and advanced to the sophisticated sixty-nine position.

Unfortunately, she got so excited and carried away she let go a little whoofer.

"Crickey, what d'yer call that?" said the country lad.

"Sorry, just an accident," she said, "It's called the sixty-nine position."

They got back to work but again she got so excited another puff of wind escaped her buttocks.

The boy scrambled out from underneath. "That's enough," he declared. "Damned if I can stand another sixty-seven of them."

SEXISM

SHOULD we be politically correct about everybody's sexual persuasion? Is it politically incorrect to make jokes about feminists, male chauvinists, lesbians, gays, big boobs and wankers?

In this section, we do.

If everyone came out of the cupboard and was proud of their declared sexual preference, including heterosexuals, then we would enjoy the jokes that follow.

THE manager was informed that the company was overstaffed and that two of his three stenographers would have to be fired. All were efficient at their work, so the problem was, which one to keep.

He decided to put $20 extra in their pay packets and be guided by their responses.

One kept the money without saying a word. Another said it was the company's mistake and she had invested it to show she had business accumen. The third gave the money back. Which stenographer kept her job?

Actually, it was the blonde with the big tits.

* * *

HOW do you know if a blonde has been baking chocolate chip biscuits?

M & M shells all over the kitchen floor.

* * *

HOW does a blonde turn on the light after sex?
   She opens the car door.
                    *   *   *
WHAT do you call a blonde who dyes her hair bru-
nette?
   Artificial intelligence.
                    *   *   *
WHAT'S the mating call of a blonde?
   "I'm soooo drunk...."
                    *   *   *
HOW do you know when your wife's a lousy cook?
   She uses the smoke detector as a timer.
                    *   *   *
WHAT do an average husband and a rodeo rider have
in common?
   They both stay on only eight seconds.
                    *   *   *
WHAT would be the best thing about electing a female
Prime Minister?
   We wouldn't have to pay her as much.

FEMINISTS

AS the feminists said to the preacher:

"So what's unusual about a man walking around and saying he was the Son of God?"

*   *   *

WHAT would the world be without men?

Free of crime, and full of fat, happy women.

*   *   *

THE men around here have obviously worked their way up from the bottom, and brought a lot of it with them.

*   *   *

THERE are no damp patches when you are on top.

*   *   *

BEFORE you meet your handsome prince, you have to kiss a lot of toads.

*   *   *

BETTER to have loved and lost than spend your whole damned life with him.

*   *   *

"FIRST I faked chastity," she said, "then I faked orgasm. And now I fake fidelity."

*   *   *

FEMINISTS will tell you that the difference between a clitoris and a pub is simple.

Most men know where to find a pub.

*   *   *

THE feminists were hailing a miracle birth.

The baby had both, a dick AND a brain.

* * *

THE modern miss stands no nonsense.

She was having a quiet drink when Larry Loud-mouth sat beside her. "Hi babe," he said. "I'd love to get into your pants."

"Why?" she replied. "There's already one arsehole there."

* * *

AUSSIE men don't suffer from piles because they are perfect arseholes.

* * *

SHE said her boyfriend wasn't a Sensitive New Age Guy, a SNAG. "No, he's more your Caring Under-standing Nineties Type," she said.

* * *

DO you know what you call that useless piece of skin on the end of a penis?

A man!

* * *

MOST Aussie men suffer from premature ejaculation because they can't wait to get down the pub and tell their mates about it.

* * *

HE said he believed in the direct approach and asked if she wanted to hear his sexual philosophy.

"I suppose so." she replied.

"Well, it's Get-It-Up, Get-It-In, Get-It-Off, and Get-It-Out," he said, "What do you think about that?"

"I think that's the Four-Get-It approach," she said coolly.

"HOW was your blind date?" asked one girl of her flatmate.

"Boring," she replied. "He was so boring I finally agreed to sit on his face just to stop him from talking."

* * *

WHAT would you call a woman who always knows where her husband is?

A widow!

* * *

HOW about herstory for a change?

* * *

IT'S a man's world. And the end is nigh.

* * *

MALE chauvinist pig's motto:
Put women's libbers behind bras.

* * *

SUPPORT Women's Lib. Get out from under.

* * *

ADAM came first. But then, men always do.

* * *

AND once you've 'Adam, you 'Eve.

* * *

A DISCERNING feminist called Ida
Said as he slipped it insider
"I'd much rather be
Underneath as 'ridee'
Than on top in the role of the rider."

* * *

CUCUMBERS are better than men because:
Cucumbers stay hard for weeks.
Cucumbers never suffer performance anxiety.
Cucumbers are there when you want them.
Cucumbers will always respect you next morning.
Cucumbers are eaten only when YOU fancy it.

Cucumbers never need a round of applause.

Cucumbers can stay up all night.

Cucumbers don't mind hiding in the fridge when mother calls.

* * *

A MAN wrapped up in himself makes a very small parcel.

* * *

GERMAN men live by the sweat of their fraus.

* * *

WHEN all that's stiff is his socks, take the money and run.

* * *

ONE man's Sunday lunch is one woman's Sunday gone.

* * *

A WOMAN who thinks the way to a man's heart is through his stomach is aiming a little too high.

* * *

IF you want a chick, go buy an egg.

* * *

A WOMAN who calls herself a bird deserves the worms she gets.

* * *

A HARD man is good to find.

* * *

NO man has ever stuck his hand up a skirt looking for a tram ticket.

* * *

"WHERE have you been all my life?" sleazed the middle-aged Casanova.

She looked up and said coyly, "Well, for the first half of it, I wasn't born."

* * *

THE waltz was invented by men, so that they could lead and step on a woman at the same time.

* * *

A WOMAN'S lot is not a nappy one.

* * *

I USED to find him boring until I stopped listening.

* * *

HI Chick!
  Hi Cock!

* * *

MEN are like toilet seats.
  They are either vacant, engaged, or full of shit!

* * *

RUGBY players suffer from breast envy.

* * *

HOW can men take themselves seriously when they have got willies?

* * *

THE birth of Venus was a misconception.

* * *

LIVE a little. Have an orgasm.

* * *

MORE women train drivers, is women's right to choo...choose.

LESBIANS

ARE you a practising lesbian?
    No. This is as good as I get.

        *   *   *

IS a lesbian a pansy without a stalk?

        *   *   *

What do lesbians recommend as the ideal birth control
for men?
    A bullet.

        *   *   *

WHAT do you call a lesbian with fat fingers?
    Well hung.

        *   *   *

HE sat next to her at the singles bar, bought her a beer
and began chatting her up.
    "Look," she said, "I'd better tell you right from the
start. I'm a lesbian."
    "What's that?" he asked in all innocence.
    "Well," she said, "See that blonde over there. She
appeals to me. In fact, I'd love to get her into bed and
get into her pants."
    "Strewth," he said, "I must be a lesbian too."

        *   *   *

AFTER the examination the gyneocologist said to her
patient, "Well, everything's neat and tidy there."
    "So it should be," said the lesbian, "I have a woman
in twice a week."

        *   *   *

IT happened some time ago, when a young man walked into a theatrical agency and said he could sing and dance. He backed it up with such a convincing demonstration that the agent knew he had a future star.

"You are great," he said. "What's your name?"

"Penis van Lesbian," answered the young hopeful.

"That's a shocker. We'll have to change that for a start," said the agent scratching his head. "I've got it. We'll call you Dick Van Dyke."

WANKERS

HE was such a wanker he used to fake orgasims during masturbation.

* * *

WHAT'S the difference between an egg and a wank?
  You can't beat a wank.

* * *

THERE is a big difference between wanking and clogs.
  You can hear yourself coming in clogs.

* * *

HE was a whimsical masturbator, with an offbeat sense of humor.

* * *

MASTURBATION is a waste of fucking time.

* * *

HE was a dysfunctional male patient and the sex therapist was advising him on the release that could be obtained through masturbation.
  "Oh, but I do get pleasure from my organ," he replied. "I frequently grasp my penis and hold it tight. It's a habit with me."
  "Well, it's a habit you'll have to shake," said the therapist.

* * *

THE doctor eyed the young man in disbelief when he said he was suffering from a square dick. Nobody has

333

a square donger, he thought, but when the lad produced it the doc was truly amazed.

"Well, that's certainly a square peg for a round hole," he said in astonishment.

He took a few measurements then reached for his prescription pad and began writing. "Is that for a lotion or something?" asked the lad.

"No," said the doctor, "I'm giving you a week off so that you can pull yourself round."

* * *

HE was such a conceited wanker he would call out his own name and come.

* * *

WHY is masturbation better than intercourse?

Because you know who you are dealing with.

Because you don't have to buy flowers.

Because you know when you've had enough.

Because you don't have to be polite.

Because you don't have to make conversation.

Because you don't have to look your best.

Because you meet a better class of person.

Because it is with someone you love.

* * *

WANKING is very much like playing bridge.

If you've got a good hand you don't need a partner.

* * *

A SHAKESPERIAN actor was being interviewed by the press.

"Did you ever have a real embarrassing experience?"

"Well, yes. One experience I will never forget was when my mother caught me playing with myself."

"Oh we all did that when we were kids."

334

"Yes, but this was last night."

* * *

LOVERS may celebrate Valentine's Day, but wankers celebrate Palm Sunday.

* * *

THE leading manufacture of imported vibrators is a Japanese firm called Genital Electric.

* * *

FRED had been stranded on the desert island for three years and had blisters on his hands. One day he grabbed his old binoculars and scanned the horizon.

"My God, a ship," he muttered to himself.

"And there, on the mast, a naked blonde, beautiful breasts, and look at those hips, wow, she is headed this way."

By now he had a roaring erection.

Suddenly he flung the binoculars away and grabbed his donk.

"Gotcha again ya bastard. There is no bloody ship."

* * *

IT was the yuppies turn to host the bridge club and although they packed their twelve-year-old son off to bed early, Junior was constantly coming downstairs and interrupting the game asking for drinks of water, wanting to go to the toilet and one excuse after another.

Finally one of the guests said she could sort the matter out and took the youngster upstairs.

When she returned the game ran smoothly and there wasn't another sound from the lad all night.

As the guests were leaving the young mother asked the guest what her secret was.

"Nothing really," she said, "I just taught him to masturbate."

GOING down to the workshed one day a father surprised his fifteen-year-old son masturbating. In an understanding manner the father explained that what the boy had been doing was natural enough for the urge for release was strong.

"But you must save all that energy and not waste it," he said. "That sperm is your life essence. Save it until you are a man and can use it in the normal manner."

The boy promised and the years slipped by.

He was given a great party on his 21st birthday and when the guests had left he thanked his dad. "I never forgot what you told me in the shed years ago," he said. "And I saved my seed like you told me to. But now I am a man and I have three barrels full. Heck Dad, what the hell will I do with it?"

*   *   *

BASIL was still pulling his pud and by his 30th birthday his father took him aside and said he would have to get married.

So Basil found himself a nice girl, got married and brought her home. Yet less than a month after the wedding the father found him whacking off in the shed again.

"What's this?" he said, "I thought this would stop once you got married."

"But Dad, the poor girl's not used to it. Her little arms get so tired."

*   *   *

THE American tourist got the shock of his life when the Mexican, brandishing a six-shooter, jumped out from behind a cactus.

"Take my money, my car, but don't kill me," said the tourist.

"I no kill you if you do what I say," said the Mexican. "Just unzip your pants and start masturbating," he ordered.

Although shocked the traveller did what he was told.

"Right, now do it again," said the Mexican.

The American protested but with the gun against his nose he managed again.

"And yet again, Gringo, or I shoot you dead."

With sweat running down his brow the American managed a final effort and fell exhausted.

"Good," said the Mexican, "now you can give my sister a ride to the next village."

* * *

"ACCORDING to the latest survey," said the sex therapist to the reporter, "only half the population sing in the shower. The other half masturbate. And do you know what the singers sing?"

"No," said the reporter.

"No, I didn't think you did."

* * *

THE single girl told her psychiatrist: "I sometimes have twenty or so consecutive orgasms during my clitoris stimulation sessions."

"That's amazing," said the normally unflappable shrink.

"Oh, I don't know," shrugged the woman, "after sixteen or so I run out of fantasies and from then on it's not much fun."

FLASHERS

FLASHER'S motto: Grin and bare it.

* * *

FLASHER'S theme song: Whistle while you lurk.

* * *

STANDING in a crowded train the pervert squeezed his body against the buxom woman and she could feel something like a coke bottle in his pocket pressed against her thigh.

She said: "I have only three words to say to you: You filthy beast."

Later, as the train approached his station he said: "I have only three words to say to you: Let go now."

* * *

A gent in a long flowing cloak
  Unzipped his fly for a joke
  An old man gave a shout
  A nun almost passed out
  And a lady close by had a stroke.

* * *

A RENOWNED art critic named Flo
  Was accosted a fortnight ago
  When the flasher unzipped
  She allegedly quipped
  "An exhibit well hung sir, good show."

* * *

338

AS the female conductor came along the train checking tickets the kinky passenger opened his raincoat with a flourish and exposed himself.

"I'm sorry," she said, "but you'll have to show me your ticket, not your stub."

*   *   *

ON the crowded train she turned to the man behind her.

"For god's sake will you stop pushing that thing at me?"

"It's only my pay packet," he said.

"Well, you must have a good job," she retorted. "You've had three rises since we left Central Station."

*   *   *

THREE old maids were on a seat in a park when a member of the raincoat brigade flashed at them.

Two had a stroke. The third was too slow.

GAYS

GAY sex is better
  Than bi-sex or hetter.

* * *

THERE was a gay guy who was so ugly he had to go out with girls.

* * *

WHY are there so many queers in the British aristocracy?
  Have you seen their women?

* * *

THE definition of an Aussie queer
  is a bloke who prefers girls to beer.

* * *

A JEWISH lawyer looked so despondent that his close friend asked him why. "I have just learned that my son is homosexual," he said. But then he added, "but the situation could be worse. At least he is in love with a doctor."

* * *

UP before the court on a charge of sodomy it was mentioned in evidence that the passive of the partners was a member of the town's philharmonic orchestra.
  "Case dismissed," said the judge.
  "Why?" asked the prosecutor.
  "I have heard them play," said the judge "and I can tell you they all need stuffing."

* * *

SEVEN survivors staggered ashore from the ship-
wreck, six women and a man. They were civilised
about it. The women decided they would each have
the bloke for one night each and he could rest on
Sundays. The bloke agreed with relish, but as the
weeks went on he realised what a physical commit-
ment he had undertaken.

Then one day he spotted a raft with a lone figure
paddling toward the island. It was a man.

Elated at finding unexpected help the bloke ran into
the shallows to help him ashore.

The guy on the raft waved a handkerchief to him
and said: "Oh, hello Big Boy!"

"Blast," said the rescuer. "There go my Sundays."

* * *

CECIL said it was true. Your entire life flashes before
your eyes when you are gone down on for the third
time.

* * *

I'LL be buggered if I'll join the British Conservative
Party.

* * *

AT prison muster one lag said: "I think my cell mate
is becoming a queer."

"How can you tell?"

"He shuts his eyes when I kiss him goodnight."

* * *

THEY were leaning on the bar. "Have you ever slept
with a gay?"

"Certainly not. But I once slept with a bloke who
had."

* * *

PUT the anal back into analysis.

341

A HUSBAND and wife were having a rowdy domestic argument in the pub. Observing the disturbance one gay said to his partner, "See. I told you those mixed marriages were no good."

*   *   *

WITH gay marriages being recognised in America it follows that divorces will be recognised as 'gay abandon'.

*   *   *

GAY pride is a group of homosexual lions.

*   *   *

CYRIL sauntered into the Interflora shop.
"Is it true that you send flowers abroad?" he asked.
"Yes," was the reply.
"Oh goody, then send me to London, I'm a pansy."

*   *   *

CHAP went to the doctor because he had a pain in the bum.
"No wonder," said the doc. "You've got a bunch of roses jammed up there."
"Really?" said the patient excitedly. "Who are they from? Can you read the card?"

*   *   *

DAISIES of the world unite.
You have nothing to lose but your chains.

*   *   *

DID you hear about the gay tattoo artist who had designs on several sailors?

*   *   *

CECIL got a parking ticket for being too fast in the parking lot. The cop caught him at sixty-nine.

*   *   *

AN alligator walked into a menswear shop.

"Do you have any shirts with little faggots on the pocket?" he said.

* * *

A GAY masochist is a sucker for punishment.

* * *

TWO very contented Irish gays were Thomas Fitzpatrick and Patrick Fitzthomas.

* * *

THE new card game at the Gay Club is called camp poker.

Queens are wild and straights don't count.

* * *

OVER the years a lawyer became concerned that his son was doing poorly at university. Each year his marks seemed to be worse so the lawyer eventually rang the dean.

"Well, I have good news and I have bad news," said the dean. "Your son has failed most of his exams because he is a blatant homosexual."

"Good God," said the lawyer, "then what is the good news?"

"He's been voted Queen of the May," said the dean.

* * *

THERE was an airline steward whose colleagues considered him a sexual pervert. He went out with women.

* * *

IF horse-racing is the sport of kings,
    drag-racing is the sport of queens.

* * *

AS a football coach Cecil was in great demand by teams who wanted to know how to win by coming from behind.

* * *

CECIL the ballet star was relating the day's exciting event to his room mate. A society matron had stopped her car, offered him a lift and driven him to her apartment.

"Then she took all her clothes off and said I could have anything I wanted."

"How exciting, what did you do?"

"I took the car. None of her clothes suited me."

* * *

OLD fairies never die. They merely blow away.

* * *

HOW did it feel when you first discovered you were a homosexual?

It was quite a blow.

* * *

DID you hear about the girl whose bloke didn't drink, didn't swear and never made a pass at her?

He also made his own dresses.

* * *

WHEN two judges found they were gay they decided to try each other.

* * *

TWO words that will clear the gent's room, even at the interval break at the theatre.

"N-i-i-ice dick!"

* * *

THE old actor said the queers in town were the ugliest he had ever encountered. "But then, buggers can't be choosers," he said.

* * *

TWO old boys met at the club after years apart. "How's your son making out in life?" asked one.

"Oh he's the top car salesman of a nationwide franchise. Going so well he topped the sales chart and they gave him a brand new Mercedes," said the proud father. "But he gave it away. Can you imagine that, gave it away."

"That's amazing," said the other old chap. "My son's in real estate and development. Clinched the biggest deal on the Gold Coast and they gave him a penthouse, but he gave it away. Can you imagine that?"

Right then a third old boy came in. "How's your son?" they asked him.

"Bit disappointing really," he said. "He's turned out to be a raving poofter. But still, he's managing quite well. One of his best friends gave him a Mercedes last week, and another gave him a penthouse."

*   *   *

THE publican was considering hiring a barman who had just been sacked from the pub next door. He was fired because he had his hand in the till, was often late and was suspected of being gay.

"I'll take you on," said the publican, "but you had better not be one cent short and never late. Now give me a kiss and get to work."

*   *   *

THE travelling salesman's car had broken down and he had staggered for miles to the proverbial farm-house. He finally struggled to the porch and knocked on the door.

The farmer said the salesman was welcome to food and water and he could stay the night. "But I must warn you, I don't have any daughters for I am a bachelor," he said.

"Oh gawd," said the salesman, "how far to the next farm?"

* * *

THEN there was the Scottish gay, Ben Doon.

He was found in the bush with nothing but an old Mackintosh on him.

* * *

AND the Greek soldier who re-enlisted because he didn't want to leave his mate's behind.

* * *

IN the days of the Roman Empire many Romans thought that sex was a pain in the arse.

* * *

WHY are there so many gays in Italy?

If you were brought up with so many ugly woman what else could you be?

* * *

TWO fellows in a gay bar had a misunderstanding.

They went outside and exchanged blows.

* * *

DARREN was in the mood for the Gay Mardi Gras.

"I want to eat, drink and be Mary," he said.

* * *

THE Gay Lib recruiting vehicle was seen patrolling the red light district. One couldn't miss it. It was mauve in color with registration plate: RU 1-2.

* * *

A GAY lad who came from Yeppoon
Took a lesbian up to his room
They argued a lot
About who would do what
And how and with which and to whom.

346

GOD save the Queens
* * *
IS camping loitering within tent?
* * *
HAVE Gums, Will Travel — Prairie Fairy.
* * *
MY mother made me a homosexual.
   (If I get her the wool will she make one for me?)

BOOBS

MUM arrived at the function looking the best she had for years. "You look great," said her husband. "You should always leave your bras at home."

"How did you know?" she asked.

"Because you've lost all the wrinkles from your face, " he said.

* * *

THE pop concert was about to start when a female streaker raced down the aisle.

She was caught by the bouncers and chucked out.

* * *

DOLLY Parton has just had a single come out.

* * *

A YOUNG husband watched his flat-chested wife try on her new brassiere.

"Why did you buy that for?" he said. "You've nothing to put in it."

"Listen," she said, "I don't complain about you buying underpants."

* * *

SIGN on Fred's door: 'Knock firmly. I like firm knockers'.

* * *

AN old man was the only other occupant of the train compartment and he had fallen asleep, so the young mother had no qualms about breast-feeding her baby.

However, he woke halfway through the process.

"What a lovely child," he said, "what do you feed him on?"

"Just milk and orange juice," she replied.

The old man thought about this for a moment. "Which one is the orange juice?" he asked.

* * *

SHE was always trying to enlarge her breasts. "I might try silicon implants," she said.

"Costs too much," said her laconic husband.

"Just get some tissue and rub it along your cleavage."

"Will that make them larger?"

"It did a good job on your arse," he said.

* * *

"JOHNNY," said the English teacher, "can you show me the meaning of the word paranoia?"

"It's not a word, Miss, it's several words,"

"Oh?"

"It's like the topless waitress said to her envious rival: 'Pardon me, but does my paranoia?'"

* * *

HER cynical husband asked why she was so bright and cheerful.

"I saw my doctor today and he said I had firm breasts like an eighteen-year-old."

"Yes," said the husband, "but what did he say about your forty-five-year-old arse?"

"Your name wasn't mentioned," she said.

* * *

THERE was a young woman called Clair
   Who possessed a magnificent pair
   Or that's what we thought
   Til we saw one get caught

On a thorn and begin losing air.

* * *

A TABLE top dancer called Valerie
   Started to count every calorie
   Said her boss in disgust
   If you lose half your bust
   Then you'll be getting just half of your salary.

* * *

THE foundation garment store unveiled its latest model brassier called the Sheepdog. It rounds them up and points them in the right direction.

* * *

"DID she blush when her shoulder straps broke?"
   "I didn't notice."

* * *

IT was such a hot day Miss Prim took a cold shower and was relaxing on the sofa in the nude when there was a knock on the door.

"Who is it?" she said in alarm, frantically looking for a gown.

"Just the blind man," said the voice outside.

Relieved at the news she opened the door slightly with one hand while reaching for her purse with the other. It was enough for Fred to barge in.

"Great set of norks, lady," he said, "but where do you want these venetians hung?"

* * *

THERE was once a maid from Assizes
   Whose boobs were two different sizes
   One was so small
   It was nothing at all
   While the other was large and won prizes.

* * *

WHILE they were cuddling under the trees
  She said to her boyfriend: "Oh please,
  It would give me such bliss
  If you play more with this
  And give less attention to these."

* * *

SHE was a buxom young woman with a baby in her arms and when she walked into the clinic the doctor asked what the problem was.

"It's the baby," she said, "he seems under-nourished."

The doc carried out an extensive examination of the baby but could find nothing wrong.

"Is he bottle or breast fed?" asked the doc.

"Breast fed," she replied.

"Then I'd better check you too. Strip off to the waist please."

She looked rather embarrassed but did as she was told to reveal a perfect pair of boobs. The doctor weighed each one lightly in his hand, then gave the nipples a gentle squeeze and a tug.

"That's the problem." he said "You are not giving any milk."

"I'm not expected to," she said. "I'm the baby's aunt, but it's been very nice to meet you."

* * *

SHEILA the feminist insisted on attending the church hatless and wearing a see-through blouse.

"You can't enter the church like that," said the priest.

"I have a divine right," persisted Sheila.

"By what I can see your left is divine too, but you still can't come in."

351

PERCY the pervert was a short bloke and used to enjoy riding home on the subway in peak hour when, more often than not, his head would be jammed between the breasts of so many buxom office girls.

Once he was nose to nipples with a tall tough blonde.

"Listen Joe," she sneered, "how would you like a bust in the gob?"

"Oh, you mind reader you," said Percy.

* * *

AT a city hotel a waiter was dismissed for having his thumb in the soup and a topless waitress was dismissed for two similar offences.

* * *

THERE was an argument at the topless bar when the president of the Beer Appreciators' Society complained that the beer was okay but his waitress was flat.

* * *

A TAXI driver who undid his lady passenger's bra was charged with exceeding the limits in a built up area.

* * *

TO his bride said the sharp-eyed detective
   "Can it be that my eyesight's defective?
   Has your east tit the least bit
   The best of the west tit?
   Or is it a trick of perspective?"

* * *

THE party girl was so proud of her boobs she always chose a dress to show them off to best advantage.

Trying on a low cut dress she checked it in the mirror and then asked the shop assistant if she thought it was cut too low.

"Do you have hair on your chest?" asked the shop assistant.

"Of course not."

"Then this dress is too low," she said.

* * *

HE placed his stethoscope on the young women's chest and said, "Big breaths, my dear"

"Yeth," she said, "And I'm only thixteen."

* * *

A MOUSE dashed up a girl's leg, passed her navel and came to rest snugly in her cleavage.

She looked down and said: "You must be a tit-mouse."

"No," he replied, "I'm a Mickey Mouse. I just overshot the mark."

* * *

TWO blokes entered a noisy pub and were surprised to see a buxom waitress bouncing from table to table and getting her boobs felt at each stop.

"Looks like a friendly pub," said one, so they sat down and waited until she reached their table.

"Can I have feel?" said one.

"Certainly not," she replied.,

"But those other blokes did."

"They didn't ask," she replied.

* * *

THE two gossips noticed the young mother in the park.

"Is that hussy breast-feeding again, right out in public?"

"It's her, right enough," said the other sticky-nose, "and look, the boy is at least twenty-five and not even her son."

A BUXOM young miss from Valetta
   Loved to parade in a sweater
   Three reasons she had
   To keep warm was not bad
   But the other two reasons were better.

* * *

AND lastly, as all parents well know, a baby is something that must have a bottle or bust.

FAT, BALD AND SHORT

Just so you won't feel discriminated against or ignored, our friends who are fat, bald or short get a guernsey in this section.After all the vast majority of jokes are levelled at normal people and if it ever reaches the stage where normal people seek political protection from jokes, then we are wll and truly "stuffed".

WHEN Cheryl finally broke the news that she was going steady, her parents were relieved that this might be the 'Mr Right' to take her off their hands. After all, she was forty-two!

But they got the shock of their lives when she introduced them to a short, fat, balding man.

Cheryl's mum quickly took her aside.

"He's not exactly a young man," Mum whispered to her daughter. "He's fat, he's bald, he's short and he's pretty old, isn't he?"

"There's no need to whisper, Mum," said Cheryl, "he's bloody deaf as well."

* * *

DID you hear about the dwarf who joined the nudist colony and was poking his nose into everybody's business?

The problem was solved when he entered the nudist rock and roll contest and was clubbed to death.

*   *   *

THE judge admonished the woman suing for divorce.

"You knew your husband was extremely short when you married him," he said.

"Yes," she replied, "but when it came to sex there were problems. When we were nose to nose his toes were in it and when he was in it, he disappeared altogether and I had no one to talk to......and I'm sick and tired of him putting a bucket on my head and swinging on the handle."

*   *   *

SHE only hires short people as waiters so the sandwiches look bigger.

*   *   *

MITCH the midget complained to the doctor that every time it rained, he had a terrible pain and rash in his groin.

"Come back next time the weather is bad," said the doctor.

Three days later Mitch trudged through the rain to the clinic.

"Ah, yes, I see the trouble," he said.

And he cut thirty centimetres off the top of his gumboots.

DEFINITIONS

ABSENTEE: A missing golfing accessory.

ABUNDANCE: A local hop usually staged in a barn.

ACME: Pimples on the face running towards the top.

ADAMANT: The very first insect.

ADIEU: Hymie Finklestein.

ADORN: What comes after the darkest hour.

ADVERTISEMENT: Something that makes you think you've longed for it for years, but never heard of it before.

ALIMONY: A mistake by two people paid for by one.

ALPHABET: Not quite the complete wager.

ANTI-FREEZE: When you don't talk to your uncle's wife.

APEX: The female of the gorilla species.

AROMATIC: An automatic longbow.

ARTFUL: A painting exhibition.

AUTOBIOGRAPHY: The car's logbook.

AUTOMATIC SHIFT: When the driver moves closer to his girlfriend.

AVAIL: Helpful for ugly women.

AWESTRUCK: Being hit with a paddle.

BACTERIA: A modern self-service TAB.

BADMINTON: The reason the lamb tasted off.

BALANCE: Something you lose if the bank pushes you.

BARBARIAN: The man who cuts your hair.

BIGAMIST: A fog over Italy.

BIGOTRY: An Italian redwood.

BLUNDERBUSS: A coach which goes from Melbourne to Sydney, via Port Augusta.

BOOKCASE: Litigation about a novel which ensures wide sales.

BOXER: A bloke who stands up for the other fellow's rights.

BRAZIER: Something to warm your hands on.

BRUSSELS SPROUT: A world famous statue found in that city.

BURLESQUE SHOW: Where attendance falls off if nothing else does.

CABBAGE: The fare you pay a taxi driver.

CLIMATE: The best thing to do with a ladder.

CONDOM: An item to be worn on every conceivable occasion.

CONDOM: A sock in the puss.

CONDOMS: Homes for Retired Semen.

CONSCIENCE: The thing that aches when everything else feels good.

COPULATE: What an Italian police chief says to an officer who doesn't get to work on time.

COWARD: A man who thinks with his legs.

DETEST: The West Indies playing India.

DIAPHRAGMS: Trampolines for dickheads.

DUCK DICK: A game warden.

ECSTACY: It's the feeling you feel when you feel you are going to feel a feeling you have never felt before.

ELECTRICIAN: A switch doctor.

ENGLISH GENT: One who gets out of the bath to piss in the sink.

EUNUCH: Massive vassel with a passive tassel.

FASTIDIOUS: A girl who is fast and hideous.

FAUCET: What you have to do if the tap won't turn.

FELLATIO: The French Connection.

FETE: A boring picnic worse than death.

FLOOSIE: A sweet girl with the gift of the grab.

GALLERY: A hostel for young women.

GAY MILKMAN: Dairy Queen.

GRANARY: A home for senior female citizens.

HEBREW: a male teabag.

HEN'S PARTY: A bunch of birds cackling about who is laying whom.

HIGH FIDELITY: A drunk who always goes home to his wife.

HORIZON: Callgirl getting up in the morning.

HUMBUG: A singing cockroach.

HYACINTH: A yank greeting a gal called Cynthia.

IDOLISE: Eyes that refuse to look at anything.

INCOME: What you have to make first, because you can't make it last.

INNUENDO: An Italian suppository.

JEALOUSY: The friendship one woman shares with another.

JEWISH DILEMMA: Free pork.

LACTIC: A grandfather clock which doesn't work.

LIBERAL: A Conservative who's been arrested.

LESBIAN COCKTAIL LOUNGE: Her-She Bar.

LESBIANS: Insurmountable odds.

LESBIAN: A manic depressive with illusions of gender.

MADAM: One who offers vice to the lovelorn.

MARCONI: The first man to send a message through a length of spaghetti without it touching the sides.

MINE SHAFT: What a German calls his dick.

MONOLOGUE: A discussion between man and wife.

NONDESCRIPT: A television play.

ODIOUS: Not very good poetry.

ORGY: Grope Therapy.

PARENTS: Couples who practice the Rythym Method.

PEDESTRIAN: A motorist with teenage sons.

PIMP: Nookie Bookie.

PIMP: Public relations man for a public relations girl.

PORNOGRAPHY: Cliterature.

PREMATURE EJACULATION: The come before the scorn.

RACIAL DISPUTE: When the course judge calls for a photo.

RED RIDING HOOD: A Russian condom.

REFLECTION: What a girl looks at, but is not given to.

SAGE: A bloke who knows his onions.

SITTING PRETTY: Sitting Bull's gay brother.

SNOW JOB: How a woman defrosts her man.

SNUFF: Sufficient unto the day.

SONATA: A song sung by Frank.

SPECIMEN: An Italian astronaut.

STALEMATE: A husband who has lost his ardour.

TEAR JERKER: A bloke who cries while wanking.

TRUE LOVE: An injection with affection to the mid-section from a projection without objection.

VICE SQUAD: The Pussy Posse.

VICE VERSA: Dirty poetry from Italy.

VIRGIN: A girl who whispers sweet nothing doings.

VIRGIN: A girl who won't take in what a guy takes out.

VIRGIN: Any Hicksville girl who can outrun her brothers.

VIRGIN SQUAW: Wouldn't Indian.

WELSH RAREBIT: A Cardiff virgin.

WET DREAM: A snorgasm.

ANTI-CLIMAX: Bore-gasm.

CORPORATE VIRGIN: New girl in the office.

DESPERATE STRAIGHTS: Sex-starved heterosexuals.

GAELIC: An Irish Lesbian.

INCEST: Relatively boring.

LIFE: A Sexually-transmitted terminal disease.

LUBRICATED CONDOMS: Bedroom slippers.

MASTURBATION: I-balling.

SELF-DECEPTION: Faking an organism during masturbation.